W9-BYK-684

Teach Yourself
VISUALLY™

Bridge

Teach Yourself VISUALLY™

Bridge

Visual®

by David Galt

BICENTENNIAL
1807
WILEY
2007
BICENTENNIAL

Wiley Publishing, Inc.

Teach Yourself VISUALLY™ Bridge

Copyright © 2008 by Wiley Publishing, Inc., Hoboken, New Jersey. All rights reserved.

Published by Wiley Publishing, Inc., Hoboken, New Jersey

For general information on our other products and services or to obtain technical support please contact our Customer Care Department within the U.S. at (800) 762-2974, outside the U.S. at (317) 572-3993 or fax (317) 572-4002.

Wiley also publishes its books in a variety of electronic formats. Some content that appears in print may not be available in electronic books. For more information about Wiley products, please visit our web site at www.wiley.com.

Library of Congress Control Number: 2007921823

ISBN: 978-0-470-11424-7

Printed in the United States of America

10 9 8 7 6 5 4 3 2 1

Book production by Wiley Publishing, Inc., Composition Services

Praise for the Teach Yourself VISUALLY Series

I just had to let you and your company know how great I think your books are. I just purchased my third Visual book (my first two are dog-eared now!) and, once again, your product has surpassed my expectations. The expertise, thought, and effort that go into each book are obvious, and I sincerely appreciate your efforts. Keep up the wonderful work!

—Tracey Moore (Memphis, TN)

I have several books from the Visual series and have always found them to be valuable resources.

—Stephen P. Miller (Ballston Spa, NY)

Thank you for the wonderful books you produce. It wasn't until I was an adult that I discovered how I learn—visually. Although a few publishers out there claim to present the material visually, nothing compares to Visual books. I love the simple layout. Everything is easy to follow. And I understand the material! You really know the way I think and learn. Thanks so much!

—Stacey Han (Avondale, AZ)

Like a lot of other people, I understand things best when I see them visually. Your books really make learning easy and life more fun.

—John T. Frey (Cadillac, MI)

I am an avid fan of your Visual books. If I need to learn anything, I just buy one of your books and learn the topic in no time. Wonders! I have even trained my friends to give me Visual books as gifts.

—Illona Bergstrom (Aventura, FL)

I write to extend my thanks and appreciation for your books. They are clear, easy to follow, and straight to the point. Keep up the good work! I bought several of your books and they are just right! No regrets! I will always buy your books because they are the best.

—Seward Kollie (Dakar, Senegal)

Credits

Acquisitions Editor
Pam Mourouzis

Project Editor
Suzanne Snyder

Copy Editor
Marylouise Wiack

Technical Editor
Peter Bonfanti

Editorial Manager
Christina Stambaugh

Publisher
Cindy Kitchel

Vice President and Executive Publisher
Kathy Nebenhaus

Interior Design
Kathie Rickard
Elizabeth Brooks

Cover Design
José Almaguer

Photography
Matt Bowen

Photographic Assistant
Andrew Hanson

Special Thanks...

To the following companies for granting us permission to reproduce photographs and screen captures.

- American Contract Bridge League
- Bridge Base Online (www.online.bridgebase.com)
- Game Zone Bridge (www.zone.msn.com)
- OKbridge (www.OKbridge.com)
- SWAN Bridge (www.swangames.com)
- Yahoo Bridge (www.yahoo.com)

About the Author

David Galt, a professional bridge teacher and game designer, is a native New Yorker with BA and MA degrees from Yale, as well as a doctorate in education from Claremont. He began playing bridge at the age of 14, and in 1972 attained the rank of Life Master. An expert player, he is on the staff of the Manhattan Bridge Club in New York City.

He is an authority on playing cards and board games, and owns a considerable collection of historical items in both areas. His column *It's in the Cards* appears 6 times annually in *Knucklebones* magazine. He is also the author of *All-Time Favorite Card Games*, *101 Great Card Games*, and *Card Games for One or Two*.

To ask David Galt questions on bridge topics, please email him at galtbridge@yahoo.com

Acknowledgments

Bridge is a game of multi-layered complexity, rivaled perhaps only by writing a book about it. In putting together this book, I want to first thank Pam Mourouzis, who recruited me to the task and helped shape the contents. Suzanne Snyder provided continued and valuable guidance throughout the entire course of the project, as well as clarity and delineation to each chapter and section. Peter Bonfanti's careful scrutiny of bridge matters large and small were of major use throughout. Marylouise Wiack offered many appropriate comments on language and matters of expression. Joni Burns and Rashell Smith ably constructed the many visual elements needed. And Christina Stambaugh and Cynthia Kitchel served significantly in managing and scheduling this project.

In addition, Charlotte Nad and Marcia Nad contributed technical support along with ongoing encouragement, while Adam Alexander frequently supplied welcome input. Maya Galt assisted me significantly on important research tasks, and further aided me by reading through an entire version of the manuscript. Tracey Yarbro and Paul Linxwiler of the American Contract Bridge League alerted me to key information as well as to available historical bridge photos. Special thanks go to Margo M. Maier and Thomas Bourreau, my online bridge partners. I am also in deep gratitude to Christopher Rivera, who played a crucial role in helping me maintain my outlook at a critical period. Finally, I feel a debt of appreciation to Howard Schenken, whose 1973 autobiography *The Education of a Bridge Player*—which I finally read about 5 years ago—planted the idea of mixing apt bridge deals within a larger narrative.

This book is dedicated to Alvin Roth (1924–2007) whom I met only very briefly a few times. He was a great player, and quite a contributor to the game.

Table of Contents

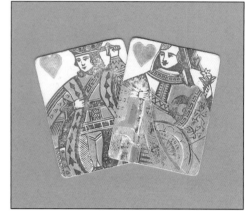

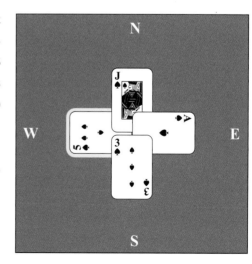

chapter 3 Rubber Bridge Playing and Scoring

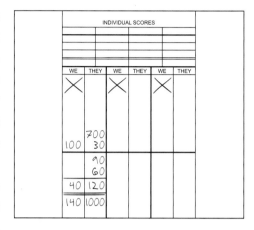

chapter 4 Hand Evaluation and the Opening Bid

Very, very good hand.

chapter 5 Responding to Opener's Bid of 1-of-a-Suit

chapter 6 Responding to 1NT

| Jacoby Sequence 1 | | | |
South	West	North	East
1NT	pass	2♦	pass
2♥	pass	?	

chapter 7   **Declarer Play**

chapter 8   Competing in the Auction

West	North	East	South
1♣	pass	1♥	?

chapter 9 — Opener's Rebid and Beyond

Relative point-count ranges of opening one-level bids

1-of-a-suit

11   21   26

0 HCP   40 HCP

26: the combined HCP needed to expect a good play for game.

1NT

15 17   26

0 HCP   40 HCP

chapter 10 — Defensive Play

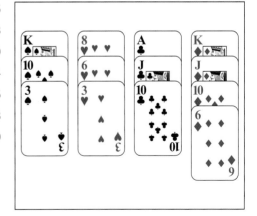

chapter 11 Preemptive Bids

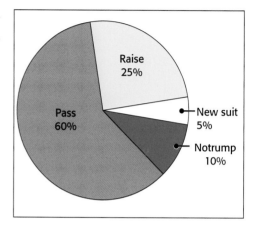

chapter 12 2♣ and 2NT Opening Bids

1♣ 1♦ 1♥ 1♠ 1NT
2♣ 2♦ 2♥ 2♠ 2NT
3♣ 3♦ 3♥ 3♠ 3NT
4♣ 4♦ 4♥ 4♠ 4NT
5♣ 5♦ 5♥ 5♠ 5NT
6♣ 6♦ 6♥ 6♠ 6NT
7♣ 7♦ 7♥ 7♠ 7NT

chapter **13** **Three Popular Bidding Conventions**

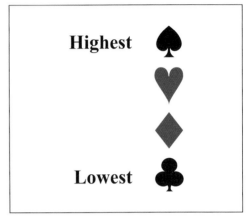

Highest ♠

♥

♦

Lowest ♣

chapter **14** **Strong Hands and Slam Bidding**

500 – 750   1000 – 1500
Small Slams   Grand Slams

chapter 15 Play Duplicate Bridge

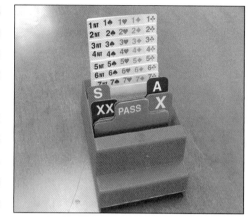

chapter 16 The World of Online Bridge

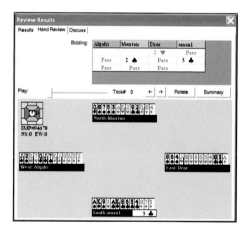

chapter 1

The Game of Bridge

Bridge is a challenging card game that never ceases to fascinate. One of its unique features is that you are not alone. Instead, you have a partner sitting across the table from you, and the two of you play together against another pair.

You may not be a star bridge player the first few times you play. However, the more time you can put into learning and practice, the better player you'll be and the more you'll enjoy each new deal. In this chapter, you will get your first glimpse of the game as you pick up a few basic concepts.

A Universal Game

The game of contract bridge—or simply bridge—has been popular for more than 80 years and is played by millions of people around the world. You can enjoy it whether you are young or old, big or little, rich or poor.

A typical game involves four people playing at home. People also play bridge in bridge clubs, filling large rooms with many tables of four players.

Of course, with a computer you can play bridge whenever you want. You can play on your own, using installed software, or play online with both friends and strangers.

Most major newspapers also publish a regular bridge column. Chances are you may have seen such columns in your local newspaper and wondered what was going on in them. After reading a few chapters of this book, you'll be able to follow them yourself. Reading the bridge columns is great for learning about the game!

Bridge is widely enjoyed both at home and at tournaments attended by many.
Right photo courtesy of the American Contract Bridge League.

In the 1600s people played a 13-card ancestor of bridge called *ruffe & honours*. By the 1700s this game had evolved into the popular *whist* (see photo). In the 1880s a more sophisticated whist became known as *bridge whist*, then simply *bridge*. In the early 1900s bridge added an auction where all four players had a say as to which suit would be trumps. By the mid-1920s *auction bridge* evolved into an even better game, *contract bridge*—the game we know today.

WHIST (from "The Compleat Gamester," 1674).

Ruffe & honours was mostly a game of luck. Hearts were the supreme *trump suit* (see Chapter 2) in early whist; in later years the last card turned up decided trumps. The dealer named the trump suit or declared no suit trump in bridge whist. In early bridge, the first team to win two *games* earned a *rubber* (see Chapter 3). Bridge also borrowed from *dummy whist*— where a player's hand is placed openly on the table and the player's partner chooses cards to be played from it (see Chapter 2).

Although auction bridge was itself a great leap forward, contract bridge was even more exciting. Credit for popularizing contract bridge's new scoring method, which greatly added skill to the *auction* part of bridge, goes to Harold S. Vanderbilt, a leading sportsman and industrialist of the day. Contract bridge also introduced *vulnerability*, a key factor within this new scoring scheme (see Chapter 3).

Harold S. Vanderbilt.
Photo courtesy of the American
Contract Bridge League.

Bridge is a game for four people, two playing against two. Traditionally, partners sit across from each other at a square table about 30–33 inches per side. Of course, any table will do, and you can even play outdoors if it's not windy.

You'll need a regular deck of 52 cards, but having two decks available is even better. You'll also need pencil and paper to keep score during the game. You can buy pre-printed score pads, which divide each score sheet into columns headed WE and THEY. The left-hand column (WE) is for your side and the other is for the opponents (THEY). Usually at least one player on each team keeps score, however, all four players may well want to keep score. See Chapter 3, "Bridge Scoring," for more about keeping score.

One pair can oppose the other pair the whole time, or the four players can *rotate* partnerships, with everyone getting to play with everyone else. If picking partners, a tradition from the days of whist is for each player to turn up one card from the pack. Those drawing the two high cards play against those with the two lower cards. In the figure below, the two players drawing the high cards, ace and king play against the two drawing the lower cards, jack and deuce.

TIP

Have a side table or two nearby for snacks and drinks. This will help keep both the playing surface and cards clean.

While many numbers are important in bridge, the number 13 is the most important of all. For starters, each suit contains exactly 13 cards. Shown here is a fan of the 13 cards in the diamond suit: ace down to deuce.

13 Cards: Dealt (Unsorted) and Sorted

In bridge, each player is dealt a hand of 13 cards. Usually a player rearranges—or *sorts*—his or her 13-card hand into suits, alternating red and black. This makes it easy for the player to see all 13 cards at once. That way, the player knows how many cards he or she possesses of each suit, and makes it easy to find or select a card to play. It also makes it easier to count total high card points (see Chapter 4 for more on high card points). Of course, you are free to arrange your cards in any way you choose.

A dealt hand, unsorted.

The same hand, sorted.

There are also 13 *tricks* in a game of bridge. You'll learn about tricks in Chapter 2, "Basic Bridge."

FAQ

Should I always order my suits the same way in my hand?
No. It's good practice not to always sort your hand the same way each time. For instance, don't put one particular suit always on the left, or your longest suit always on the right. If your opponents know your sorting habits, they might even take advantage of it! Some players don't sort their cards at all. In this book, suit order changes with each new chapter. You should vary your suits more often than that, however!

There are right and wrong ways to hold your cards at bridge. Your basic concern is that only you see the cards that you hold. Don't let either opponent see your cards.

All players are holding their cards correctly at this table.

Because bridge is quite interesting, people like to watch it being played. Onlookers are called *kibitzers*, one of several terms in bridge's unique vocabulary.

Often a group of 5 or 6 can be involved in a game of bridge, although only four play actively at once. Anyone who's out can sit at a table corner and watch—or *kibitz*. Kibitzing can be a good way to learn about the game. As long as it's okay with all four players, anyone can be a bridge kibitzer.

Bridge even seems to have its own language. In fact, observing your first game, you may feel a bit confused and overwhelmed! Many familiar words like *open, jump, lead, make,* and *signal* have their own meanings in bridge, which you will learn in upcoming chapters of this book.

Meanwhile don't worry about memorizing vocabulary. As you learn and play bridge, its language will become quite familiar to you.

TIP

If you are kibitzing, watch only one player, and don't talk to or distract any player during the game.

2

Basic Bridge

In this chapter, you will be observing your first bridge hand. You will be a *kibitzer*, seeing what bridge players do. However, before that happens, you need to know a few more things about the game—you need to know about *tricks*, *trumps*, and *bids*.

The first dealer is decided by cutting the cards. The player who draws the highest card deals first and gets his or her choice of seat! After the first hand, each new deal moves to the player on the left.

Partners sit directly across from each other. It's standard bridge lingo to refer to the two partnerships directionally: *North* and *South* play against *East* and *West*.

To start a bridge hand, the dealer deals out the whole deck around the table, one card at a time. The first card goes to the player at the dealer's left. The deal then continues clockwise until it ends with the dealer getting the last card.

Once the cards have all been dealt, players pick up their hands of 13 cards, and sort them into suits.

TIP

Good bridge etiquette is to wait until all 13 cards are dealt before you pick them up!

Bridge is all about taking *tricks.* A trick consists of four cards, one card from each player's hand, played one at a time to the center of the table. The cards played to a trick may even touch each other in the center of the table.

Because each player has 13 cards to begin with, every bridge deal has 13 tricks to be played.

In every bridge deal, 13 tricks are played, to be won or lost, One of the 4 cards played to each trick counts as the high card, or the winner, of that trick. The game of bridge is all about how many tricks each side wins. To a newcomer, all those tricks played one after another may be remembered as not much more than one continuous blur of cards.

First trick

Last trick

TIP

At first, don't be surprised if you can't remember which cards have already been played. In fact, your memory of tricks played may be almost a total blank, like the cards on this page.

CONTINUED ON NEXT PAGE

HOW TO WIN A TRICK

Cards 10 and above are called *honor cards* in bridge. Deuces through nines are usually called *spot* cards or *small* cards.

Cards *rank* from the ace to the two, or *deuce*. The ace is the highest card in each suit, while the deuce is the lowest.

In general, a trick is won—or *taken*—by the highest card played of the suit that is led to start the trick.

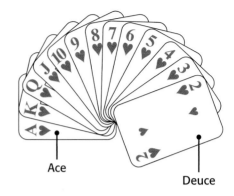

Ace

Deuce

SAMPLE TRICK 1

Let's look at a few tricks. In the figure, the highlighted card indicates the card that is led to begin the trick.

The trick shown starts with the West player, who begins it by leading the ♠5. The North hand then follows with the ♠J, East plays the ♠A, and South the ♠3.

The *East* player wins the trick with the ♠A and then gathers in all four cards, turning them over in a small pile. This face-down pile represents a taken trick.

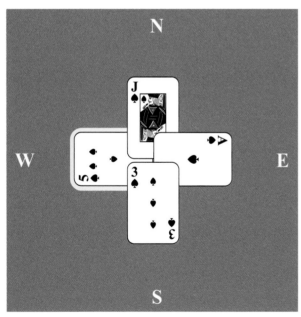

Highlight indicates card led.

Packet of 4 cards in a trick taken by East–West.

SAMPLE TRICK 2

In the next example of a trick, East leads the ♦10, South plays the ♦Q, West follows with the ♦K, and North completes the trick by playing the ♦2.

East reaches out again and gathers in the taken trick. Because East and West are a partnership, it's okay for either partner to gather in the tricks, even though in the second trick example, the high card on the trick was West's ♦K.

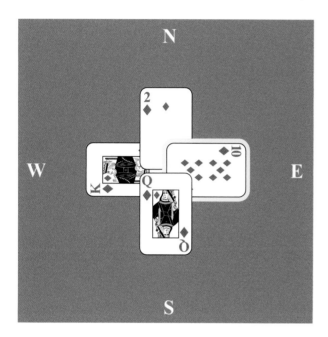

Following Suit and the Power of Trumps

An essential rule of bridge is that each player must *follow suit*. Following suit on a trick means that, if possible, every player plays a card of the same suit as the card that began the trick. In the two tricks illustrated so far, everybody has followed suit.

Trump Suit

When you do not hold a card of the suit that was led, however, you may play any card you choose. This may allow you a special privilege. In bridge—as in a number of card games—one suit becomes identified as the *trump* suit (or *trumps*), reigning supreme over all other suits.

The chosen trump suit is decided by the players, deal by deal, as the result of an *auction*, which begins after everyone picks up their cards. You will learn more about auctions in the next few pages.

TRUMPS TAKE TRICKS

A card in the trump suit played on a trick wins the trick, unless there's a *higher* trump card on that same trick.

For the purposes of this example, let's say that clubs are *trump*. West leads the ♠K, North follows with the ♠2, East plays the ♠7, and South, who has no more spades, *trumps* with the ♣4.

Because clubs are trump, South's ♣4 captures the trick. South gathers up the four cards of the trick into a small face-down pile.

Note: *South was not required to play a club on the trick, but playing the trump card won the trick. If South had instead discarded—by playing a diamond or heart—West's ♠K would win the trick instead.*

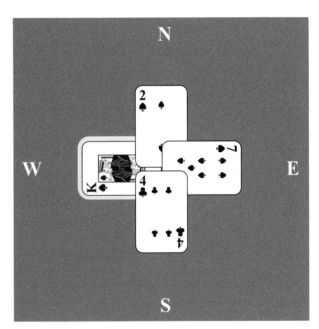

TRICKS AND TRUMPS: TWO MORE EXAMPLE TRICKS

Spades are trump in this example. North leads the ♥8, East plays the ♥K, South trumps with the ♠8, and West overtrumps with the ♠10 (to overtrump is to trump with a higher trump than any already played on a trick). West wins the trick.

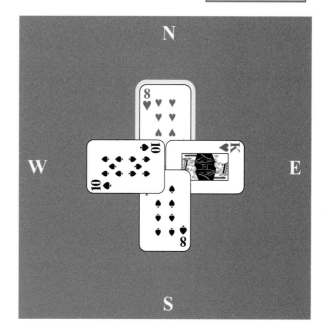

Here's an example where hearts are trump. West leads the ♣3, and North follows by playing the ♣9. East trumps with the ♥6, and South discards the ♦10. East's trump card, the ♥6, wins the trick. Note that South's ♦10, though higher in rank than a nine or a six, cannot win the trick because it is not a trump.

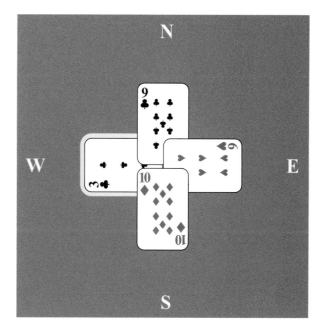

The Auction and the Meaning of Bids

Before the play of 13 tricks begins, the players conduct an *auction* to determine which suit, if any, will be the trump suit. The purpose of the auction is to reach a final contract, the highest bid any player is willing to make.

Starting with the dealer, each player in turn takes part in the auction either by making a bid, or by declining to make a bid. To make a bid, you say a number from one to seven, followed either by the name of a suit—clubs, diamonds, hearts, or spades—or by the words "No trump." If you don't make a bid, you can just say "Pass."

Two other words can also occur in the auction, *double* and *redouble*. Don't worry about them at all, right now. You'll meet up with them later.

Beginning with whist, the basic goal of games in the bridge family is to win more tricks than the other side wins. Because a bridge deal consists of 13 tricks, you and your partner need to win at least *seven* tricks to win more tricks than the other side wins.

In the auction, the first *six* tricks needed are "understood" (see chart) and may be referred to as a *book*. For example, a bid in the auction of "one"—1♣, 1♦, 1♥, 1♠, or 1NT (1 no trump) means a promise to win the first six tricks plus *one* more trick—that is, a total of seven of the 13 tricks.

First six tricks "understood" in the bidding

1♣	1♦	1♥	1♠	1NT
2♣	2♦	2♥	2♠	2NT
3♣	3♦	3♥	3♠	3NT
4♣	4♦	4♥	4♠	4NT
5♣	5♦	5♥	5♠	5NT
6♣	6♦	6♥	6♠	6NT
7♣	7♦	7♥	7♠	7NT

Chart of bridge bids translates each side's desires to win between 7 and 13 tricks.

FACT

Bridge *bids* are written with the *number* first, followed by the suit-sign (or NT). Examples: 6♦ (six diamonds), 2NT (two notrump). Bridge *cards* are instead designated by *suit-sign* first, followed by the number (or letter). Examples: ♦6 (diamond six, or six of diamonds), ♠A (ace of spades, or spade ace).

Another way to view it is that any bid at the *1* level translates to a *contract* to win seven tricks at least. Similarly, a bid at the *2* level is a promise or a contract to take at least eight tricks. A bid at the *5* level seeks to win 11 out of 13 tricks. A bid at the highest level—a bid of 7♣, 7♦, 7♥, 7♠, or 7NT—is a commitment that your side take all 13 tricks! The diagrams below show tricks taken by the bidding, or declaring, side. In each case, the vertical stack at the left contains 6 tricks already gathered in, or "book."

Seven tricks.
Book (6 tricks) + 1 trick.
Fulfills a 1-level contract.

Eight tricks.
Book + 2 tricks.
Fulfills a 2-level contract.

Eleven tricks.
Book + 5 tricks.
Fulfills a 5-level contract.

Thirteen tricks.
Book + 7 tricks.
Fulfills a 7-level contract.

Bidding Higher in the Auction

In the auction, every bid after the first must be a *higher bid* than the bid preceding it. Look over the bid chart and notice that it starts at the lowest possible *bid*, 1♣, and ends with the highest possible bid, 7NT (7 notrump).

RANK OF SUITS IN THE BIDDING

Use the chart as a reference. Once a bid is made you can make any bid to the right on the *same* level—ending with NT— or you can make *any* bid at *any* higher level.

At each level of bidding, *clubs* is the lowest-ranking suit, followed by diamonds, hearts, and spades. This means that a bid of 1♣ can be outbid by any other suit at the one-level: 1♦ is a higher bid than 1♣, 1♥ is higher than 1♦, and 1♠ outbids 1♥.

TIP

> Knowing the order of suits should soon be automatic, but for a key to remembering their order, try *Clam Diggers Hear Splashes, Clean Dishes Have Sparkle,* or *Climb Down Here Soon* for Clubs-Diamonds-Hearts-Spades. Or just make up your own mnemonic!

1♣	1♦	1♥	1♠	1NT
2♣	2♦	2♥	2♠	2NT
3♣	3♦	3♥	3♠	3NT
4♣	4♦	4♥	4♠	4NT
5♣	5♦	5♥	5♠	5NT
6♣	6♦	6♥	6♠	6NT
7♣	7♦	7♥	7♠	7NT

To make a higher bid in a lower-ranking suit, you must bid at a higher level. Compare these two auctions:

West	North	East	South
1♥	pass	1♣	

Wrong

West	North	East	South
1♥	pass	2♣	

Right

A bid of 1NT is higher than a bid of 1♣, 1♦, 1♥, or 1♠. Indeed, at every level, a bid of notrump outbids any suit bid. For example, 3NT *outbids* 3♥. At any bidding level, a bid in notrump is higher than a bid of a suit at the same level.

West	North	East	South
1♥	1NT		

North's bid of 1NT is the highest bid at the 1 level, equivalent to a contract to win 7 of 13 tricks. Any further bids must be at the 2 level or higher, where 8 or more tricks must be taken to fulfill the contract.

By the way, *notrump* means just what it suggests: that no suit is trump over another suit. In a notrump contract, only a card in the suit that is *led* to a trick can win the trick. No card in one suit can take a trick that is started by a card in another suit.

Once the bidding starts, it doesn't end until three players pass consecutively. The last bid made becomes the final contract. The final contract establishes which suit is trump, if any, and tells how many tricks the declaring side must take in order to *fulfill* the contract.

EXAMPLES OF COMPLETED AUCTIONS AND FINAL CONTRACTS

The dealer begins the auction by bidding or passing. Once somebody has bid, three consecutive passes end the auction and the last bid becomes the final contract. (See the examples below.)

In Auction A, West's 2♠ bid becomes the final contract. West needs to make eight tricks, with spades as the trump suit for the entire hand.

Auction A			
East	*South*	*West*	*North*
pass	1NT	2♠	pass
pass	pass		

In Auction B, South's 3♥ bid becomes the final contract. North–South must win 9 tricks for the contract to succeed.

Auction B			
South	*West*	*North*	*East*
1♥	1♠	2♥	2♠
3♥	pass	pass	pass

In Auction C, each player passes on the first round. The cards are thrown in, and North deals the next hand.

Auction C			
West	*North*	*East*	*South*
pass	pass	pass	pass

West's bid of 3NT ends a long auction, as 3 passes follow it. East–West have contracted to make 9 tricks with no suit as a trump suit. Note, also, that it is quite all right to bid after passing first, as both East and South have done. You may also skip levels as West has done.

Auction D			
North	*East*	*South*	*West*
pass	pass	pass	1♣
pass	1♦	1♥	1♠
pass	1NT	pass	3NT
pass	pass	pass	

Reminder: *The words double and redouble can also be part of the auction, but you will learn their meaning later in this book.*

Now it's time to kibitz your first deal to find out what bridge players do when they bid and play a hand.

You sit down next to the player sitting in the South seat, whose sorted hand you can see. East is the dealer, and so East is the first to bid in the auction. East can either pass or make the *opening*, or first, bid.

East commences the auction, and you hear him open the bidding by saying "Two diamonds." South (whom you are watching) says "Two spades." West says "Pass." North (South's partner) calls "Three spades."

Now it's East's turn again, and East says "Pass." Once again it is South's call again, and this time South bids "Four spades." After this, West, North, and East each say "Pass."

With these three passes, the auction ends. A *final contract* of 4♠ (four spades) has been reached. This means that North–South are seeking to win ten tricks, with spades as the trump suit.

The South player's hand.

To review the bidding, East dealt, and the auction went like this (see auction at right):

With the bidding completed, it's time for the play of the hand to get underway!

East (D)	South	West	North
2♦	2♠	pass	3♠
pass	4♠	pass	pass
pass			

THE PLAY OF THE FIRST TRICK: LAYING DOWN THE DUMMY

West, sitting at South's left, begins the first trick of the hand by playing the ♦A, placing it toward the center of the table.

North, you are surprised to see, now places her entire hand of 13 cards on the table! First North puts down spades, which are trumps. Next, North places a red suit, diamonds, then clubs, and then the other red suit, hearts. Each suit has been put down in a column headed by the highest card it contains. South now says to North, "Thank you, partner."

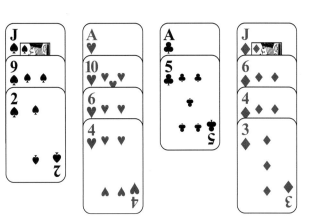

Everybody can see the 13-card hand that North has face up on the table. This hand, which remains on the table, is called the *dummy*. (It can also be referred to simply as the *table* or the *board*.)

South reaches across the table and plays the ♦3 from dummy, following suit to the card led on opening lead, the ♦A. South may well actually touch that card to the ♦A to make clear that it is the card South has selected from dummy to play on the trick.

Note: *South, who controls play of both his hand and dummy's hand, is called the declarer. On each trick, the declarer—and only the declarer—picks the card to be played from the dummy. The player who originally held the dummy hand no longer has any say in choosing which card to play from it.*

To complete the trick, East plays the ♦10 and South the ♦8.

The ♦A, played by West, wins the trick. That player gathers in the four cards played, turns them over into a single packet, face down.

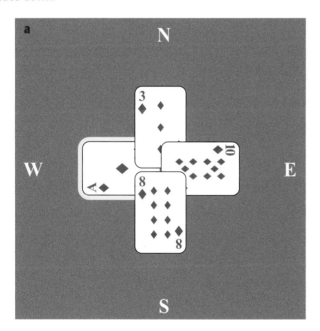

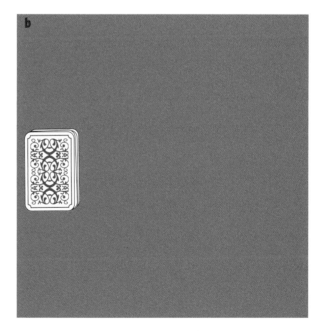

CONTINUED ON NEXT PAGE

A LOOK AT THE ENTIRE DEAL

For this first hand, you'll get a special privilege. You'll have a view of all four hands at once, as if you were kibitzing all four players together!

Note: *You will not often get a privilege like this. A kibitzer is usually only allowed to look at one player's hand.*

You will remember that East, the dealer, opened the bidding with 2♦. South next bid 2♠, and West passed. North *raised* her partner's bid to 3♠. East then passed, South bid 4♠, and the next three players each passed.

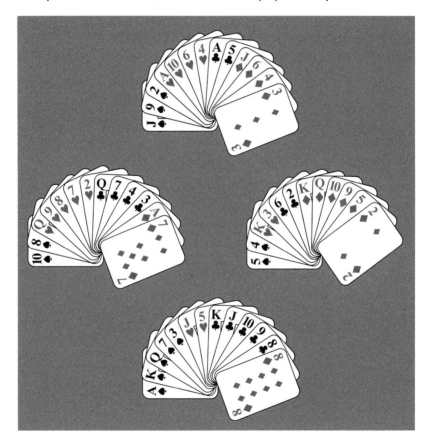

WATCHING THE NEXT FEW TRICKS

West has taken the first trick, and so now leads to the second trick, playing the ♦7 toward the center of the table. South plays the ♦4 from dummy (the North hand), East plays the ♦9, and South trumps with the ♠3. "No diamonds, partner?" asks North, the dummy. "That's right," says South, "No diamonds."

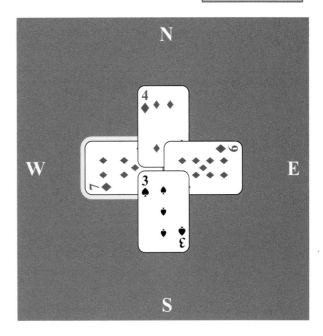

South, having won the second trick, gathers it in and leads the ♠7 to the third trick. West follows with the ♠8, South plays the ♠J from dummy (North), and this card wins the trick as East follows with ♠4.

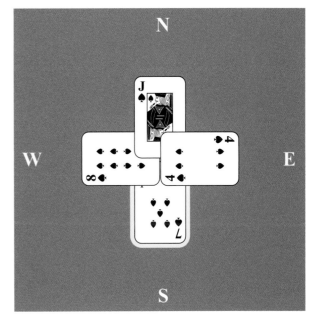

CONTINUED ON NEXT PAGE

South now leads the ♠2 from dummy to the next trick, East plays the ♠5, South puts in the ♠K, and West plays the ♠10. South wins this trick and, to the next trick, he leads the ♠A. West—having no more spades—discards the ♥2, and the North and East hands each then follow with their final spade card.

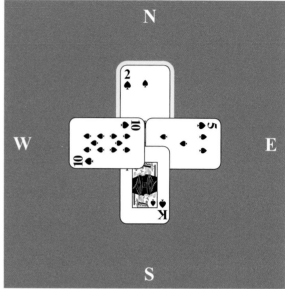

TRICKS SIX THROUGH NINE

The first five tricks have been played, with North–South winning four tricks, and East–West winning one. Each hand now has eight cards remaining. Having won the previous trick, South, the declarer, is now "on lead." South decides to lead the ♣8 to begin the next trick, West follows with a low club, and dummy's ♣A wins the trick, with East following with the deuce of clubs (♣2).

South now plays the last club from dummy, and when East follows with the ♣6, South plays the ♣J, which loses to West's ♣Q. West leads the ♥7 to the next trick. South plays low from dummy, and East plays the ♥K, winning the trick. East now leads the ♦K, and South trumps with the ♠Q, as West discards a heart and South follows suit from dummy's hand with the ♦6.

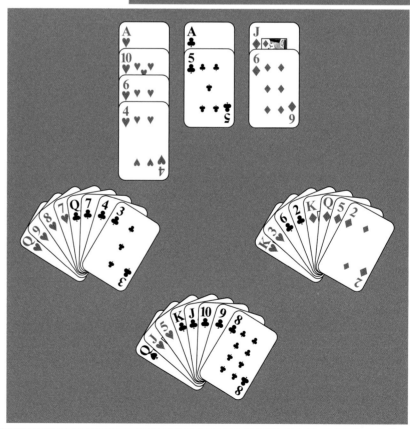

TRICKS TEN THROUGH THIRTEEN

Now each player has four cards left.

South is on lead, and wins the next three tricks with the ♣K, ♣10, and ♣9. East–West, who have no more trumps (their trumps were removed by tricks played earlier), have no way to capture these three club tricks. For the thirteenth and final trick, South has the ♥J remaining in hand, which is won by dummy's ♥A, saved, of course, for the last trick.

South has taken ten out of 13 tricks, and has made his contract of 4♠—a ten-trick contract. East and West have taken only three of the 13 tricks.

"Well played, partner. We made game," says North, jotting down a number on a score sheet.

And as you sit in silent admiration, South writes down the number 120, on a scoresheet. (This is a bridge *score*, something you'll learn a lot more about when you turn to the next chapter.)

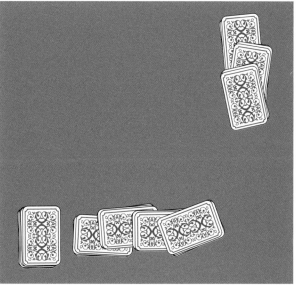

INDIVIDUAL SCORES					
WE	THEY	WE	THEY	WE	THEY
✕		✕		✕	
120					

It's not unusual for bridge players to talk about a hand just completed. So, let's look at the same hand again. This time, you'll view it the way a bridge deal typically appears in print. The experience may seem like an instant replay in sports!

East opens the auction with a surprising bid of 2♦—a contract that would require winning eight tricks for success. South then bids 2♠. West passes and North raises to 3♠. After East passes, South bids 4♠. After 3 more passes, that bid becomes the final contract .

This has been the bidding:

East	South	West	North
2♦	2♠	pass	3♠
pass	4♠	pass	pass
pass			

West makes the opening lead of the ♦A, and continues at the next trick by leading his remaining diamond, the seven. South trumps East's ♦9 with the ♠3. Next, South leads his ♠7—won by dummy's jack—and then follows with two more rounds of spades, with West discarding the ♥2 on the third spade trick.

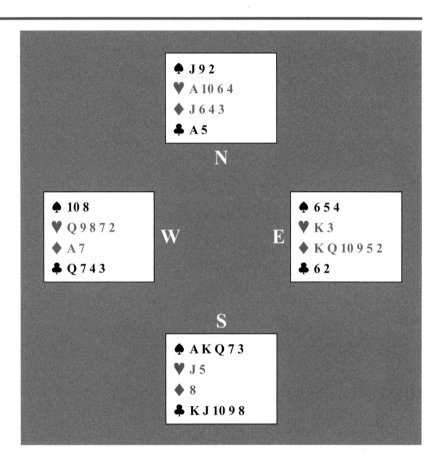

N
♠ J 9 2
♥ A 10 6 4
♦ J 6 4 3
♣ A 5

W
♠ 10 8
♥ Q 9 8 7 2
♦ A 7
♣ Q 7 4 3

E
♠ 6 5 4
♥ K 3
♦ K Q 10 9 5 2
♣ 6 2

S
♠ A K Q 7 3
♥ J 5
♦ 8
♣ K J 10 9 8

TIP

To help follow the play of a bridge hand in a book, or in a newspaper, get a deck of cards and deal them out just as shown. Then, as tricks are played, simply remove the cards played.

At this point, five tricks have been played and these cards remain: South, the declarer, now leads the ♣8 to dummy's ♣A, winning the trick in dummy. South then plays dummy's last club, and puts in the ♣J when East follows with the ♣6. West wins with the Q♣ and returns the ♥7, won by East's ♥K after dummy plays low.

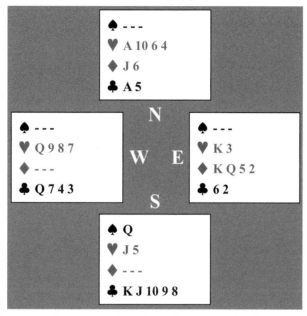

Now five cards are left for each player. East leads with the ♦K. South trumps with the ♠Q, and then wins three clubs tricks, saving dummy's ♥A to take the final trick. The defense has taken three tricks: the ♦A, ♣Q, and ♥K. Declarer has captured the other ten tricks, and has made his 4♠ contract.

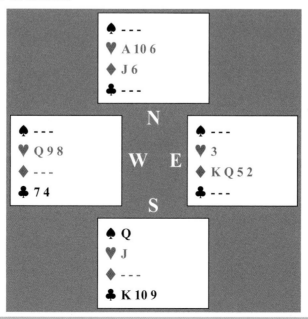

Rubber Bridge Playing and Scoring

A key element of bridge is the score your side or your opponents' side records after the play of a hand ends. Although complicated, bridge scoring is something you need to know. But, you don't have to memorize all its details. In fact, most of the bridge decks for sale toss in an extra card with a compact scoring guide on it!

The score for any bridge hand depends on how many tricks the declaring side takes in the play of the hand. This chapter will show you how to compute the scores both for successful contracts (those that the declarer makes) as well as for unsuccessful, or *defeated*, contracts.

You will find out what a trick is worth, what it means to earn a *game*, and how to win a *rubber*. You will also learn how to enter the scores correctly on a score sheet.

A rubber bridge *score sheet*, used by bridge players at home, is basically just two columns on a piece of paper. You can buy pads of bridge score sheets at many stationery stores, but a pencil and an ordinary sheet of paper can do. The score sheet is where you record points scored for contracts that declarer makes, as well as points scored by the other side for contracts declarer *doesn't* make. Calculating that score usually requires just a little easy multiplying and adding.

After all 13 tricks of a hand have been played, and the outcome agreed upon, it's time to enter an appropriate point score on the score sheet. As you remember from Chapter 1, each score sheet is typically divided into columns marked alternately WE and THEY. Each pair of such columns counts as a rubber. The score sheet might have just one pair of columns, or—more commonly—it has two or three.

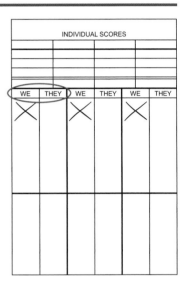

Whenever your side wins points on the hand, you write a score under the left column, headed WE. Of course, if your opponents earn the score, then write it in the right-hand or THEY column.

The object is to score enough points to earn a game. The first side to score *two* games wins the rubber. A rubber can be completed in two deals, or it may take many.

Note: *The word* **rubber** *is an ancient gaming term, the first recorded use of which (around the year 1600) was for the English lawn game of bowls. A rubber means a short series of games, usually 3. Whichever side wins the majority of games wins the rubber. As early as 1749, players of whist (see Chapter 1) scored in rubbers. The term is also nowadays routinely used in baseball, where teams mostly play 3-game series. If each team has won one game, the third and series-deciding game is called the rubber game.*

THE PARTS OF THE SCORE SHEET

Before learning how to figure the scores, it helps to understand the different areas of the score sheet. (You've already learned in which column your side's scores belong.)

- **The Line.** The horizontal line at mid-score sheet is very significant to the scoring. Quite appropriately, this line is called the *line*.

- **Below the Line.** When a contract succeeds, a *trick score* goes below the line for the successful declaring side. Points for tricks bid and made are the only points that go *below the line*.

- **Above the Line.** All other scores go *above the line*. These include points earned for defeating contracts (*undertricks*), points for taking tricks beyond your contract (*overtricks*), as well as a variety of bonus and other scores. You'll be meeting the complexity of bridge scoring in the pages directly ahead.

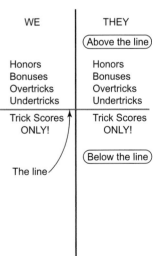

The score for making a contract varies from contract to contract. A particular score will depend both on the number of tricks bid for as well as whether the contract was in clubs, diamonds, hearts, spades, or notrump.

MINOR SUIT CONTRACTS

In bridge, clubs and diamonds are the two *minor* suits. If your side succeeds at a club or diamond contract, you receive 20 points below the line for each trick bid. (Remember that no score is given for the first six tricks taken! Those first six tricks are considered *understood* in the meaning of a bid, as you saw in Chapter 2).

Example: Your side wins the auction at 3♣, and takes nine tricks at that contract, making the contract exactly. As a result, for making the three tricks you bid for (beyond the first six that are *understood*) your score is $3 \times 20 = 60$ points. Write that number *below* the line, in your column of the pad.

INDIVIDUAL SCORES					
WE	THEY	WE	THEY	WE	THEY
60					

MAJOR SUIT CONTRACTS

Hearts and spades are the *major* suits. Rather than 20 points, if the final contract is hearts or spades, you receive 30 points for each trick bid and made. Here are some examples. In both cases, these points are written below the line.

INDIVIDUAL SCORES					
WE	THEY	WE	THEY	WE	THEY
90					

For bidding 3♥, and taking exactly nine tricks, you score $3 \times 30 = 90$ points.

INDIVIDUAL SCORES					
WE	THEY	WE	THEY	WE	THEY
120					

For bidding 4♠, and taking exactly ten tricks, the score is $4 \times 30 = 120$ points.

Trick-Scores at Notrump Contracts

When you succeed at a notrump (NT) contract, trick scoring is a little more complicated. The first trick counts 40 points, and then each additional trick counts 30 points. You can find a useful scoring chart at the end of this chapter.

This page shows trick-score points entered on the scoresheet for contracts of 1NT, 2NT, 3NT, and 6NT.

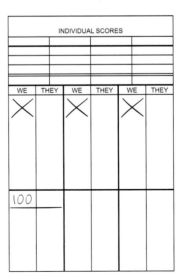

	INDIVIDUAL SCORES				
WE	THEY	WE	THEY	WE	THEY
✕		✕		✕	
40					

A 1NT contract, bid and made, scores 40 points.

	INDIVIDUAL SCORES				
WE	THEY	WE	THEY	WE	THEY
✕		✕		✕	
70					

A 2NT contract, bid and made, scores 40 + 30 = 70 points.

Note that when 100 or more points are scored, you draw another line underneath.

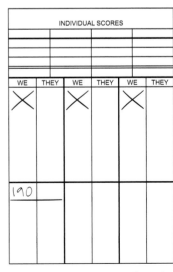

	INDIVIDUAL SCORES				
WE	THEY	WE	THEY	WE	THEY
✕		✕		✕	
100					

A 3NT contract, bid and made, scores 40 + 30 + 30 = 100 points.

	INDIVIDUAL SCORES				
WE	THEY	WE	THEY	WE	THEY
✕		✕		✕	
190					

A 6NT contract, bid and made, scores 40 + 30 + 30 + 30 + 30 + 30 = 190 points.

EARNING GAME

100 points earned in trick-scores equals one *game*. A partnership can do this in a single deal, with a bid of 3NT (40 + 30 + 30 = 100), 4♥ or 4♠ (4 × 30 = 120), or 5♣ or 5♦ (5 × 20 = 100).

Remember, in rubber bridge, the goal is to win two games before your opponents do. Whenever you total 100 points below the line, this counts as one *game*.

Here are some important scoring terms:

- **Part-score contracts.** A contract whose trick-score is less than 100 points is called a *part-score.* Two or more successful part-scores can be combined to attain the 100 points needed for game.

- **Game contracts.** A contract whose trick-score is 100 points or more is called a *game contract.* Examples of game contracts are 3NT (100 points), 4♥ or 4♠ (120 points), and 5♣ or 5♦ (100 points).

  You can also make game by combining trick-score points earned for 2 or more successful lower-level contracts.

- **Slam contracts.** A contract at the 6 level is called a *small slam* (or little slam). A contract at the 7 level is called a *grand slam*. In addition to providing enough points to earn a game, either successful slam bid earns a large extra bonus (see under Slam Scoring, later in this chapter).

- **Vulnerability.** When a side has earned one game towards winning the rubber, it is said to be *vulnerable*. A side which has not earned a game is *not vulnerable*.

  The line drawn under a game score is an indicator of vulnerability. You can see examples of this line on the previous and following pages.

Note: Vulnerability is an important concept in bridge, because—as you'll soon see--some scores change depending on whether your side is vulnerable, or not vulnerable!

The word **slam,** for winning *all* the tricks on a deal, goes back about 400 years ago to the ancient game of *ruffe & honours*. The concept of making a small slam (just 12 of 13 tricks) derives from the days of *bridge whist*.

CONTINUED ON NEXT PAGE

PART-SCORE AND GAME CONTRACT EXAMPLES

On the first deal, North–South bid and make 2♣ for a score of 40 points below the line (20 × 2, the number of tricks bid). As a result, North–South have earned a 40-point *part-score* towards game (100 points).

On the second deal, North–South bid and make 2NT for a score of 70 (40 for the first trick at NT, plus 30 for the next trick). Because the two scores combine to add up to 110, North–South have earned enough to score a *game* by way of two part-score contracts.

To show that a game has been earned, draw a line across both columns beneath these two part-score contracts.

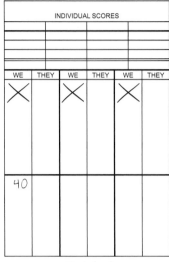

First deal

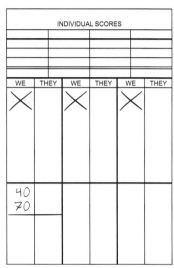

Second deal

On the third deal, East–West bid and make 4♥, worth 4 × 30 = 120 points. Write 120 on the THEY side of the score sheet, below the line drawn earlier. Then mark another line beneath the 120 score, which again signifies a game score earned.

Having each tallied a game, both sides now are vulnerable. Whoever wins the next game wins the rubber!

TIP

If one side has a part-score, and the other side then earns a game, the line drawn across both columns also "wipes out" the first side's part-score. The points earned for that part-score may no longer be combined with further part scores to reach the 100 points for game.

Third deal

Overtricks are any extra tricks your side takes beyond those needed to make your contract. Each overtrick is worth a small additional score. In a minor suit (clubs or diamonds), the value is 20 points per trick, and in a major suit (hearts or spades)—or at notrump—30 points per trick.

On the score sheet, put overtrick points *above the line*. Points scored in overtricks do NOT count towards the 100 needed for *game*.

EXAMPLES OF OVERTRICK SCORES

Example 1: North–South make a 3♦ contract with 2 overtricks, a total of 11 tricks taken. This scores 60 *below the line* and 40 *above the line*. You can also refer to the result as 3♦ *making five.*

Example 2: East–West are in 1NT *making four*—that is, making the contract plus 3 overtricks—a total of ten tricks taken. This scores 40 below the line and 90 above the line.

	INDIVIDUAL SCORES				
WE	THEY	WE	THEY	WE	THEY
✕		✕		✕	
40					
60					

3♦ making 5.

	INDIVIDUAL SCORES				
WE	THEY	WE	THEY	WE	THEY
✕		✕		✕	
90					
40					

1NT making 4.

BONUS FOR WINNING THE RUBBER

The side that first scores two games *wins the rubber* and earns a large bonus score. When the rubber is won two games to one, that bonus score is 500 points. When the rubber is won two games to none, the rubber bonus score rises to 700 points.

In the graphic to the right, the THEY side wins the rubber 2 games to none, and earns a 700 point bonus. THEY win a rubber adding to a total of 920 points.

	INDIVIDUAL SCORES				
WE	THEY	WE	THEY	WE	THEY
✕		✕		✕	
	700				
	120				
	100				

When declarer doesn't win enough tricks to fulfill a contract, that contract has failed. The other side—the defenders—earn a score, written *above* the line. Each trick by which declarer falls short of his contract is called an *undertrick*. Defenders score points for each undertrick. Such scores, going above the line, *cannot* count towards the 100 needed for game.

FIGURING THE SCORE FOR UNDERTRICKS

When calculating the score for setting (defeating) a contract, it does NOT at all matter whether the hand was played in clubs, diamonds, hearts, spades, or notrump! Also, the *level* of the defeated bid does not matter. Instead, the penalty you collect for setting the opponents' contract depends upon these three factors:

- **Number of undertricks:** By how many tricks did the contract fail?
- **Vulnerability:** Was the declaring side vulnerable, or not vulnerable?
- **Doubling:** Was the final contract doubled, or—possibly--redoubled?

WHAT IS DOUBLING (AND REDOUBLING)?

The last factor in the above list brings up a very important concept in bridge: *doubling*. The idea of one side doubling the other goes back to the whist era, and refers to doubling the amount of money at stake for the deal. At whist, the object was simply to take more tricks than the other side took. If one side declared that they would take the majority, either player on the other side could then *double* the stakes, feeling that *their* side would instead capture the trick majority. The declaring side naturally then had the right to double the stakes again, to re-double.

In bridge today, each player is permitted a similar privilege during the auction, merely by saying the word "double" following an opponent's bid. On occasion the final contract will be one that has been *doubled*. This means the amount of points at stake will be increased, though no longer exactly just doubled. Every once in a while the declaring side will *redouble* a doubled contract. The redouble does basically indeed multiply the score by 2 a last time.

Note: Right now, don't worry about the ins and outs of doubling and redoubling. Just be aware that it's an important factor in the scoring, and useful to know about. You can always return later to this chapter to re-study the scoring details included!

BASIC UNDERTRICK SCORES

When calculating the undertrick score, it does not matter whether the contract has been played at a minor suit, at a major suit, or at notrump. It is the number of tricks by which the contract is defeated that determines the score. The basic undertrick score is 50 points per undertrick when the defeated side is *not vulnerable*, and 100 points per trick when it is *vulnerable*. Example: 3NT vulnerable, down one, scores 100 points above the line for the defenders. 2♥ down three not vulnerable is worth 150 points above the line for the defenders.

DOUBLED AND REDOUBLED UNDERTRICKS

When the final contract is doubled or redoubled, undertricks increase in score. Here's how to figure their worth. For the first undertrick, doubling simply doubles the penalty score earned. For each extra undertrick, the increase in point score is more than twice as much!

If the declaring side is vulnerable, all extra doubled undertricks after the first one count 300 points! Not vulnerable, the second and third doubled undertricks cost 200 points each, with every further undertrick worth 300 points! Should the contract be redoubled, simply multiply the doubled undertrick penalties by two.

Refer to the chart for finding doubled and redoubled undertrick scores.

Scores for Setting Doubled and Redoubled Contracts						
	NOT VULNERABLE			**VULNERABLE**		
Tricks Set	**Undoubled**	**Doubled**	**Redoubled**	**Undoubled**	**Doubled**	**Redoubled**
1	50	100	200	100	200	400
2	100	300	600	200	500	1000
3	150	500	1000	300	800	1600
4	200	800	1600	400	1100	2200
5	250	1100	2200	500	1400	2800
6	300	1400	2800	600	1700	3400

As you can see, some of the biggest scores come from doubling the opponents and setting them, especially if they are vulnerable!

Making Doubled and Redoubled Contracts

The most complicated bridge scoring comes when a doubled or redoubled contract is made. Even experienced bridge players sometimes take extra time to figure out the correct score. You needn't concern yourself about remembering all the possible bridge scores that can occur; instead, you can learn these scoring details as you get real playing experience. In case you are interested now, however, here is how to compute scores for doubled and redoubled contracts.

- For starters, doubling (or redoubling) a final contract doubles (or redoubles) the basic trick-score for tricks bid when the contract is made (succeeds). As trick-scores, enter them *below* the line for the declaring side. These will vary for minor suits, major suits, and notrump.

- After that, in case you make extra tricks beyond your contract, doubled overtricks are worth 100 points each if not vulnerable, and 200 points each if vulnerable. Redoubled overtricks count 200 points each if not vulnerable, and 400 points each if vulnerable. (These points score above the line.) When computing doubled or redoubled overtricks, suit or NT is irrelevant.

- Finally, you receive an additional 50-point bonus for making a doubled contract, or a 100-point bonus for making a redoubled contract. These small bonuses also go above the line.

Example: Your opponents, who are vulnerable, bid 4♠, you double and they redouble. Your opponents make 11 tricks at 4♠ redoubled—their contract plus one overtrick. They score 480 points in trick-score (120 × 4, entered below the line), 400 points for the redoubled vulnerable overtrick (entered above the line), and 100 more points for making a doubled contract, also entered above the line. Of course, your opponents also win the rubber bonus of 500 or 700 points.

Making 4♠ redoubled, with an overtrick, vulnerable.

Below the line: 4 (tricks bid) × 30 (per trick in a major) × 4 (doubled and redoubled) = 480

Above the line: 400 (1 redoubled overtrick) + 100 (bonus for making a redoubled contract) + 500 or 700 (bonus for winning the rubber).

TIP

The threat of a doubled contract then being redoubled increases the risk of doubling a contract that you only hope to set. When you double a contract without having enough tricks to beat it, the opponents can *redouble* and increase their score greatly for making the contract.

As stated previously in this chapter one side is occasionally able to take 12 tricks, or even all 13 tricks. When your side bids *and* makes a 12-trick contract (any bid at the 6 level), you have made a *small slam*. When your side bids all the way to the 7 level *and* wins all of the tricks, you make a *grand slam*.

Each of these high-level bids earns a big bonus, scored above the line. A *small slam* earns you a 500-point bonus if you are not vulnerable at the time of the bid, and a 750-point bonus if you are vulnerable. The grand slam bonus is 1000 points when not vulnerable, and 1500 points if vulnerable.

Of course, a successful slam bid contains enough in trick-points (more than 100) to count as one of the two games needed to win the rubber.

INDIVIDUAL SCORES					
WE	THEY	WE	THEY	WE	THEY
✕		✕		✕	
1000					
140					

On the first deal, your side bids and makes 7♣—a Grand Slam! You score 140 below the line in trick-score, plus 1000 points above the line for the non-vulnerable grand slam bonus.

Honor Scores

Honor scores in rubber bridge can be traced back to bridge's ancestors: ruffe & honours, whist, bridge whist, and auction bridge (see Chapter 1), where a side scored points merely for the luck of being dealt a certain number of high cards, or *honors*, in the trump suit. (See also the discussion of honor cards in Chapter 2.) The scoring impact of honor scores in those games was much greater than it is in today's contract bridge, but it is still a part of the scoring.

Bonuses for Honors

Scoring for honors is primarily a reward for luck. If you are dealt the top *five* trumps—AKQJ10—you score 150 above the line. If you are dealt any *four* of the top five honors in the trump suit, you receive 100 points above the line. If you are dealt all *four* aces and the contract is played at notrump, you can claim a 150-point bonus. Any scores you earn for honors go above the line, and do not count towards the 100 points needed to earn a game.

Honor scores are tallied whether the contract has succeeded or not. Honor scoring is also not affected by whether or not a final contract has been doubled. And, either the declaring or the defending side may receive the premium, or bonus, for honors.

Note: *Honors divided between the partnership do not count—all honor combinations must be held in a single hand. Example: East has the AQ10 of trumps, and West the KJ. Since neither hand contains 4 or 5 of them, they receive no honor score.*

In order to get credit for honors, you must claim them before the next hand starts.

Five top trumps, all in one hand: 150

Four of five top trumps (clubs are trumps), all in one hand: 100

 TIP

Usually a player claims honors during a hand, as soon as their possession has become obvious to all of the players.

All four aces in one hand, in a NT contract: 150

When a rubber ends, you add up the points in each column. Whoever has more points wins the point difference. Traditionally, rubber bridge is played with something at stake. It could be a prize, but more often it's money. Rubber bridge can be played for any stakes that are agreed upon (usually the stakes are small).

In the rubber shown, the first game consisted of two part-score bids by the THEY side. WE then earned a 40-point part-score.

The second game was worth 120 points to THEY (no doubt it was 4♥ or 4♠). Along the way, the WE side scored a 100-point set, and the THEY side got credit for an overtrick worth 30 points. By winning the rubber two games to none, the THEY side got a 700-point bonus above the line.

INDIVIDUAL SCORES					
WE	THEY	WE	THEY	WE	THEY
✕		✕		✕	
	700				
100	30				
	90				
	60				
40	120				
140	1000				

Adding each column, THEY beat WE by 860 points. Playing for a penny a point, the THEY pair would be ahead by $8.60. However, if the stakes were higher, say $1 a point, THEY would be up $860 after just one rubber!

Usually more than one rubber is played. Assuming that the partnerships remain the same, the 860 score is *carried over* to the start of the next rubber as shown here.

Note: *In case play must end before the rubber is won, a pair that has scored one game gets a 300-point bonus to settle the scoring.*

INDIVIDUAL SCORES					
WE	THEY	WE	THEY	WE	THEY
✕		✕		✕	
	700		860		
100	30				
	90				
	60				
40	120				
140	1000				
	−140				
	860				

Chicago-Style Bridge Scoring

Because it can sometimes take many deals for one side to earn two games and end a rubber, many players favor Chicago-style bridge scoring, scored in groups of four deals.

A regular score sheet is used, but vulnerability is determined ahead of time for all four deals. On the first deal, neither side is vulnerable. On the second and third deals, the dealing side is vulnerable. On the fourth deal, both sides are vulnerable. As usual, the deal passes to the left with each new hand.

Game is still 100 points, and part-scores can be added together to make those 100 points. There's no bonus for winning a rubber though. Instead, you get an immediate 300-point bonus if you make a game when not vulnerable, and a 500-point bonus if you make a game when vulnerable. An X design at the top of the score helps keep track of the deal number.

You are vulnerable on the second deal of a bridge game scored Chicago-style. On the first deal, you made 2♥ with an overtrick. If you can add a small part-score to that on this deal, you will earn an immediate 500-pt. bonus for a vulnerable game.

In some versions of 4-Deal Bridge, part-scores do not carry ahead to the next deal, but instead merely get an immediate 50-point bonus, vulnerable or not.

The trick-score, for each trick bid and won, goes *below* the line.

	Undoubled	Doubled	Redoubled
♦ or ♣ (minor suits)	20	40	80
♠ or ♥ (major suits)	30	60	120
Notrump, first trick bid	40	80	160
Each additional trick bid	30	60	120

Overtrick Scores, Each Trick			
	Undoubled	Doubled	Redoubled
Not Vul	same as trick-score	100	200
Vul	same as trick-score	200	400

All other scores go above the line.

Bonuses		
	not Vulnerable	Vulnerable
Small Slam	500	750
Grand Slam	1000	1500
For making a doubled contract	50	
For making a redoubled contract	100	
For winning the rubber 2 games to 1	500	
For winning the rubber 2 games to 0	700	
For one game in an unfinished rubber	300	

For Defeated Contracts						
Number of Tricks Set	Undoubled		Doubled		Redoubled	
	nonVul	Vul	nonVul	Vul	nonVul	Vul
1	50	100	100	200	200	400
2	100	200	300	500	600	1000
3	150	300	500	800	1000	1600
4	200	400	800	1100	1600	2200
5	250	500	1100	1400	2200	2800
6	300	600	1400	1700	2800	3400
7	350	700	1700	2000	3400	4000
etc.						

Honor Scores	
Any 4 of 5 trump honors, all in one hand	100
5 trump honors, all in one hand	150
4 aces at a NT contract, all in one hand	150

4

Hand Evaluation and the Opening Bid

In bridge, every hand you pick up is unique. The laws of probability assure that, card for card, you'll never get dealt that exact hand again. It's up to you to decide what to do. Will you bid with this hand, or not? And if no one has bid yet, will you be the first one to bid?

In this chapter, you'll learn how to rate a bridge hand for bidding, mostly based on the high cards it contains. You'll also learn the key guidelines for making the first, or opening bid of the auction. For the moment, we'll consider just 1-level opening bids. Opening bids at higher levels will be dealt with in chapters 11 and 12.

You bid at bridge because you expect to win tricks after the play starts. With some hands, it will be pretty easy to see whether you will be winning tricks—or not winning them!

Because this hand has high cards in every suit, it is certain to take many tricks. Trick by trick you will likely play a higher card than the opponents can play. You anticipate bidding with this hand to a contract that would earn all the trick-points for game, such as 3NT or 4 of either major suit, hearts or spades.

Very, very good hand.

Conversely, with this hand it's likely that on no trick will a card of yours be the highest card of any suit led; however, if diamonds are trumps, your hand might actually win a trick or two! With this extremely weak hand, you should probably pass, and not bid in the auction.

Of course, your partner could have very good cards. Your partner may decide to bid. And your partner's cards could win tricks for your side during the play.

Very, very bad hand.

Although you *will* certainly get hands like these two, they are extreme examples. Most of the time, you'll have hands in between such extremes. Wouldn't it be great to have a way to judge just how good—or bad—any hand might be?

HAND EVALUATION IN BYGONE DAYS

Though you won't be using this method yourself, it's interesting to see how players first approached hand evaluation. In the early years of contract bridge, players rated their hands using an intelligent though primitive approach that primarily hinged upon the highest ranking cards, *honor cards* (aces and kings), the cards most likely to win tricks. These high cards were translated into units of *honor tricks*. An ace counted as one honor trick, and an ace and king of the same suit counted as two honor tricks.

A combination of king and queen together in a suit (second and third highest cards together) was also valued at one honor trick, since as soon as the ace in that suit was played to capture one of those two cards, the other was promoted to top card in the suit, a winner. An ace and queen in the same suit counted as 1½ honor tricks, and a king with any supporting card or cards was rated as ½ honor trick.

Seventy-five years ago, to make the first bid of the auction—the *opening* bid—the advice was that you needed an honor trick total of 2½ or more. Various further bids also were based on honor trick considerations

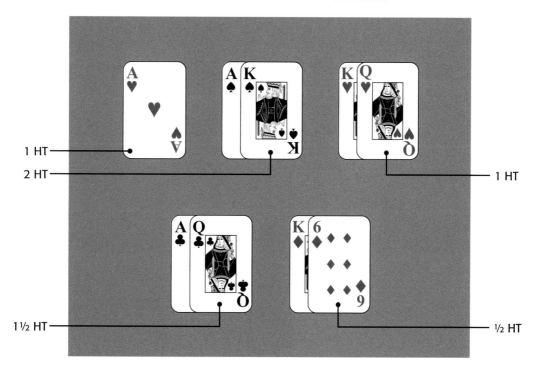

Other Honor Trick Combinations

AKQ 3 HT	KQJ 2 HT
AKJ 2½ HT	KQ10 1½ HT
AQJ 2 HT	KJ10 1 HT
AJ10 1½ HT	QJx ½ HT
	(x = any small card)

Counting High Card Points

These days, bridge players have found a better way to rate their hands than by the honor trick method described on the previous page. The *high card points* or point-count method is much more accurate than the old honor trick approach, and helps you get to better final contracts. Using very basic concepts, it's as easy as 1-2-3-4!

To understand evaluation by high card points (HCP), consider just the aces, kings, queens, and jacks of the pack. Value each ace in your hand at 4 HCP, each king at 3, each queen at 2, and each jack at 1. Since every suit contains one ace, king, queen, and jack, each suit has 10 total HCP (4 + 3 + 2 + 1).

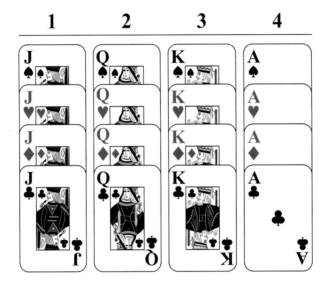

Because the entire deck has four suits, the deck contains 40 HCP; in other words, 10 HCP per suit, times 4. Much thinking in bridge revolves around high card points. They are certainly a key in bidding—in fact, totalling the high card points that you hold is your main bidding tool. HCP guidelines help you decide both *whether* to bid and *what* bid to make. A small but necessary chore, counting HCPs will soon become routine for you to do.

TIP

The numbers 4, 3, 2, and 1 are as vital to learning about bridge as they are to playing the game. You'll be counting and adding up these little numbers all the time. The better you can do it, the better player you will become!

Practice in Counting HCPs

If you want to play bridge well, you will need to add up your HCPs on *every* hand. Here are some hands for practice in counting and adding up HCPs. To check your math, the correct HCP total is listed underneath each hand.

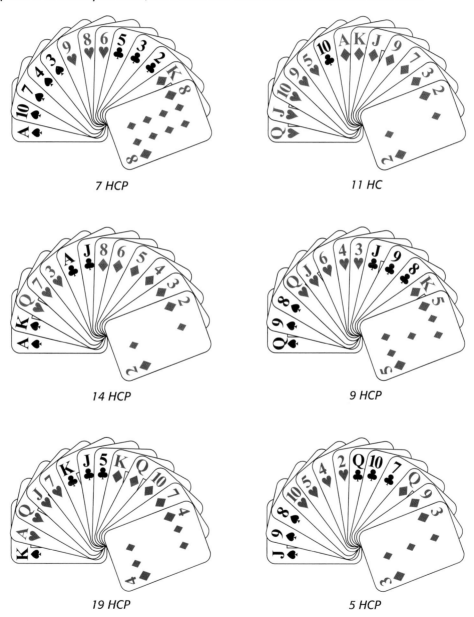

7 HCP

11 HC

14 HCP

9 HCP

19 HCP

5 HCP

The Importance of *Distribution*

In deciding whether or not to bid, you must first total up your HCPs. To select which suit to bid—or whether to bid notrump—you also need to look at the *shape* or *distribution* of your hand. The distribution of your hand is a summary of the number of cards you have in each suit.

TYPES OF DISTRIBUTION

Count the number of cards you have in each of the four suits. The breakdown into these four numbers—which add up to the 13 cards you have—gives you the *shape* or *distribution* of your hand. For example, 4-4-3-2 distribution means that you have a hand with four cards in one suit (any suit), four cards of another suit, three cards in a third suit, and two cards in the remaining suit.

FREQUENCY OF "BALANCED" DISTRIBUTIONS

The most common shape of a bridge hand is 4-4-3-2 distribution (with *any* 2 suits as the 4-card suits). You will be dealt a hand of that distribution 21.6 percent of the time. The second most likely shape is 5-3-3-2, which you will get 15.5 percent of the time. After that come hands with distributions of 5-4-3-1 and 5-4-2-2. Curiously, the most even or *balanced* distribution, 4-3-3-3, is only the fifth most likely. Hands with 6-card, 7-card, and even longer suits are quite possible, although less frequent.

5-4-3-1 distribution

4-3-3-3 distribution

SOME HANDY DISTRIBUTIONAL TERMS

- *Void:* No cards dealt in a suit
- *Singleton:* One card dealt in a suit
- *Doubleton:* Two cards dealt in a suit
- *Tripleton:* Three cards dealt in a suit
- *Freak Hand:* A hand with wild distribution; for example, 6-6-1-0, 7-5-1-0, 8-4-1-0

FACT

Every bridge hand has to have at least one suit at least four cards long.

DISTRIBUTION VS. HCP

To illustrate the influence of distribution, compare these two hands. Each has 10 HCP, the average point-count for a bridge hand. Let's assume spades are trump.

<table>
<tr><td align="center">*Hand A*</td><td align="center">*Hand B*</td></tr>
</table>

With Hand A, you might take one or two tricks—maybe even three. With Hand B, you would expect to win ten tricks—nine in spades and one more in hearts. Keep in mind that with the same hand, if diamonds or clubs were trump, this hand might not win any tricks at all!

Note: *Excellent distribution can make up for lack of high cards—if your side gets to choose the contract.*

JUDGING DISTRIBUTIONAL STRENGTH

Most hands with seven-card or longer suits have distributional value and should probably take part in the bidding. Unless you are extremely low in high card points, you should probably make a bid with such a hand as soon as you can. In addition, the following hand patterns can also be dynamic in terms of taking tricks—assuming that you are able to steer the auction to end at a favorable contract. The most dynamic hand-pattern is at the top of the first column.

EXCELLENT	GOOD	FAIR
6-6-1-0	6-4-2-1	5-4-3-1
6-5-2-0	6-3-3-1	5-4-2-2
6-5-1-1	5-5-3-0	4-4-4-1
6-4-3-0	5-5-2-1	
	5-4-4-0	

Relative value of distributional hand patterns (hands containing no 7-card or longer suit).

A hand with great shape can play a varying role in the auction. It's up to you to decide how and when you'll take part. Starting in this chapter, you'll learn the key guidelines for entering the auction.

Any hand with a nine-card suit is very rare, and a hand with 9-4-0-0 distribution is much rarer. You might play bridge your entire life and never be dealt a hand with that shape.

Opening 1-Level Bids: Function and Guidelines

Although the first player to bid in the auction can choose any bid, most auctions begin with a bid at the 1 level: 1♣, 1♦, 1♥, 1♠, or 1NT.

FUNCTION

An opening 1-level bid starts an auction that may go to a much higher level. Where it goes depends on what others at the table do when their turns in the auction come. Most of the time, the auction will advance to a higher-level contract.

A big benefit of the opening bid is that the opener's partner can begin to consider her and her partner's hands combined. It's okay to know the defining criteria of your partner's bid. In fact, it's recommended that partners play and bid according to a shared and agreed method. Chapter 5 focuses on the important the role played by the opening bidder's partner.

Note: *When the bidding starts at the 1 level (highlighted), plenty of higher bids remain.*

(First six tricks understood)

1♣	1♦	1♥	1♠	1NT
2♣	2♦	2♥	2♠	2NT
3♣	3♦	3♥	3♠	3NT
4♣	4♦	4♥	4♠	4NT
5♣	5♦	5♥	5♠	5NT
6♣	6♦	6♥	6♠	6NT
7♣	7♦	7♥	7♠	7NT

THE BETTER-THAN-AVERAGE HAND

An opening bid of 1-of-a-suit (1♣, 1♦, 1♥, or 1♠) should be based on a hand worth 13 to 21 HCP.

The minimum count for an opening bid, 13 HCP, is a hand that's about a king (3 HCP) better than an average hand (the 10 HCP that an A, K, Q, and J supply).

OPEN THE BIDDING WITH A BETTER-THAN-AVERAGE HAND

With a total of 40 HCP in the deck, the *average* hand has 10 HCP. The math is easy: 40 divided by four people is 10. To open the bidding with 1-of-a-suit, you should have a better than average hand. Because 13 is the recommended minimum count, you can think of it as about a king better than an average hand's 10 HCP (king = 3 HCP; see the previous figure). As a result, the minimum requirement of 13 HCP to open means a hand worth about a king more than an average hand.

With a hand of 12 or fewer HCP, you generally should pass, rather than open the bidding. Of course, if the hand has distributional strength, pass may not be your best call.

Usually you open the bidding in the longest suit in your hand.

The *top* amount of HCP for an opening bid is around 21 HCP. Very powerful hands with 22 or more HCP are opened at a higher level of bidding (see Chapter 12).

With a 1-level bid, your side needs to win only seven of the 13 tricks. Your side may well take seven tricks with about 20 HCP, half of the 40 total HCP.

If you have a minimum opening hand of 13 HCP, the three other hands have 27 HCP among them. If your partner has the average share of those 27 HCP, or 9 HCP, you should be able to make a low-level contract. Together, you will (on average) have 22 HCP to your opponents' 18 HCP. Of course, you still have to play the hand after the auction, and win the number of tricks needed.

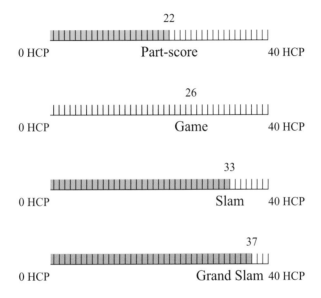

If your partner has a *better*-than-average hand, you may have enough strength to make a *game* contract—3NT, 4♥, 4♠, 5♣, or 5♦. Making a *game* in a single deal (with 100 or more points in trick-score) is what every bridge partnership would *like* to do!

To have a good play—that is, a good chance—for making game at 3NT, 4♥, or 4♠, you and your partner need together about 26 HCP of the 40 possible HCP.

Note: Bridge is not an exact science, and being dealt 26 HCP is not a guarantee that you will bid or make game.

To make a small slam, you need about 33 HCP, and for a grand slam, about 37 HCP. (Find more on slam bidding, and the big scores they earn, in Chapter 14.)

TIP

Remember: At any level of bidding, dynamic distribution can compensate for a lack of high cards.

We'll start by considering the essential ingredients for a 1♥ or 1♠ opening bid.

1♣	1♦	**1♥**	**1♠**	1NT
2♣	2♦	2♥	2♠	2NT
3♣	3♦	3♥	3♠	3NT
4♣	4♦	4♥	4♠	4NT
5♣	5♦	5♥	5♠	5NT
6♣	6♦	6♥	6♠	6NT
7♣	7♦	7♥	7♠	7NT

Opening 1♥

To open 1♥, you need at least 13 HCP and five or more hearts. For example, open 1♥ with these hands:

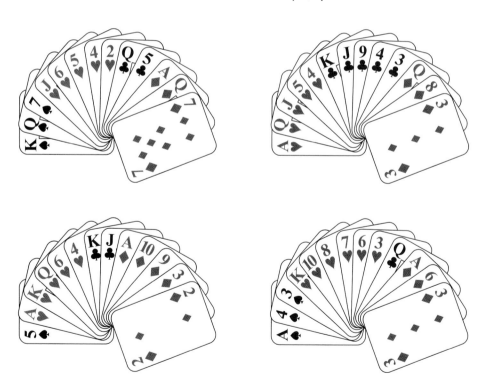

Opening 1♠

To open 1♠, you need at least 13 HCP and five or more spades. For example, open 1♠ with these hands:

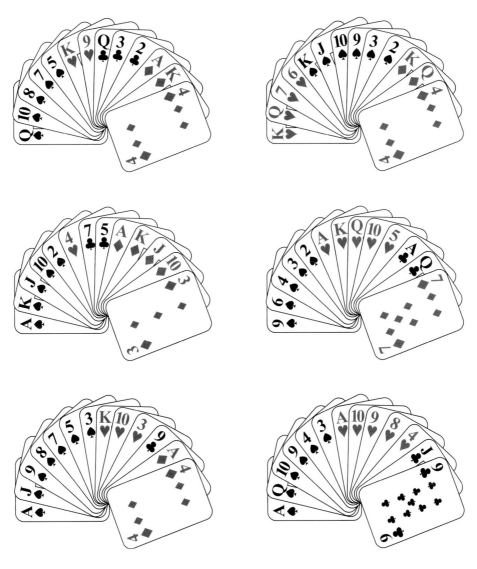

CONTINUED ON NEXT PAGE

Tips for Opening 1♥ and 1♠

♠96432
♥AKQ105
♦7
♣AQ

With five spades and five hearts, open 1♠—even when your hearts are much better than your spades. You can then plan to bid hearts at your next turn in the auction. It's worth giving up the score for *100 honors* in hearts if you can learn in the bidding that your partner's hand has spades, but *not* hearts.

♠AK1085
♥2
♦A
♣KQ10763

When holding a five-card major and a six-card minor, it's usually better to open the bidding in the longer suit. With the hand in this example, you should open 1♣. You plan to bid spades later in the auction—perhaps twice—to suggest this dynamic 5-1-1-6 shape.

However, some players welcome the chance to be a little tricky in the bidding. They might open 1♠ and be able to keep a secret of the long club suit.

FACT

An Historic Note about "Five-Card Majors"

In the early days of contract bridge, it was common to open 1♥ or 1♠ with just a four-card holding in the suit. Even today, there's no "rule" to stop you from doing so.

However, about 40 years ago, bridge players all over the world began to embrace the trend toward *five*-card major suit opening bids. This book supports this preference.

The "requirements" for opening 1-of-a-minor suit (1♣ and 1♦) differ from those for major-suit openings.

1♣ 1♦ 1♥ 1♠ 1NT
2♣ 2♦ 2♥ 2♠ 2NT
3♣ 3♦ 3♥ 3♠ 3NT
4♣ 4♦ 4♥ 4♠ 4NT
5♣ 5♦ 5♥ 5♠ 5NT
6♣ 6♦ 6♥ 6♠ 6NT
7♣ 7♦ 7♥ 7♠ 7NT

Opening 1♣

To open 1♣, you need a minimum of 13 HCP and at least three clubs. Sometimes clubs will not even be the longest suit in your hand, but 1♣ will be your best opening bid. That's because hands with no 5-card major are very often opened with 1-of-a-minor suit.

Open 1♣ with hands such as these:

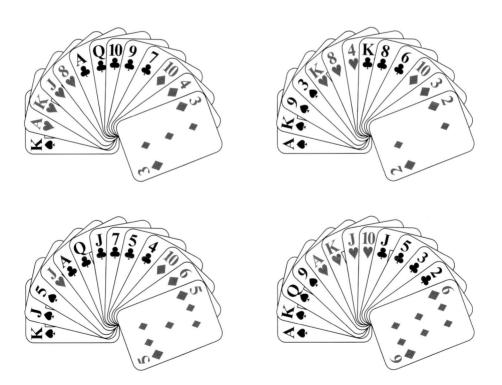

CONTINUED ON NEXT PAGE

Minor Suit Opening Bids:
1♣ and 1♦ *(continued)*

Opening 1♦

To open 1♦, you need 13 HCP and at least three diamonds. Sometimes diamonds will not even be the longest suit in your hand, but 1♦ will be your best opening bid. This is because hands with no 5-card major are opened with 1-of-a-minor suit.

Open 1♦ with hands such as these:

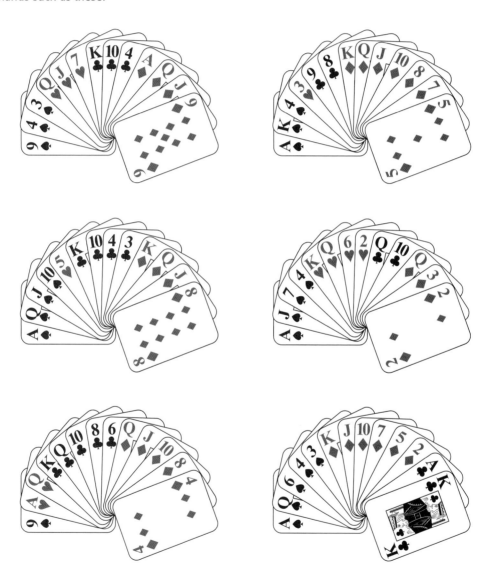

Tips for Opening 1♣ and 1♦

An opening bid in a minor suit can lead to a contract in any suit, or in notrump. The minor suit will give your partner a great number of possible choices in response to your opening bid. For this reason, it's okay to open 1♣ or 1♦ even when it's not your best or longest suit.

♠A4
♥986
♦J873
♣AKJ9

With four diamonds and four clubs, most players prefer to open 1♦ —even if the clubs are better than the diamonds. Others, when holding 4-4 in the minor suits, prefer to open the better suit.

♠A74
♥A862
♦KQ10
♣J83

With three diamonds and three clubs, most players prefer to open 1♣ —even if the diamonds are better than the clubs. Others, when holding 3-3 in the minor suits, prefer to open the better suit.

♠A
♥975
♦KQ32
♣KQ432

With four diamonds and five clubs, open 1♣. As you play more, you may find, however, that you prefer to open 1♦ with a hand like this.

REQUIREMENTS FOR OPENING 1NT

HCP and Distribution

To open 1NT, you need 15 to 17 HCP and a hand with balanced distribution. It should follow one of these patterns:

4-3-3-3
4-4-3-2
5-3-3-2
5-4-2-2
6-3-2-2

HAVING STOPPERS

Because your opponents may lead any suit at NT, it's helpful to have cards in every suit to stop them from winning trick after trick. A suit holding of a card or cards that prevents the opponents from taking all the tricks in a suit is called a *stopper*.

Sure stoppers (sometimes also called *full stoppers*) are ace, KQ, QJ10, or J1098. With KQ in a suit, for example, you must be able to win the first or second trick of that suit. However, you won't always be dealt sure stoppers. Likely stoppers also do very well, such as K103, QJ5, Q106, and J974.

Ideally, you should have a stopper in each suit when you open the bidding with 1NT, but it is not mandatory.

Sometimes all you may have in a suit is a small doubleton (two low cards in a suit) or tripleton (three low cards in a suit). Even so, 1NT is probably the best bid if you have 15 to 17 HCP. In bridge, you are always taking chances.

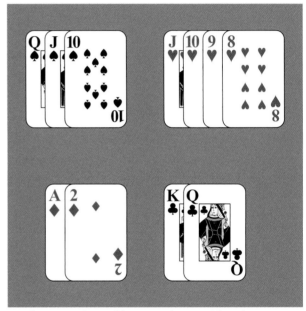

Each group pictured here can be considered a stopper.

DON'T OPEN 1NT WITH A SINGLETON OR VOID

It's not advisable to open 1NT with a singleton or void in a suit, because when you open 1NT, you give your partner the impression that you have a balanced hand. Hands with extreme shortness in one suit will nearly always win more tricks if one of the *other* three suits becomes the trump suit. If that is the case, a hand with a singleton or void can win the first or second round of the "short" suit by playing a trump. If the final contract is in notrump, the opponents may be able to take a number of tricks in that suit—even when your singleton is the ace.

Your partner can feel secure, expecting a balanced hand when you open 1NT. Partner will be able to rely on you to have at least 2 cards in every suit!

Opening 1NT

Open 1NT with hands such as these:

CONTINUED ON NEXT PAGE

TIP

Note to the Kibitzer

Many years of bridge experience teach players that a 1NT opening bid works best with a narrower point-count *range* than a suit opening bid at the 1 level. That's why 1NT is limited to, or has a *range* of, 15 to 17 HCP.

TIPS FOR OPENING 1NT

♠K43
♥Q98
♦83
♣AKQJ4

Here even though the strength of your hand is in clubs, 1NT is a better bid than 1♣. Unless one of your opponents also holds five clubs (unlikely), your club holding should take 5 tricks, and just 2 more tricks is enough to score 1NT, worth 40 points below the line in trick-score. You'd have to bid 2♣ (an 8-trick contract) to earn a 40 score at clubs! Of course, you'd have to play at clubs to get the 100-pt. bonus for "100 Honors" (4 of 5 top trumps in one hand).

A long minor suit can be a nice part of a 1NT opening bid.

BIDDING 1NT VERSUS 1-OF-A-MAJOR SUIT

♠QJ9
♥KQJ98
♦K103
♣A10

With 15 to 17 HCP and a five-card major suit (hearts), your hand can open either 1♥ or 1NT. Experience shows that although you might get better results opening 1NT with such a hand, opening 1♥ is not a mistake and some players just feel happier opening in the major suit. Bridge is often a game of differences of opinion and feeling.

It's okay to open 1NT when you have a 5-card major suit.

Here are a few more general tips for the opening bidder:

- **Watch for Part-Score Situations.** If your side has a part-score, another part-score can complete a game. That means your side may not have to bid very high to earn the remaining trick-points for game.

  Under these circumstances, opening the bidding with a slightly lighter hand than usual (fewer than 13 HCP) can pay off. For example, with a 90 part-score, you might well open the bidding a bit light just to get your side off to a good start, threatening to complete a game. Because any part-score will give enough more for game—even 1♣ or 1NT—your partner can pass with ease, and your opponents may also choose not to bid either. You might be able to score what is called a "cheap" game.

  Similarly, when your opponents own a part-score, you might also open a little bit on the light side to make it more challenging for them to win the auction at a low level, which is all they need to do to complete their game.

- **Consider "Light" Opening Bids Carefully.** Not all bridge players bid the same. Some have a more aggressive style and open the bidding with hands that other players would pass with.

  For example, with a hand such as

  ♠AK93
  ♥K84
  ♦1032
  ♣K86

  (13 HCP), most players will open the bidding (with 1♣). Change the hand to

  ♠AK93
  ♥Q84
  ♦1032
  ♣K86

  (12 HCP), and many players would choose to pass, while others will still think they are just about close enough to shade the traditional 13 HCPs that are a wise guideline.

  If you are in the first or second seat, it is better to pass with such hands.

- **Consider "Light" Opening Bids In the Third Seat.** When your partner has passed, you know that your partner has a hand limited to 12 HCP. In the third seat, it becomes okay to open the bidding light if you can comfortably pass when your partner responds. For example, you would pass as dealer or in second position a light balanced hand like

  ♠AK93
  ♥Q84
  ♦1032
  ♣K86

  (seen just above). But you can open this hand as a tactical move in third position. You could open 1♣, or even try a 4-card major, and open 1♠. You will simply pass your partner's next bid, since you have a few cards in any suit that might be bid. (Be sure that your partner is aware of this strategic opening bid too, so that it won't be a surprise. It's okay to discuss such things in advance.)

- **Notice and Be Aware of the Vulnerability.** Another factor in opening a borderline hand is *vulnerability*. When *not* vulnerable, your risk is reduced. When vulnerable, the risk of defeat is greater—especially if your final contract is doubled! Just take a quick glance back to Chapter 3 to see the points you lose going down a few tricks in any doubled contract.

- **Bid with Confidence.** Make your opening bid—and every other bid—in a clear and steady voice. Whether you are making a questionable bid, a very sound bid, or a light bid, speak confidently. If you have doubts about your bid, it's not fair for your partner to know it—and you don't really want your opponents to realize it, either!

Good bidding is a partnership venture. Partners who understand each other's bids in the auction can achieve good final contracts. They can correctly judge how high to go in the auction, and also whether to play in a suit or notrump contract.

The opening bid is the first step, and the response to it is the meaningful next step toward a final contract. Occasionally, the final contract to reach will be clear in one or two bids. At other times, a series of bids back and forth may be needed to complete a fuller picture of the two hands and reach the partnership's desired final contract.

Together, two players strive to find out the following: Can we make a part-score? Can we make a game? Can we possibly even make a slam?

Of course, you and your partner are not always left alone to settle on a final contract. Often, one or both opponents enter the auction. For the time being, let's assume that your opponents are very cooperative. They remain "silent"—and simply pass at each turn. No need to worry about them...for now!

Partners have a chat toether at a casual bridge game at home.

Types of Responses

When you *respond* to an opening bid, the requirements are very different than they are for *making* the opening bid. Of course, you still use guidelines based on the high card point (HCP) count, where ace = 4, king = 3, queen = 2, and jack = 1. However, the standard of a 13 HCP minimum for the opening bidder doesn't apply at all to the responder. With a minimum of just 6 HCP, the responder can almost always bid in reply to partner's opening bid of 1♣, 1♦, 1♥, or 1♠. In rare cases, the responder can bid with even fewer points!

The responder selects from these four types of responses to their partner's opening 1-of-a-suit bid:

1. Pass.

2. Raise partner's suit. To *raise,* or *support,* is to bid partner's suit at a higher level. A raise can be at the next level of bidding (simple raise), or by jumping one or more bidding levels (jump raise).

3. Bid a new suit.

4. Bid NT.

Remember that with 24–25 or fewer combined HCP, a part-score may be the partnership's limit, although distributional power may help you achieve game in a suit. With 26 or more HCP, your side should have a good chance to make a game. With 33 HCP or more, you could be scoring a slam bid.

As to the choice of final contract, you want to end up in a trump suit that your side has plenty of. You prefer your side's trumps to outnumber the enemy's trumps by at least 8 to 5. If you are lucky and bid correctly, you will often find that your trumps outnumber their trumps by 9 to 4, 10 to 3, or even 11 to 2!

Bridge Lingo

Drop the "the." When talking about bridge, language can get streamlined. Opener, responder, declarer, dummy, partner, dealer, overcaller, doubler—you can usually speak these words comfortably without use of a "the"!

When partner opens 1-of-a-minor, either of the bids highlighted in the chart, a great many higher possible bids remain. Since partner's minor suit opening bids often have a 4-card major suit that may actually be better than the minor suit already bid, responder needs to bid carefully. That way the partnership can find its best fit, and reach its best contract too.

1♣	1♦	1♥	1♠	1NT
2♣	2♦	2♥	2♠	2NT
3♣	3♦	3♥	3♠	3NT
4♣	4♦	4♥	4♠	4NT
5♣	5♦	5♥	5♠	5NT
6♣	6♦	6♥	6♠	6NT
7♣	7♦	7♥	7♠	7NT

Responder can select from these four types of responses to partner's opening bid of 1♣ or 1♦.

PASS

♠J83 ♥109 ♦Q8764 ♣965

North	East	South	West
1♣	pass	pass	

South, as responder, shows 5 or fewer HCP, by passing.

RAISE

Single Raise

♠104 ♥A52 ♦K10853 ♣J74

North	East	South	West
1♦	pass	2♦	

South's raise to 2♦ shows 6–10 HCP and usually 5-card+ support for partner's suit.

Jump Raise

♠K103 ♥A9 ♦A75 ♣KQ952

North	East	South	West
1♣	pass	3♣	

With a jump raise to 3♦, South shows 13+ HCP and 5-card+ support for partner's suit.

This bid commits the partnership to a game contract. It is *forcing to game*.

BID A NEW SUIT AT THE 1 LEVEL

♠QJ32 ♥A102 ♦864 ♣Q72

North	East	South	West
1♣	pass	1♠	

South's 1♠ response shows 6+ HCP and 4+ cards in the suit bid. Bid your longest suit. If you have suits of equal length, then bid the higher-ranking suit first if they are both 5 cards or longer. Bid the lower- or lowest-ranking suit first if none is more than 4 cards long.

This leaves each partner the chance to show (at least) four cards with each new suit bid at the one level. Every deal is different, but often the best suit for the partnership to bid as a final contract is one where they each have 4 cards. A careful eye to making 1-level bids helps the partnership discover when such a 4-4 "fit" may exist.

In the bidding, the player learning of a 4-4 suit can, as a next bid, raise that suit (that is, bid it), at a higher level of bidding.

Note: *The first time a suit is raised signals to both partners that this may be a good suit for the final contract.*

♠Q ♥J9765 ♦KQ2 ♣KQJ6

North	East	South	West
1♦	pass	1♥	

South responds 1♥, a bid in South's longest suit.

BID 1NT, 2NT, OR 3NT

1NT Response

♠932 ♥KJ10 ♦QJ5 ♣J942

North	East	South	West
1♣	pass	1NT	

South's 1NT response promises 6–10 HCP, with balanced distribution.

CONTINUED ON NEXT PAGE

2NT Response

♠J104
♥AQ
♦J1087
♣K986

North	East	South	West
1♦	pass	2NT	

South's 2NT response shows 11–12 HCP, with a balanced distribution and no 4-card major. This is not forcing to game, and North may pass next.

3NT Response

♠Q108
♥AJ9
♦Q73
♣AJ82

North	East	South	West
1♦	pass	3NT	

South's 3NT response shows 13–15 HCP, with a balanced distribution and no 4-card major. South has *stoppers* or likely stoppers in each unbid suit.

Note: *See Chapter 4 for more about stoppers.*

Bridge Lingo

To describe any hand in spoken words, start in spades and work down in suits, using ordinal numbers for your count. For example, to describe ♠Kxxx ♥Axx ♦Qx ♣J10xx, say "King fourth, ace third, queen doubleton, and jack-ten fourth." Often 10s or 9s are important, so mention them. Refer to ♠---- ♥A98x ♦Q10x ♣AJ109xx as "Void, ace-nine-eight-fourth, queen-ten third, and ace-jack-ten-nine-sixth."

Examples of Responses to 1♣

PARTNER OPENS 1♣, NEXT PLAYER PASSES

A

♠A986
♥10932
♦Q1032
♣9

Bid 1♦. Partner will next have the chance to bid 1♥ or 1♠ with a 4-card suit. This gives the partnership its best chance to find an 8-card *fit*. That's where your side has eight trumps to their five trumps.

B

♠K9853
♥AQJ76
♦103
♣K

Bid 1♠. With equal suits that are at least 5 cards or longer, bid the higher-ranking suit first.

C

♠42
♥Q943
♦J72
♣J82

Pass. You need 6 HCP to reply to partner's opening bid. This hand has only 4 HCP.

CONTINUED ON NEXT PAGE

D

♠86
♥97
♦Q103
♣QJ10875

Bid 2♣. You normally want at least 6 HCP for this bid, but the sixth club makes up for that.

E

♠AQJ5
♥92
♦J2
♣Q10952

Bid 1♠. You will have a chance to bid again, and can then bid in support of clubs if you want.

F

♠KQ8
♥5
♦A732
♣KQJ107

Bid 3♣. This move alerts your partner to the chance of a slam in clubs, and is forcing to game.

Examples of Responses to 1♦

PARTNER OPENS 1♦ AND THE NEXT PLAYER PASSES

A

♠QJ4
♥654
♦KJ107
♣Q32

Bid 1NT.

B

♠A1098
♥J643
♦K4
♣J95

Bid 1♥. Bid 4-card suits *up the line* (that is, lowest ranking suit first), at the 1 level. If the opener has four spades, then the opener will bid 1♠ and the 8-card spade fit will become known to the partnership.

C

♠98432
♥AKQJ
♦8
♣K32

Bid 1♠. Even though the hearts are very strong, bid your longest suit first. You will have another chance and may want to bid hearts next.

CONTINUED ON NEXT PAGE

D

♠AK9
♥10
♦Q63
♣KQJ1074

Bid 2♣. Over 1♦, a 2♣ bid promises at least 10 HCP and a 4-card suit—this hand has much more than the minimum of 10 HCP!

E

♠6
♥10876
♦A102
♣KJ873

Bid 1♥ in response to 1♦. You haven't the strength for a 2♣ bid.

F

♠K4
♥A52
♦K10853
♣AJ4

Bid 3♦. This bid is forcing to game and might even lead the partnership to a worthwhile slam-level contract.

Tips for Responding to 1♣ or 1♦

TRUMP SUPPORT

Because partner sometimes has 3 cards in a minor suit, you prefer to have 5-card support to raise. Sometimes, you will support with only 4 cards because it is the best bid.

♠2
♥1063
♦AK87
♣97642

Raise partner's 1♦ bid to 2♦.

BID 4-CARD SUITS "UP THE LINE"

Because a minor suit scores only 20 points per trick, look to play in a higher-scoring contract. As the responder, bid 4-card suits *up the line* at the one level. That is, start by responding in your lowest-ranking 4-card suit.

Partner opens 1♣.

♠AK87
♥AK98
♦J842
♣7

Respond 1♦.

♠AQJ2
♥10876
♦Q43
♣53

Respond 1♥.

BID HIGHEST-RANKING OF 5-CARD SUITS FIRST

♠AQ873
♥AQ983
♦J8
♣7

Respond 1♠ to 1-of-a-minor. You can bid hearts at your next turn, and perhaps again at the following turn, depending on how the auction goes. This will tell partner that you have at least 5 spades and at least 5 hearts.

PART-SCORE SITUATIONS

If you already have a part-score, your choice of bid and level may be changed. For example, suppose your side has a 60 part-score, and partner opens 1♦. With

♠K98 ♥Q92 ♦K4 ♣K1086

you might ordinarily bid 2♣ or even 2NT. In this case, with a 60 partial, you need only 40 points more for game, and you can bid just 1NT. No need to risk bidding to any higher-level contract!

Suppose instead your side has a 40 part-score and partner opens 1♣. In this instance, you would raise partner to 3♣. Normally, this would show 13+ HCP in support of clubs. Because a 3♣ contract scores 60 points, that's a game bid, and partner will bid no more. Your side may then complete the 100 points in trick-score needed for game.

CONTINUED ON NEXT PAGE

Making a Game at Notrump

Dealer: East

North–South Vulnerable

THE BIDDING

East	South	West	North
pass	pass	pass	1♦
pass	2NT	pass	3NT
pass	pass	pass	

Opening lead: ♥6

After three passes, North opens the bid-ding 1♦ in fourth seat. South, with 12 HCP and a balanced hand, responds 2NT. North, with 14 HCP and a useful 5-card suit, raises to 3NT, a game contract, know-ing that her side has the necessary 25 points for game. South, declarer at 3NT, needs to win nine tricks for the contract to succeed.

All play low on West's heart lead, and South wins in hand with the ♥9. Declarer sees that if West has ♦K, it can be cap-tured. South leads ♦Q and West covers with ♦K. Dummy wins the trick with ♦A. Now South leads ♦3 from dummy and wins with ♦J in hand.

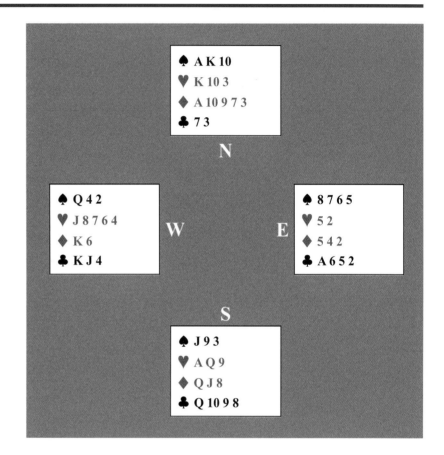

This is now the position:

South has taken the first three tricks and can already see more than enough tricks to make the contract: three more diamond winners, two more heart winners, and the two top spades. That's ten tricks.

South decides to go for 11 tricks and plays the ♠3 from hand. When West follows with the ♠2, South inserts the ♠10 from dummy. Because West has the ♠Q, not East, the ♠10 wins this trick! South takes 11 tricks in all. The defenders win just the final two tricks.

South makes 3NT, with two overtricks!

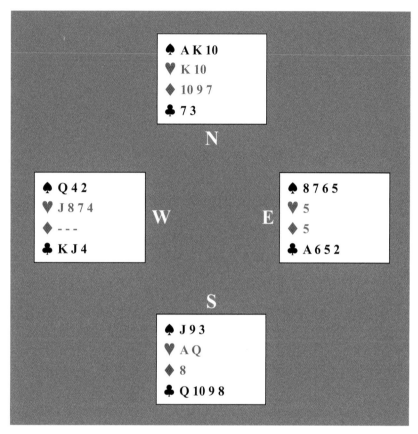

WE	THEY	WE	THEY
✕			
60			
100			

Partner's major suit opener—which shows at least a 5-card suit—might or might not be the partnership's best trump suit. The partnership may instead end up choosing another suit, or playing notrump. Further bidding determines this.

1♣	1♦	**1♥**	**1♠**	1NT
2♣	2♦	2♥	2♠	2NT
3♣	3♦	3♥	3♠	3NT
4♣	4♦	4♥	4♠	4NT
5♣	5♦	5♥	5♠	5NT
6♣	6♦	6♥	6♠	6NT
7♣	7♦	7♥	7♠	7NT

Responding to a **major** suit opening differs from responding to a **minor** suit opening. That's because partner's opening bid of 1♥ or 1♠ promises a 5-card suit. By comparison, a 1♣ or 1♦ opener can be made on a 3-card suit. When partner opens in a major, you can expect a five-card suit, and you can immediately determine whether your side has 8 or more cards in that suit. That would make opener's major suit a good suit for a final contract if you have as few as 3 cards of support in it.

On the other hand, if you have fewer than 3 cards in partner's major, you may be looking for another place to play the hand. As you can see, some bids lie ahead, but not as many as over a minor-suit opening bid.

Also, over the 1♥ or 1♠ opener, responder has to go up to the 2 level to bid clubs or diamonds. In contrast, in response to 1♣ or 1♦, responder can often bid in a new suit and remain at the 1 level.

Responder can select from these four types of responses to partner's opening bid of 1♥ or 1♠. In all cases, you are South.

PASS

♠42
♥532
♦1098
♣KQ983

North	East	South	West
1♠	pass	pass	

South's pass shows 5 HCP or fewer.

RAISE

Single Raise

♠854
♥932
♦Q9
♣AQJ82

North	East	South	West
1♠	pass	2♠	

South's raise to 2♠ shows 6–10 HCP and 3-card+ support for partner's suit.

Jump Raise

♠A4 ♥K865 ♦AQJ ♣10983

North	East	South	West
1♥	pass	3♥	

South's jump raise to 3♥ shows 13+ HCP and 4-card+ support for partner's suit.

This bid commits the partnership to a game contract—it is forcing to game. Note that a single raise, to 2♥, requires only 3-card support; the game-forcing jump raise requires at least 4-card support.

BID OF A NEW SUIT

♠QJ96 ♥J ♦87532 ♣Q63

North	East	South	West
1♥	pass	1♠	

Bid 1♠ in response to partner's 1♥ opening bid. South has 6+ HCP and 4+ cards in the suit bid.

♠A76 ♥Q4 ♦1053 ♣KQ932

North	East	South	West
1♥	pass	2♣	

Bid 2♣, a new suit at the 2 level. South shows 10+ HCP and 5+ cards in the suit bid. (Occasionally it may be a 4-card suit.)

♠J ♥104 ♦AKQJ98 ♣A543

North	East	South	West
1♠	pass	2♦	

Your 2♦ bid has considerably more than 10 HCP. It will be your duty to make sure the partnership reaches at least a game contract.

CONTINUED ON NEXT PAGE

BID NT (1NT, 2NT, OR 3NT)

♠932
♥J
♦Q106
♣KJ9743

North	East	South	West
1♥	pass	1NT	

South's 1NT response shows 6–10 HCP. Hand shape can vary widely. South usually has fewer than four spades and fewer than three hearts (the suit bid by partner).

♠Q7
♥AQ109
♦Q986
♣K107

North	East	South	West
1♠	pass	2NT	

South has 12–14 HCP, balanced distribution, and a doubleton in partner's suit. South also is prepared for the opponents to lead any unbid suit. This bid is forcing to a game contract.

♠KJ8
♥J10
♦J975
♣AKQ2

North	East	South	West
1♥	pass	3NT	

South's 3NT bid shows 15–17 HCP, balanced distribution, and just a doubleton in partner's suit. South is also well prepared for the opponents to lead any unbid suit. It's just about the same sort of hand South would have opened 1NT had South been the opening bidder!

Examples of Responses to 1

In each case, partner opens 1♥ and the next player passes . . .

A

♠AK765
♥8
♦9
♣AK7654

Bid 2♣, not 1♠. Respond when possible in your longest suit. Clubs, 6 cards long, should be bid first. You can assume that you will have more chances in the auction to bid perhaps re-bid spades, your 5-card suit, and communicate your hand-shape to your partner.

B

♠9
♥J643
♦A8752
♣1098

Bid 2♥. Even though you have only 5 HCP, you have 4-card support and nice shape.

C

♠J943
♥A8
♦Q7432
♣63

Bid 1♠. This is better than 1NT, and you do not have the strength needed to bid 2♦.

CONTINUED ON NEXT PAGE

D

♠8
♥KQ108
♦K432
♣AJ92

Bid 3♥. This bid is forcing to game.

E

♠A82
♥95
♦K1084
♣A983

Bid 2♦. You are too strong for 1NT but not quite strong enough for 2NT. The only alternative is to bid a 4-card minor suit at the 2 level, showing 10+ HCP.

F

♠J4
♥A10963
♦3
♣K10652

Bid 4♥! Dynamic shape—in this case, 2-5-1-5—can make up for your lack of high cards. A game contract is a good bet! You might not *always* take ten out of 13 tricks when you make such a bid, but your chances will usually be excellent.

Examples of Responses to 1♠

In each case, partner opens 1♠ and the next player passes. . .

A

♠10543
♥62
♦AQJ65
♣93

Bid 2♠. You do not have enough HCP to bid 2♦.

B

♠K6
♥976
♦973
♣KJ832

Bid 1NT, simply because the hand qualifies for no other bid. If left to play 1NT, you might win quite a few tricks with your long club suit. A 2♣ bid, which would promise 10 HCP is out, because you have only 7 HCP.

C

♠5
♥J32
♦1064
♣Q86432

Pass. Even though you have only 1 card in partner's suit, you have too few HCP to make a bid.

CONTINUED ON NEXT PAGE

D

♠J1096
♥A52
♦AJ5
♣A87

Bid 3♠. This game-forcing raise of partner's opener promises at least 4-card trump support, with slam potential.

E

♠J9
♥K542
♦AQJ65
♣K3

Bid 2♦. Responder knows that together the hands have game-level strength. Further bidding will indicate whether to go for game in diamonds, hearts, spades, or NT. Because you have bid a new suit, your partner will bid again.

F

♠4
♥KQJ84
♦AKQ63
♣KQ

Bid 2♥. Your side may have a good play for slam. Because you have bid a new suit, your partner will bid again.

Sample Hand

Dealer: North

Neither side vulnerable.

THE BIDDING

North	East	South	West
1♥	pass	1♠	pass
2♠	pass	pass	pass

Opening lead: ♣K

North opens the bidding 1♥, and South responds 1♠. North raises to 2♠, which becomes the final contract after three passes. South makes no further bid, because South promised six points by bidding 1♠, and has "nothing more to say." South, declarer at 2♠, needs to win eight tricks for the contract to succeed.

West wins the first trick with the ♣ K. At trick two, West shifts to a trump, leading the ♠2, and South, playing low from dummy, captures East's ♠10 with the ♠Q. South next plays the ♥J to dummy's ♥A.

South leads the ♥2 from dummy on the following trick and *ruffs* (trumps) it in hand with ♠6. South leads ♣6 and ruffs with dummy's ♠8.

Again in dummy, South leads ♥4 and ruffs in hand with ♠9, as East and West continue to follow suit helplessly. South next leads the ♣Q and ruffs West's ♣A with dummy's ♠K.

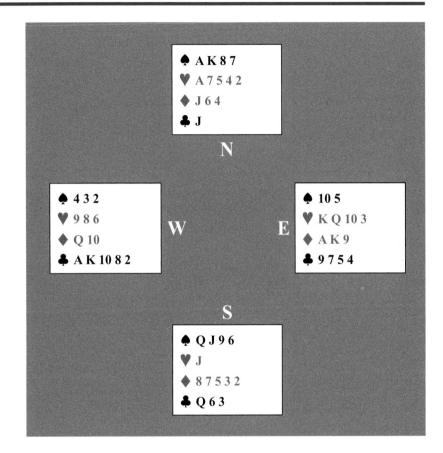

♠ A K 8 7
♥ A 7 5 4 2
♦ J 6 4
♣ J

N

♠ 4 3 2
♥ 9 8 6
♦ Q 10
♣ A K 10 8 2

W

E

♠ 10 5
♥ K Q 10 3
♦ A K 9
♣ 9 7 5 4

S

♠ Q J 9 6
♥ J
♦ 8 7 5 3 2
♣ Q 6 3

CONTINUED ON NEXT PAGE

The situation now is as follows:

Dummy is on lead, and South has taken six tricks so far—the spade trick that West led, the ace of hearts, and four consecutive ruffs back and forth.

South now leads ♥5 from dummy and ruffs with ♠J for their seventh trick. Eventually, dummy's ♠A wins a trick, and South's 2♠ contract is a success.

South has made North–South's contract, taking the ace of hearts and seven tricks using trumps. Six trump tricks were winners on 6 separate tricks, by using the technique called a *cross-ruff*. In it, declarer won trumps on individual tricks by coordinating leads between his hand, and dummy's. The lead of a suit is ruffed in one hand, which then leads a card in another suit for the other hand to ruff. This ruffing, by crossing back and forth between hands, gives the name cross-ruff.

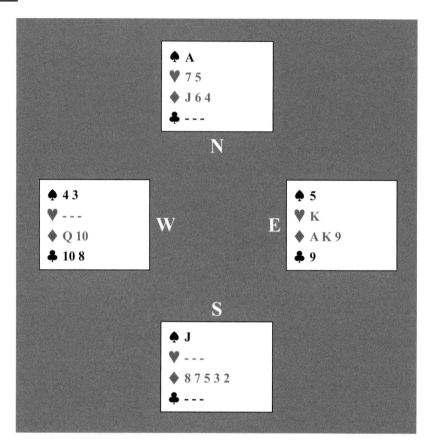

WE	THEY	WE	THEY
✕			
60			

	Bid Chart for Responder		

RESPONDER'S CALLS

Opening Bid	PASS	Single RAISE	Jump RAISE (game-forcing)
1♣	0–5	6–10 5+ trumps	13 and up, 5+ trumps
1♦	0–5	6–10 5+ trumps	13 and up, 5+ trumps
1♥	0–5	6–10 3+ trumps	13 and up, 4+ trumps
1♠	0–5	6–10 3+ trumps	13 and up, 4+ trumps

RESPONDER'S CALLS

Opening Bid	New Suit at 1 level	New Suit at 2 Level	1NT	2NT	3NT
1♣	6 and up, 4+ cards	********	6–10	11–12	13–15
1♦	6 and up, 4+ cards	2♣ =10 and up	6–10	11–12	13–15
1♥	6 and up, 4+ cards	10 and up	6–10	12–14	15–17
1♠	----------------	10 and up	6–10	12–14	15–17

Notes:

Numbers in green indicate high card points (HCP).

Numbers in black indicate suit length.

Jump raises are considered game-forcing bids.

A jump bid by responder in a new suit can be used to show a very strong hand as well as a powerful suit. This bid would be forcing to game and with an interest in slam, But, the jump also might make it harder for the opening bidder to make a comfortable and informative second bid (simply because fewer bids remain to choose from). It may serve the partnership better for responder to bid a new suit without jumping any bidding levels. Opener will bid again anyway.

A new suit at 2 level should be a 5+card suit, although you may be okay with 4 cards.

A 2♥ response to 1♠ should be a 5+card suit.

Strategies and Tactics for the Responder

Here's a chance to follow the sort of tactical thinking that occurs at the bridge table.

IMMEDIATE JUMP TO GAME

An immediate jump to game does not show a strong HCP hand. It shows a very distributional hand, with lengthy trump support, which should give the contract a good chance for success.

♠K7543
♥Q9642
♦A7
♣4

Opposite partner's 1♠ opener, bid 4♠. This contract should have a great chance of succeeding.

♠6
♥—
♦KJ98743
♣K10743

Opposite partner's 1♦ opener, bid 5♦. It should also have a great chance of succeeding.

PART-SCORE SITUATIONS

If your side or the other side has a part-score, it can affect your bid selection. For example, say you have a 60 part-score toward game. Holding the hand shown here, you have a good chance to complete the game.

♠AQ98
♥104
♦J43
♣Q654

If partner opens 1♣, 1♦, or 1♥, rather than bidding 1♠, you may choose to bid 1NT instead.

That contract needs only seven tricks to succeed and scores the 40 points needed to convert the part-score to game. Concealing the presence of your good spades may help you as declarer at 1NT!

RESPONDING IN A NEW SUIT

When you respond in a new suit, your partner knows your HCP minimum but also knows you might well have a very good hand. Therefore, you can rely on your partner, who opened, to bid again if you respond in a new suit. It's even possible for you to have 20 HCP or more when partner opens!

When you reply in a new suit at the 1 level, you could have 6-20+ HCP. Partner will bid again, in case you have more or much more than a minimum hand in response

♠AKQJ65 ♥Q96 ♦A3 ♣J8

Partner opens 1♣. With 17 HCP in your hand, you expect 4♠ to be an easy contract. If you want to bid 4♠, you can, and partner will not be disappointed when you score up the game.

Because you have thoughts of slam, it's okay to bid 1♠ first. Knowing that you might have a good hand, partner will bid again. Partner's choice of bids may help you decide whether to try for slam.

RESPONDING TO THIRD SEAT OPENER

Partner's third position opening bid at times may be a bit lighter than the usual 13 HCP standard for first and second seat openers—especially if your side isn't vulnerable. This may influence your choice of calls.

Example: partner in third position bids 1♥.

♠AJ10 ♥Q43 ♦Q93 ♣J976

You have 10 HCP and certainly could bid 2♣ or 2♥. The safest bid is probably 1NT.

If partner has opened with a light hand in third position, that contract will be high enough, and partner will pass. If partner has a very good hand and bids again, you may then steer the partnership toward a game contract in hearts or notrump.

When Opponents Enter the Auction

This chapter's guidelines for responding are for times when partner opens and the next hand passes. However, if the next hand bids, your considerations change. For example, you may now decide to pass with hands you would have bid on.

There's more on the topic of both sides bidding in chapters 8, 11, and 13.

chapter 6

Responding to 1NT

When your partner opens 1NT, that bid shows 15 to 17 high card points—a pretty good hand. If you have enough strength yourself, the partnership may be able to bid a game and make it. As responder, you have a large responsibility. The care you take in responding to 1NT is the key to reaching the best final contract.

In this chapter, you'll learn both how and when to continue bidding after your partner opens 1NT. Along the way, you'll be introduced to two key "artificial" or "conventional" bids that you and your partner should agree to play together.

Responder's Choices

When your partner opens 1NT, what you do as responder is pivotal to your success. *You* are the player who can most quickly appreciate the worth of the partnership hands together. Since partner shows 15–17 HCP in a balanced hand, you can judge what your own hand adds to that.

North	East	South	West
1NT	pass	?	

2♣ 2♦ 2♥ 2♠ 2NT
3♣ 3♦ 3♥ 3♠ 3NT
4♣ 4♦ 4♥ 4♠ 4NT
5♣ 5♦ 5♥ 5♠ 5NT
6♣ 6♦ 6♥ 6♠ 6NT
7♣ 7♦ 7♥ 7♠ 7NT

Partner's 1NT opener still leaves you many bids, starting at the 2 level.

Often responder determines that a part-score is the limit of the hand. As a result, responder is in a position to comfortably *pass* the opening 1NT bid. A responding hand that would have taken a bid if partner had opened 1♣, 1♦, 1♥, or 1♠ may very appropriately *pass* a 1NT opening bid!

An opening bid of 1NT can easily become the final bid. If no other player has a hand suitable for bidding higher, all will pass. Those three passes put an end to the auction.

East	South	West	North
1NT	pass	pass	pass

Responder's Three Basic Choices

As the responder, you have three basic alternatives when your partner opens 1NT and the next player passes:

1. **Passing.** If the next player passes too, then 1NT becomes the final contract.

2. **Raising NT.** You may raise to 2NT, 3NT, 4NT, 5NT, 6NT, or 7NT.

3. **Making a suit bid.** Any suit bid is permitted—from the 2 level all the way up to the 7 level. However, very high level responses to 1NT are rare.

Your hand's shape and HCP total are both important factors when choosing a reply to 1NT. The next sections examine responder's choices more closely.

On balanced and semi-balanced hands with 0 to 7 HCP and no 5-card (or longer) major suit, pass is the call to make. At most, your side has 24 points and so a game contract is questionable. Much of the time, you will also pass when you have 8 balanced or semi-balanced HCP.

Do not view passing partner's 1NT opening bid as anything to be ashamed of. Making 1NT can be a nice result. Whenever your partner can take at least seven tricks declaring that contract, your side will score 40 points below the line toward the 100 needed for game. Now a part-score of 60 on a following deal is all that you need for game.

WE	THEY	WE	THEY
✕			
40			

Pass 1NT with any of these hands:

As the responder, with a balanced hand of at least 8 HCP, you will often raise the 1NT opening bid by also bidding notrump, at a higher level. For example, you may think your side is strong enough to take nine tricks at notrump. To earn the 100 points in trick-score below the line for taking those nine tricks, you must bid for them. You cannot pass 1NT; instead your side must bid 3NT.

When you think your side might win 12 or 13 tricks at notrump, again your side must bid 6NT or 7NT to earn a big slam bonus score.

Note: *Contracts of 4NT and 5NT—for 10 and 11 tricks—don't earn any added bonuses, although they still count as a game if you make the contract. There's no point in bidding 4NT or 5NT as a final contract if you can win the auction at 3NT.*

2NT RAISE

When you have a balanced hand and 8 or 9 HCP, bid 2NT.

North	East	South	West
1NT	pass	2NT	

South's 2NT raise is an *invitational* bid. The 2NT bid invites the opener to bid a game (3NT) with a maximum 1NT opener (17 HCP), or to pass with a minimum 1NT opener (15 HCP). With 16 HCP, opener will choose whether to bid on, or not, a bid she can make based on her individual judgment and experience.

Bid 2NT with 8 HCP only when you have extra features such as a 5-card suit or useful 10s and 9s.

With a hand like this, you should raise 1NT to 2NT (8 HCP).

But with a hand like this, you should pass 1NT (also 8 HCP).

3NT RAISE

With 10 to 15 balanced or semi-balanced HCP and no 4-card or longer major suit, raise immediately to 3NT.

North	East	South	West
1NT	pass	3NT	

North will pass South's 3NT response. This is a rather common auction in bridge.

Raise directly to 3NT with any of these hands:

TIP

"Extras" at Notrump

For both opener and responder, the difference between bidding further in notrump and passing can come down to a matter of having "extras." Suit quality, suit length, and the presence of 10's and 9's can influence your decision to bid on to a notrump game or slam.

Suit quality	K10987 is better than K6432, yet they have the same HCP.
Suit length	QJ1092 is better than QJ109, yet they have the same HCP.
Presence of 10s and 9s	10s and 9s are better than 3s and 2s, yet they have the same HCP.
	A1092 is a better holding than A432, yet they have the same HCP.

CONTINUED ON NEXT PAGE

4NT RAISE

With a good 15 HCP or 16 HCP, a balanced hand and no 4-card or longer major, raise to 4NT.

♠Q109 ♥AK4 ♦QJ1084 ♣A9

North	East	South	West
1NT	pass	4NT	

South's 4NT call requests opener to bid 6NT with a *maximum* 1NT opener (17 HCP), or to pass with a *minimum* (15 HCP). With 16 HCP, opener again uses judgment and feel based on the hand's shape and quality.

6NT RAISE

(**Note:** *The 5NT raise will come next.*)

With a balanced or semi-balanced hand of 17–19 HCP, raise to 6NT.

♠J109 ♥KQJ ♦AQ432 ♣A10.

North	East	South	West
1NT	pass	6NT	

Opener will pass your 6NT bid.

5NT RAISE

With 20 or 21 balanced HCP, bid 5NT.

♠AQ10 ♥AK4 ♦QJ1084 ♣A9

North	East	South	West
1NT	pass	5NT	

This call requires partner to bid 7NT with a *maximum* 1NT opener, or to bid 6NT with a *minimum*. Notice that 5NT, which invites a grand slam, is a stronger bid than 6NT!

7NT RAISE

With 22+ HCP, bid 7NT.

♠AQ5 ♥KQJ965 ♦K ♣AK10

North	East	South	West
1NT	pass	7NT	

To bid 7NT, your hand doesn't need to be balanced.

Raising NT: Example Hand

Dealer: East
Neither Side Vulnerable

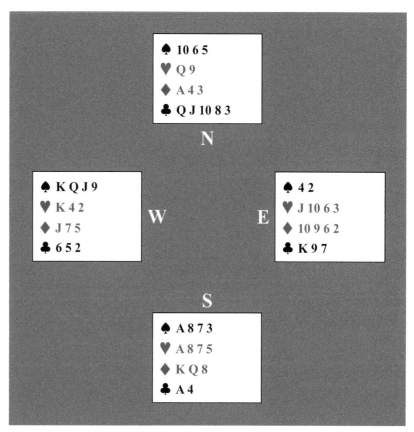

N
♠ 10 6 5
♥ Q 9
♦ A 4 3
♣ Q J 10 8 3

W
♠ K Q J 9
♥ K 4 2
♦ J 7 5
♣ 6 5 2

E
♠ 4 2
♥ J 10 6 3
♦ 10 9 6 2
♣ K 9 7

S
♠ A 8 7 3
♥ A 8 7 5
♦ K Q 8
♣ A 4

THE BIDDING

East	South	West	North
pass	1NT	pass	2NT
pass	3NT	pass	pass
pass			

Opening lead: ♠K

BIDDING EXPLANATION

South has a clear 1NT opening bid, and North's hand is certainly worth a raise to 2NT, with 9 HCP and a good 5-card club suit. Having 17 HCP, South carries on to game.

THE PLAY

West leads the ♠K, and the declarer, South, is pleased to see North's dummy hand. Thanking partner, South plays low from both hands and lets West win the first trick. West continues with the ♠Q, and this time South wins the trick with the ♠A.

South forms a plan. South sees that the dummy hand will win a number of club tricks once the ♣A and ♣K have been played. South therefore plays the ♣A at trick 3 and leads the ♣4 to the next trick, playing the ♣10 from dummy. South wants whoever has the ♣K to win it. East, however, allows the ♣10 to hold the trick.

South persists in clubs, leading the ♣Q from dummy, forcing East to win the ♣K, as South discards ♥5.

CONTINUED ON NEXT PAGE

Raising NT: Example Deal

This is now the position:

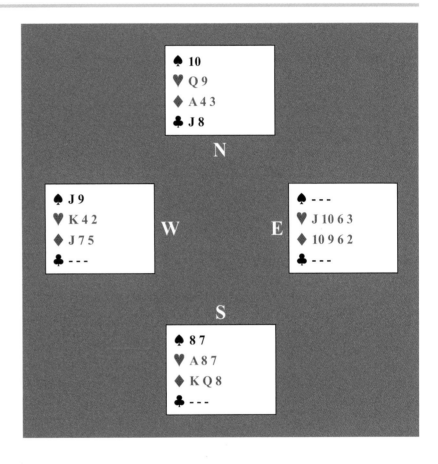

East is on lead, having won the third round of clubs. South, the declarer, has taken three tricks, while the defenders have won two.

East leads the ♥3. Counting tricks, South wants to win six more to go with the three already taken, in order to make the nine-trick contract. South can see three tricks with the ♦AKQ, and the two club winners still in dummy will take two more tricks. Needing just one more trick, South rises with (plays) the ♥A, guaranteeing the contract.

South wins that trick, as well as tricks with the ♦K and ♦Q. South next leads the ♦8 to the ♦A in dummy. With the lead now in dummy, South takes two tricks with the ♣J and ♣8. West claims the final two tricks.

South has taken the nine tricks bid for a *game,* and earned his side 100 points in trick-score, below the line.

WE	THEY	WE	THEY
✕			
100			

2♦ and 2♥ Responses: Jacoby Transfer Bids

Having begun at 1NT, a partnership often makes several further bids before settling on a final contract. Two of responder's replies at the 2 level, 2♦ and 2♥, share a name: *Jacoby transfer* bids. Jacoby transfer bids are the creation of Oswald Jacoby (1902–1984). A superb player, his fame began early as one of the *Four Horsemen of Bridge*, a team of young superstars in the early 1930s.

Oswald Jacoby. Photo courtesy of the American Contract Bridge League.

Jacoby Sequence 1			
South	**West**	**North**	**East**
1NT	pass	2♦	pass
2♥	pass	?	

North has at least 5 hearts!

Jacoby Sequence 2			
South	**West**	**North**	**East**
1NT	pass	2♥	pass
2♠	pass	?	

North has at least 5 spades!

BACKGROUND: OLD-TIME METHODS LEFT BEHIND

In bridge's early days, a 2-level suit response to 1NT showed length in the suit bid, usually a 5-card or longer. When bridge was a simpler game, responder's suit-bids in response to an opening 1NT bid showed a hand with that suit. For instance, 2♣ showed clubs, 2♦ showed diamonds, 2♥ showed hearts, and 2♠ showed spades. Each of these was a *natural* bid that showed length in the suit that was bid.

Well, those early days of simple bidding now are very passé. These days, in place of old-fashioned, "natural" suit-bid responses to 1NT, there are much better ways to use the bids you are allowed to make!

BEYOND 1NT: CONCERN FOR THE MAJOR SUITS

Remember that as the responder to 1NT, you can roughly size up the combined partnership assets. For that reason, your responsibility is either to pass—satisfied that 1NT is already the best contract—or to bid on and guide the partnership to a higher contract.

Much of bridge strategy centers around discovering whether or not your side can bid and make *game* (a contract worth 100 trick-points) in a **single** deal. When partner opens 1NT, responder's bids at the 2 level help the partnership discover whether to bid a notrump game (3NT, needing 9 tricks) or a major suit game (4♥ or 4♠, needing 10 tricks).

It might or might not matter. On some deals, your partnership's cards will be good enough for game in either notrump or in a major—or perhaps for neither. Occasionally game at notrump may be easy to make while a major suit game is difficult or impossible. Sometimes it is just the other way around!

CONTINUED ON NEXT PAGE

JACOBY TRANSFER: WHAT'S IN A NAME?

The *transfer* part of the Jacoby transfer name simply refers to the clever function the call has. You, the responder, must bid the suit that ranks just *below* a major suit that you *actually* have. Your 2♦ bid in response to 1NT asks opener to bid 2♥. Your 2♥ response to 1NT asks the opener to bid 2♠! Partner, who opened 1NT, will be the one to actually bid the suit that you have. The bidding of your suit transfers then from you to your partner.

AFTER THE TRANSFER IS MADE, THEN WHAT?

The two auctions shown on the previous page are the two basic Jacoby transfer bidding sequences (with the opponents always passing). In both auctions, North begins the transfer process by bidding the suit which ranks just below the suit she actually has. Next, South "accepts" the transfer and bids the suit North expects. South is not supposed to make any other bid than the one North wants! In effect, both parts of the Jacoby transfer sequence are "artificial" bids.

North's hand can be weak or strong—or somewhere in between. In the second auction, a transfer to spades, North might have

♠J105432 ♥6 ♦Q3 ♣Q875

and simply be planning next to pass. Or North might have a very promising hand like

♠AQ864 ♥6 ♦KQ982 ♣K2

and be at the start of a longer bidding search for a slam contract in either spades or diamonds.

THE TRANSFER BIDDER'S SECOND CALL

With North's turn to make a second call in the auction, North will have a wide range of choices. North of course may just pass, and leave partner to play a major-suit part-score. But quite often a Jacoby transfer bid is only responder's first move in getting to the best contract. After the transfer into the major has been made, responder may go in a number of directions.

As an example, let's look at the table showing North's choices for a second call in a Jacoby sequences where North's 2♥ transfer bid fetches the expected 2♠ bid from South. In general, North's further bids are natural bids.

Pass	8 or fewer HCP. North leaves it to South to play the hand at 2♠.
2NT	An *invitational* bid. 8-9 HCP with a 5-card spade suit.
	South makes the next decision, to pass, or to bid higher in spades or NT.
3♣	A strong hand with a second suit, clubs. A forcing bid, probable slam interest.
3♦	A strong hand with a second suit, diamonds. Forcing, probable slam interest.
3♥	A strong hand with a second suit, hearts. A forcing bid, probable slam interest.
3♠	An invitational hand with a 6-card spade suit, and 7-9 HCP according to shape. South passes with a doubleton spade and 15 HCP. With 3 or more spades, or with 17 HCP, South should bid on to 4♠.
3NT	A 5-card spade suit and 10-14 HCP. Asks South to choose the final contract.
	South should pass with a doubleton spade, and bid 4♠ with 3 or more spades.
4♥	A 5-card heart suit as well as 5 or 6 spades.
	South can pass and stay in 4♥ or go to 4♠.
4♠	A "sign-off" at game, with 6 or 7 spades, and 9-14 HCP, less with great distribution. South is expected to pass.
6♠	6-card suit or longer, 16-17 HCP, could be less with great distribution.

Jacoby Transfer Bids: Sample Sequences

You'll see that some of responder's second bids are *forcing* calls (new suit at the 3-level), while others are *sign-off* bids (game or slam in responder's actual major). 2NT or 3 of the major are *invitational* bids, allowing opener to pass, or continue to game. Notice that 3NT, a game bid, is not a complete sign-off. It requests opener to "correct" to 4-of-a-major, if opener wants, or if not to pass.

Here are examples of the Jacoby transfer bid in action:

NORTH
♠94
♥QJ743
♦Q85
♣AJ4

South	West	North	East
1NT	pass	2♦	pass
2♥	pass	3NT	pass
4♥	pass	pass	pass

SOUTH
♠A6
♥K105
♦A1097
♣KQ63

With 3-card support for partner's 5-card heart suit, South chooses to play in 4♥, where the partnership has an 8-card trump fit. 4♥ will be an easy contract for South, whereas 3NT will almost surely go down on a spade opening lead. (South's spade stopper, the ♠A, will soon be gone. When the opponents win the ♥A, they should be able to take enough tricks in spades to beat 3NT.)

NORTH
♠94
♥QJ743
♦Q85
♣AJ4

South	West	North	East
1NT	pass	2♦	pass
2♥	pass	3NT	pass
pass	pass	pass	

SOUTH
♠AQ10
♥105
♦AJ109
♣KQ63

This time, with just a doubleton in hearts, South passes North's 3NT bid. 3NT should be a certain contract, with declarer easily able to win at least 9 tricks. 4♥ might also succeed, but might well go down, especially if one opponent holds 4 or more hearts! Notice that North has the same hand as in the previous example.

CONTINUED ON NEXT PAGE

NORTH
♠KJ10743
♥4
♦A10
♣Q854

East	South	West	North
pass	1NT	pass	2♥
pass	2♠	pass	4♠
pass	pass	pass	

SOUTH
♠Q6
♥AKJ2
♦985
♣AJ72

Here North with a 6-card suit and game-going strength jumps right to 4♠, a sign-off bid that places the final contract. South knows to pass. The road to 10 tricks should be quite easy. Declarer should get 5 tricks in trumps, 2 top hearts, the ♦A, and at least two tricks in clubs. The defense will be made to take the ♠A and will also be given a chance to win the ♣K. And they might even win one more trick. Game at 3NT would be in jeopardy if the opponents start by leading diamonds.

NORTH
♠J87432
♥4
♦A10
♣9854

East	South	West	North
pass	1NT	pass	2♥
pass	2♠	pass	pass
pass			

SOUTH
♠Q6
♥AK92
♦985
♣AK72

This time North has a much poorer hand and passes the transfer to 2♠. Depending on how the East–West cards are placed, South will probably make 8 or 9 tricks at this contract.

ADVANTAGES OF THE JACOBY TRANSFER BID

As you get used to playing Jacoby transfers, you will grow to appreciate how well they work. These are their two big advantages.

1. The bidding is very flexible. Further bids after the major-suit transfer help the partnership reach its best contract, whether part-score, game, or slam.

2. The 1NT bidder will become declarer in responder's major suit. The transfer maneuver makes the 1NT opener be the one bidding the major suit actually possessed by responder. When this happens, declarership in that suit goes to the 1NT opener. As a result, the likely *stronger* hand—with 15-17 HCP—is the declarer. (Remember, when your side wins the contract at a suit or at NT, the partner who first bid that suit or NT becomes the declarer. Who bid the suit last doesn't matter.)

The declaring hand has an automatic edge on the first trick, and with a strong hand (15–17 HCP) that advantage will be even greater! Whoever plays the fourth (and final) card on any trick has the advantage of seeing the cards both opponents have played, and can therefore win or lose the trick with the lowest card necessary, saving any higher cards for later tricks in that suit (see in Chapter 7, ahead, "Declarer Play").

Consider one example. The 1NT bidder has

♠K53
♥AQ10
♦K432
♣K73

No matter what suit is led, declarer's task of taking tricks gets easier. If hearts, declarer can win with the lowest card needed and still retain the highest card in the suit for later. Any other suit lead gives declarer an easy chance to win the king of that suit.

Without a transfer bid, this hand might instead be the dummy hand, and play second to the opening lead, not fourth. Playing second, with one defender yet to play to the trick, the ♥Q or ♥10 or any of the kings might still be captured by an opponent who has a higher card to play!

WHAT YOU GIVE UP BY PLAYING JACOBY TRANSFERS

By agreeing to play Jacoby transfer bids, your partnership has little opportunity to play a 2♦ contract after a 1NT opening bid. That's not a lot to be concerned about. A 2♦ contract's 40 points in trick-score below the line is the same as the score for 1NT. Although there may be a few times where 2♦ succeeds but 1NT fails, most of the time 1NT will be just as easy to make as 2♦. A weak responding hand with diamonds can pass the 1NT opening bid.

WHAT IF AN OPPONENT ENTERS THE AUCTION?

In bridge your happy bidding plans may get disrupted if the opponents enter the auction too. We'll look at the general topic of both sides bidding in chapters 8 and 11. For now, it's important that you and your partner have some bidding plans in place when the auction takes one of the paths shown here:

South	West	North	East
1NT	Dbl.	?	

South	West	North	East
1NT	2♠	?	

In the first case, both of your transfer bids are still possible, and you can continue to play the Jacoby transfer bid when this occurs, if you wish. Be sure that both you and your partner agree. But if an opponent comes in with a 2♥ or 2♠ bid over 1NT, your 2♦ or 2♥ Jacoby bid is no longer a legal call!

This is a topic to be aware of now, without looking for all the answers instantly. Later on it will be worth having a discussion with your partner as to what various bids and bid sequences may mean.

 TIP

There are no minimum HCP "requirements" for making a Jacoby transfer bid. What matters is that responder wants to be in a different contract than 1NT. With

♠9875432
♥Q
♦93
♣1054

bid 2♥ in response to 1NT in order to let partner play a 2♠ contract. That's a bid that has a chance to succeed, since your side has at least 9 trumps (partner opening 1NT has at least 2 cards in any suit). Your partner will win a number of tricks with your trumps. At 1NT, those spades are not likely to take any tricks at all!

When bridge was a simpler game, responder's suit-bids in response to 1NT bid showed that suit. A bid of 2♣ meant that you had some clubs.

Today, when you respond 2♣ to 1NT, the bid has *nothing* to do with the clubs in your hand! Instead, it is an artificial, *conventional* bid, another tool for responder to use, in order to guide the partnership to its best contract. Like the 2♦ or 2♥ *Jacoby transfer* bid, this 2♣ response also has a special purpose and name: *Stayman*.

Sam Stayman and George Rapée. Photos courtesy of the American Contract Bridge League.

South	West	North	East
1NT	pass	2♣	pass
?			

The *Stayman convention* is named after Sam Stayman (1909–1993), a champion bridge player and devoted advocate of the game. In 1945, Stayman wrote an influential article describing the 2♣ convention, although the player actually to have concocted it was Stayman's bridge partner at the time, George Rapée (1915–1999). The pair was using the convention very successfully in big bridge tournaments. Without aiming to do so, Stayman received the credit and glory for the convention.

FOCUS ON THE MAJORS

Again, the focus is on the 2 major suits, hearts and spades. When you bid 2♣ (the *Stayman* convention) opposite partner's opening 1NT, you specifically want to know if partner's notrump bid includes 4-card length in either major. You want to learn if opener has a heart suit of at least 4 cards, or a spade suit of at least 4 cards (occasionally an opening 1NT bid includes a 5-card major).

By learning about opener's major suit holdings, responder can tell when each partner has 4 cards of the same suit, and guide the partnership to play in that suit. A 4-4 fit (in any suit) can be a good *trump fit* for a partnership's final contract.

OPENER'S REPLY TO STAYMAN 2♣ BID

When using a *Jacoby transfer* bid (2♦ or 2♥), responder gets one specific bid back from the 1NT opener. By contrast, the Stayman 2♣ response to 1NT gives the opener a few choices of calls.

The Stayman 2♣ response simply asks opener to bid a 4-card major suit. Only in response to an opening 1NT bid does 2♣ have this meaning.

With 4 or more spades, opener bids 2♠.

South	West	North	East
1NT	pass	2♣	pass
2♠			

With 4 or more hearts, opener bids 2♥.

South	West	North	East
1NT	pass	2♣	pass
2♥			

With no 4-card major, opener bids 2♦. This bid simply denies holding as many as 4 cards in either major suit. In the auction shown, South's 2♦ call is just part of the Stayman convention, and is also an artificial bid. The number of diamond cards South actually holds is not relevant to making the bid.

South	West	North	East
1NT	pass	2♣	pass
2♦			

Opener must always let responder be in charge, and must make no reply other than 2♦ or 2♥ or 2♠. Opener should not, for example, reply 2NT or 3NT to a 2♣ Stayman bid.

On responder's side, responder should not make a Stayman call unless prepared for each reply partner might make. For example, it can be tempting after partner's 1NT with

♠62
♥K654
♦732
♣K864

to bid 2♣ Stayman, looking for a 4-4 heart fit. But it would be awkward to hear a 2♠ reply, which partner might make. It's therefore wiser just to pass 1NT, a contract that stays in safer territory and should have a very good chance to succeed.

CONTINUED ON NEXT PAGE

The Benefit of the 4-4 Fit

Very often an extra trick can be won when an 8-card fit, divided 4-4 between the two hands, is trumps, rather than if that suit were *not* a trump suit—as at a notrump contract. Understanding why this is so takes a bit of study, and involves thinking about how hands are played out.

If you have 8 trumps, your opponents have 5 trumps. Usually five cards will be divided 3-2 between the opponents (but not always). Assume that they are, and that after playing three tricks in trumps (as suggested in the diagram), the opponents are out of trumps—they have all been "drawn" by the play of three rounds of trumps.

Your side, however still has one trump remaining in each hand. If you can arrange to play those 2 trump cards on separate tricks, then they win 2 tricks, not just one! By contrast, at notrumps, or if another suit were trumps, those leftover cards cannot individually win tricks.

Usually placing leftover trumps on separate tricks will be easy, as long as you can lead a suit from one hand that can be trumped in the other! Sometimes you can make more than one extra trick by trumping, or *ruffing*, a few times in each hand. If you can ruff enough times, it's possible actually to win 8 tricks with those 8 trumps! The ability to ruff in one hand, and then in the other, is called a *cross-ruff*, as we have seen in the previous chapter.

The Stayman Bidder's Further Bids

The Stayman bidder's second call can follow a number of bidding paths, partly depending upon the 1NT bidder's reply. Usually the Stayman bidder will make some further call, although on an exceptional hand like ♠J876 ♥J876 ♦J10765 ♣----, the Stayman bidder can pass any reply by the 1NT opener, including 2♦!

Here are the general guidelines, with a few examples:

A jump to game by the Stayman bidder is a sign-off, except that the 1NT opener may bid his other major over 3NT by responder.

South	West	North	East
1NT	pass	2♣	pass
2♠	pass	3NT	pass
?			

North's hand might be

♠Q10 ♥QJ103 ♦KQJ65 ♣J9

There's no point in any other bid by North, such as 3♦, since 5♦ (an 11-trick game) does not look easier than the 9-trick 3NT choice. South might still bid 4♥, which North will pass.

A bid of 2NT is invitational to 3NT, and shows no 4-4 has been found.

South	West	North	East
1NT	pass	2♣	pass
2♦	pass	2NT	pass
?			

North's hand might be

♠94 ♥Q1072 ♦Q10983 ♣AJ

North has a 4-card major suit and a very sound invitational bid of 2NT. In fact, instead of leaving the decision to partner, some holding the North will just take a shot and bid 3NT, rather than 2NT.

A raise to the 3-level of partner's major suit response promises a 4-4 fit but is invitational also, leaving opener to pass or carry on to game.

South	West	North	East
1NT	pass	2♣	pass
2♥	pass	3♥	pass
?			

North's hand could be

♠A874 ♥J1083 ♦A42 ♣109

An aggressive bidder might have bid 4♥ instead of 3♥, but here North is leaving it up to partner.

The bid of a new suit at the 3-level is forcing by the Stayman bidder, and shows length in the suit just bid along with a 4-card major.

South	West	North	East
1NT	pass	2♣	pass
2♠	pass	3♦	pass
?			

North's hand might be

♠A107 ♥AQ102 ♦KQJ65 ♣5

Slam looks like a good possibility. With 16 HCP and attractive distribution, North would like to reach a slam, perhaps in diamonds, hearts, or notrumps. Further bidding may help North choose the best place for the final contract.

CONTINUED ON NEXT PAGE

Here's a typical Stayman auction, leading to playing in a 4-4 trump fit:

NORTH
♠6532
♥AQ62
♦Q6
♣J42

SOUTH
♠AKQ4
♥K4
♦943
♣KQ86

South	West	North	East
1NT	pass	2♣	pass
2♠	pass	4♠	pass
pass	pass		

North has two 4-card majors, and enough strength to bid for game, so North uses the 2♣ Stayman convention to see if South has a 4-card major. When South replies 2♠ to show a 4-card spade suit, North brings the partnership directly to its final contract by bidding game, 4♠. In the play, South will make 10 tricks at spades if the opponents' spades divide 3-2. South's winners will be 3 top spades, 3 top hearts, 2 tricks in clubs (after the ♣A gets played), and the 2 leftover trumps to be won on separate tricks. For example, the fourth and last heart in dummy can be ruffed in declarer's hand, to put the trumps on separate tricks.

Note that even though the N-S hands each have balanced 4-4-3-2 shape, the 9-trick 3NT game will go down. The opponents should be able to win at least 4 diamond tricks plus the ♣A.

WHICH MAJOR TO BID, WHEN YOU HAVE BOTH

If you have opened 1NT, and have 4 cards in each major suit, discuss with your partnership whether to respond to Stayman first with 2♥ or 2♠. On the theory that the Stayman bidder would not bid 2♣ unless prepared to hear 2♠, bid 2♠ first. However, if you and your partner wish instead to first respond 2♥ when you have both majors, that's okay, and many pairs prefer that choice.

WHAT YOU GIVE UP BY PLAYING STAYMAN

By agreeing to play the Stayman convention, your partnership has little opportunity to play a 2♣ contract after a 1NT opening bid. That's not a lot to be concerned about. A 2♣ contract's 40 points in trick-score below the line is the same as the score for 1NT. Although there may be a few times where 2♣ succeeds but 1NT fails, most of the time 1NT will be just as easy to make as 2♣. A weak responding hand with clubs can pass the 1NT opening bid.

DON'T SAY "STAYMAN" IN THE AUCTION

Although the 2♣ bid opposite 1NT is referred to as Stayman, that word is not allowed to be heard during the auction. Just say "Two clubs" in a neutral tone of voice. Later, after the hand is over and you are discussing the bidding, it's OK to say "Stayman."

WHAT IF AN OPPONENT ENTERS THE AUCTION?

We have already mentioned in the Jacoby Transfer section, earlier, that your happy bidding plans can be disturbed by opponents who come into the auction. In fact, any bid at all by them removes the opportunity to bid 2♣.

South	West	North	East
1NT	2♦	?	

It's a topic to be aware of now, without looking for all the answers instantly. Later on it will be worth having a discussion with your partner as to what various bids and bid sequences may mean. For starters, you could bid their suit — in this case diamonds—at the next highest level (in this case North could call 3♦), and let this be your artificial way of asking partner to bid a 4-card major. That's a pretty advanced concept, though. And to make that bid you will need a hand of game strength, probably 9 or more HCP. With no 4-card major, partner will sign off at 3NT.

Dealer: East

East–West Vulnerable

THE BIDDING

East	South	West	North
pass	1NT	pass	2♣
pass	2♥	pass	4♥
pass	pass	pass	

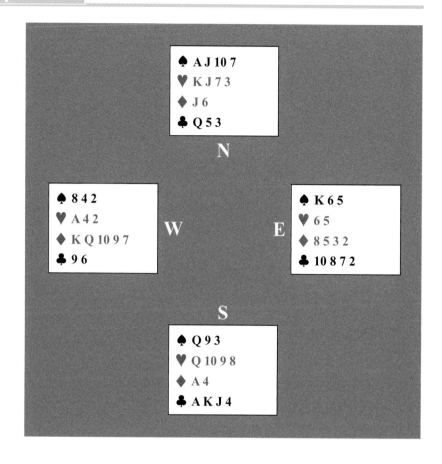

Opening lead: ♦K

BIDDING EXPLANATION

South makes a classic 16-point 1NT opening bid. North, with 12 HCP, knows the partnership has the strength to make a game contract.

North has 4 cards in each major and wants to bid the game contract that is most likely to succeed. North wants to explore the possibility of her side's finding a 4-4 trump fit in one of the major suits.

North bids 2♣, which partner recognizes as the Stayman convention, requesting the 1NT opener to bid a 4-card major suit. South, holding four hearts, obediently bids 2♥.

North now sees a likely game contract in hearts, the partnership's 4-4 suit fit. Consequently, North promptly bids 4♥, which ends the bidding as the next three players pass.

THE PLAY

West leads the king of diamonds. South, the declarer, thanks North warmly as the dummy hand is placed on the table.

South wins the opening lead with the ♦A and immediately attacks the trump suit, hearts, at trick 2, leading the ♥Q. West wins the ♥A and plays the ♦Q to win a second trick for the defense. West may already realize this contract will probably not be beaten!

At trick 4, West exits by leading a small trump. South chooses to win this trick in dummy with the ♥K as East follows suit.

CONTINUED ON NEXT PAGE

Declarer, knowing that the defenders started with a total of five trumps, has seen four of them played, and so draws the opponent's final trump, leading the ♥7 from dummy, and overtaking with the ♥9, as East discards a diamond.

With five tricks already played—two rounds of diamonds and three rounds of hearts—the position is as follows:

South is on lead, and can win all the rest of the tricks if West has the ♠K! South leads ♠Q and when West and North both play low, East wins with the ♠K.

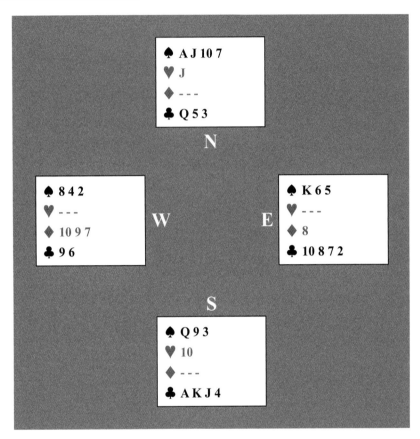

That makes the third—but final—trick for the defense. No matter how East continues, South wins all the remaining tricks with high cards in trumps, spades, and clubs. South makes a total of ten tricks, and game in hearts.

WE	THEY	WE	THEY
✕			
120			

You may be amazed at how well your 1NT auctions can proceed just by passing, raising, and knowing the use of the *Stayman* convention (2♣) and the *Jacoby transfer* bids (2♦ and 2♥). Of course, responder to 1NT can make higher-level suit bid calls as well. Very briefly, let's look at those too, with a brief guideline for the use of each:

Response to 1NT	Meaning or Purpose
2♠	Rather than make a 2♥ Jacoby transfer bid, you will be the ♠ declarer.
3♣, 3♦	Strong, suggesting slam, at least 5 cards of the suit bid.
3♥, 3♠	Strong, suggesting slam, though you could also start with a transfer bid.
4♣	A special bid, see Chapter 14.
4♦	A bid with little usefulness.
4♥, 4♠	Direct jump to game, with a good chance to make, no interest in slam.
5♣, 5♦	Direct jump to game, with a good chance to make, no interest in slam.
6 of any suit	Direct jump to slam, usually a hand with great distributional strength.

Responder's 3-level suit-bid shows a strong hand where even slam may be possible. The 1NT bidder must bid again.

1NT opener must pass after responder's jump to a game or slam contract.

1NT opener must pass after responder's 2♠. This is a bid without high usefulness, since responder with spades can just transfer to 2♠ via a 2♥ Jacoby transfer bid.

EXAMPLE: PARTNER OPENS 1NT

♠AJ4
♥----
♦KQ54
♣QJ7653

You should bid 3♣. A contract of 3NT might be defeated when opponents attack by leading hearts.

♠AJ4
♥Q4
♦K4
♣QJ7653

By contrast, now you should bid 3NT. Here you have less concern about your opponents' heart strength, because your ♥Q could be a very helpful value.

CONTINUED ON NEXT PAGE

♠K2
♥----
♦A1093
♣QJ108543

Bid 5♣.

Keep in mind that while 5♣ is not a guaranteed contract, neither is 3NT. 3NT could be at risk if your partner is weak in hearts, so five of your long minor looks like the safer game to bid.

As with this hand, your leap to a minor suit game should be based on dynamic, unbalanced distribution, with about 7 to 12 HCP. You should usually have a 7-card suit or longer, but it might also be appropriate at times with a 6-card suit.

An immediate bid of slam in a suit, although rare, is also possible and appropriate if you foresee a good possibility of 12 tricks for your side to win.

♠A106
♥----
♦KQ108543
♣AQJ

Bid 6♦.

This contract is very likely to succeed facing a 1NT opening bid.

For more on slam bidding, see Chapter 14.

IF YOU HAVE A PART-SCORE

Let's say your side has a 60 part-score, and partner opens 1NT. The 40 points in trick-score for making that contract already are enough to add to *game*—100 points scored below the line. With a hand such as the one shown, you should just pass. You need not raise to 2NT or bid 3NT. Having a 60 partial, it won't matter that the overtrick score goes above the line!

If you hold

♠KQ9 ♥J932 ♦K8 ♣J1075

with 60 toward game, you should just *pass* your partner's 1NT bid.

True, without a part-score you would head to a 3NT game—or possibly 4♥ by using Stayman. But with a part-score, 1NT already provides the 40 trick-score points needed to complete your game. If your opponents decide to compete with you in the bidding, they suffer the risk of being doubled and losing a big penalty score.

If instead you have a 40 part-score, you might raise 1NT to 2NT on a hand where you would have simply passed 1NT. Because 2NT is enough for game (partner will pass), with 40 toward game, you would raise to 2NT on a hand with as few as 6 HCP.

With

♠Q8 ♥J107 ♦K865 ♣J975

you should raise 1NT to 2NT.

BID 3NT WITH LONG MINOR AND ENOUGH POINTS

With

♠72 ♥863 ♦AKQ983 ♣97

game in diamonds (11 tricks) is probably unlikely, whereas game in NT (9 tricks) should be very likely.

Consequently, even though your diamond suit is excellent, there's no real point in bidding that suit! Why let the player on opening lead know where your strength lies?

STAYMAN RESPONSE WITH 5-4 IN MAJORS

When you have a 5-card major, you can use a *Jacoby transfer* so that partner bids the suit. However, when you also have 4 cards in the other major, it's better to use the Stayman convention instead.

With

♠KQ65 ♥J9753 ♦2 ♣832

start with 2♣, the Stayman convention. If partner bids 2♥ or 2♠, you will pass either bid and be in a very good contract. But if partner bids 2♦ —showing no 4-card major—just bid 2♥. Partner should pass and leave you to play in this part-score contract that you are likely to make.

This two-level call is a sign-off bid. With a stronger hand (turn the ♦2 into ♦A), you would instead jump a bidding level to 3♥, which would be a forcing bid.

chapter 7

Declarer Play

A special feature of bridge is that one player—the *declarer*—picks the cards to play from two hands—the declarer's own hand and the dummy's. The dummy, meanwhile, watches in silence, rooting for the contract's success. That success usually hinges upon the declarer's choices of which cards to play and when to play them.

On any single deal, there may be trillions of different ways that 13 tricks could be played. Regrettably, you as the declarer get only one chance to play out the hand. This chapter shows you how to choose your best line of play.

You as Declarer

When you are declarer, your partner's dummy hand is placed on the table. You are in charge of those 13 cards as well as your own. You command the play of half the cards in the deck. This can be a great advantage to you if you know how to play your cards right!

Don't be daunted. Initially, here's what to do.

- **Say "Thank you."** Once the dummy's cards are all on the table, you say, "Thank you," or "Thank you, partner." While this statement has no effect on the play, it's a solid tradition that experienced players almost always follow.

- **Pause and view.** Your next move as declarer is to carefully look over the dummy hand on the table. Take a brief moment to size up the two hands' combined trick-taking potential. This is also your last time—and everybody else's—to see the dummy's full hand. This habit of pausing and viewing the dummy works in your favor, because it helps you plan the full play of the hand. When you pause and view, later on you will more easily recall dummy's full 13-card hand, even after many cards are gone from it.

Declarer's partner laying out dummy hand.

- **Play bridge often.** Of course, the declarer must watch carefully in order to remember all that happened during the play. The more often you play, the better you'll get at this key skill: to be a keen observer. Take the time to watch the cards played and keep them in your memory. Also with continued play comes the comfort of successfully performing the mental chores that declarer needs to do time after time, hand after hand.

At first, you may not recognize whether your contracts are easy, or whether they require careful technique in play. Becoming a *good* declarer usually takes plenty of bridge experience. If you can, it helps to make a commitment of time to playing bridge. The more you play, the more your skills improve. The more you get to declare, the better you become at this challenging component of the game.

- **Develop essential declarer skills.** Pausing, observing, and remembering are the foundation of every declarer's responsibilities. To be a good declarer, you also need to *count, plan, know technique,* and *know your odds.* You'll be taking a closer look at each of these skills in the section, "Essential Skills for Declarer."

TIP

When the dummy's cards are put down, all 26 cards that you control are in full sight for you—and *only* you—to see. This first moment is also the last moment you will see your combined assets all together. Make the moment count!

When you are the declarer, your partner, the player who is the *dummy,* can help you in a few limited ways.

- Dummy may indicate to you whether the lead is in your hand or in the dummy hand.

- When you do not follow suit to a trick, dummy may ask you if you are *sure* that you have no cards of the suit led. For example, if diamonds are led, but you play a heart, dummy might ask, "No diamonds, partner?" If it turns out that you do have a diamond to follow suit with, then dummy has saved you from *revoking* (not following suit when you could follow suit). You can then play a diamond and put the heart back in your hand.

  Note: *Remember, not following suit when you could have followed suit—that is, revoking—is a violation of bridge rules. The penalty for a revoke is usually two tricks.*

Dummy's partner, declarer, reaching to lead a card from dummy.

- You can ask dummy for his/her physical assistance in the play of the dummy cards. Instead of reaching across the table each time to play the cards you want, you might prefer to *call* the card you want from the dummy hand. Dummy is expected to play the card you call for.

  Note: *Whenever you call for dummy to play a card you designate, be very clear about which card you want.*

Other than these ways, dummy may *not* assist you. Dummy is not permitted to aid you in deciding or planning the play of the hand, or in counting or remembering cards that have been played. Nor can dummy indicate, point to, or select any card for you to play.

Of course, dummy is not to show reactions of approval or disapproval to your choice of plays, or to offer any verbal advice.

Keeping Track of Tricks

When a trick is completed, it is often quickly taken away and turned over, and you may not have seen it long enough to get a full view. As a result, cards played on that trick may not have really registered in your mind.

In most games, you are routinely allowed to look at the cards from the previous trick, as long as you haven't played to the next trick. Naturally, each defender receives a similar courtesy.

Turning over a trick of 4 cards.

As the declarer, after taking six tricks, it is customary to stack them up in one big pile. These first six tricks are referred to as a *book*, and each trick after these six can now be easily counted on the way to fulfilling your contract.

A book (6 tricks), plus 2 tricks taken.

Example Deal: Catching a Break

Let's take a peek at declarer in action.

Dealer: North

Both Sides Vulnerable

THE BIDDING

North	East	South	West
pass	pass	1♥	pass
2♣	pass	2♠	pass
2NT	pass	3♠	pass
4♥	pass	pass	pass

Opening lead: ♦A

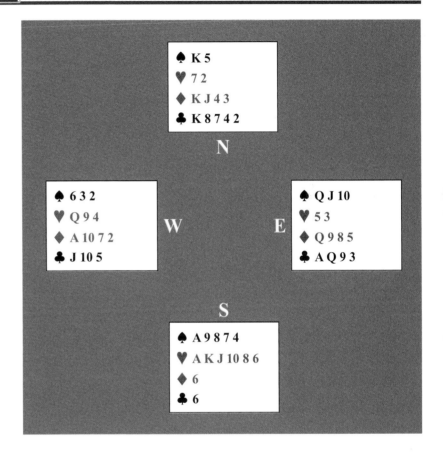

BIDDING EXPLANATION

After two passes, South, having a hand of very nice shape, opens 1♥ in third seat. North responds 2♣, showing ten or more HCP and usually at least five clubs.

Next, South bids 2♠ and North, with a stopper (good cards) in diamonds, tries 2NT. South continues to 3♠. South's bidding sequence suggests a hand with six hearts and five spades.

North now bids 4♥. North trusts that the partnership has landed in an 8-card trump fit. 4♥ becomes the final contract.

THE PLAY

West places the ♦A on the table and South, the declarer, thanks North for the dummy.

Before proceeding to the first trick, South takes a moment to look at the dummy and to form an overall plan for playing the hand. Having thought things over, declarer plays a low diamond from dummy, and all follow suit as West wins the trick.

At trick 2, West *shifts* to the ♣J. South plays a low club from dummy, and West's ♣J holds this trick, too. When West continues at trick 3 with the ♣10, South ruffs with the ♥6 and captures that trick.

South has taken the time to size up the key suits—hearts and spades. South has formed a plan to take ten tricks and land the contract.

CONTINUED ON NEXT PAGE

Let's follow declarer (South)'s thoughts on this hand in more detail.

Declarer has already viewed and counted the number of cards held in the two key suits. In trumps (hearts), declarer has six in hand plus two in dummy, for a total of eight. The opponents therefore have five trumps.

Doing the same calculating in spades, South knows that the opponents together have six cards in that suit.

South also sees that dummy has only two spades, and that once those two spades are played, dummy can trump the third round of spades. Those plays could bring down all six of the opponents' spades.

Declarer forms a plan: First win the ♠K, and then win the next trick with the ♠A. After that, continue with a *third* round of spades and ruff in dummy.

South plans to watch and count the opponents' cards in spades. South may be able to *establish* his fourth and fifth spades as winners.

So, having already taken trick 3 with the ♥6, South follows the plan. South leads the ♠4 from hand to the dummy's ♠K, and then the ♠5 back to South's ace, winning both those tricks. Declarer next leads the ♠7, and trumps in dummy with the ♥7.

Because declarer has been *observing*, *remembering*, and *counting*, declarer knows that these last three tricks have captured all of the opponents' six spade cards.

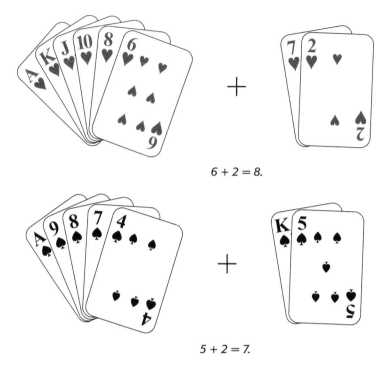

6 + 2 = 8.

5 + 2 = 7.

This is now the position:

Dummy is on lead. Declarer now leads dummy's ♥2 to his ♥J. This loses to West's ♥Q. However, South the declarer will next trump West's likely ♣5 return, and then play enough high trumps to *draw*—that is, remove—whatever remaining trumps the enemy still have. South then wins the rest of the tricks, because the ♠9 and ♠8 are established winners.

In all, South takes ten tricks: four spade tricks, five heart tricks in South's own hand, and the spade trick trumped in dummy. The defenders have won only three tricks: ♦A, ♣J, and ♥Q, not enough to defeat the contract.

South's plan is successful: to establish spades, and then collect trumps. Of course, South was lucky to find the six enemy spades divided evenly, three in each hand.

North–South score 120 below the line, 100 above the line for 100 honors, and also capture the 500-point rubber bonus.

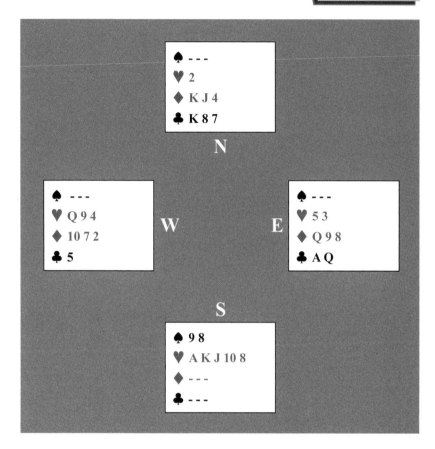

TIP

Kibitzer's Observation
If South had tried to draw trumps first, *before* playing spades, South would have lost one spade trick and not made the contract.

WE	THEY	WE	THEY
✕			
500			
100			
	60		
	60		
100			
120			

To be a winning declarer, you need to *count, plan, know technique*, and *know your odds*.

DEVELOP COUNTING SKILLS

Good bridge requires *a lot* of counting. Besides counting HCP (high card points) on every hand, you also should try to count the way each 13-card suit is dealt around the table, and also what each player's hand pattern may be. However, both of these are skills which develop over a considerable time period.

At first, the most important thing is to try to pay attention to who plays what cards so you can get a feel for how the suits were distributed. Notice especially when a player has no more of a suit—this will tell you how many in that suit the player started with—if you've been watching (and remembering) the cards.

PLAN YOUR PLAYS

As declarer overlooking two hands in play, you are in charge of most of the action. Because you control so much, the sequence of plays you choose can really matter. You choose the sequence of taking high cards, or winners. You also control playing tricks that may lose, but which will result in winning cards for tricks later in the play.

KNOW BASIC CARD-PLAY TECHNIQUE

Winning tricks involves a lot more than *hoping* that everyone else plays cards lower than yours. You need to learn *techniques* of play!

After you've played awhile, you may notice that some suit arrangements, or combinations start to come up again and again. Mastering techniques of playing familiar—or any—suit combinations is one ingredient of good declarer play.

Some suits require no technique at all in play. In suit Combination A (right), it should be very easy to play hearts for five winners. Suit Combination B requires a little bit more skillful play.

Consider the four suit combinations below. How can each be played to take the greatest number of tricks?

For each heart suit combination, what's the best play for five tricks? (The answers soon!)

A	♥AJ1087	♥KQ9
B	♥AJ1087	♥Q93
C	♥AJ1087	♥K93
D	♥AQ1064	♥987

As you become familiar with suit combinations in bridge, the opportunity to use proper playing techniques will arise over and over again.

KNOW YOUR ODDS

Luck is always a part of bridge. The cards played may fall nicely for you, or not, according to chance alone. If you know something about probability—odds and percentages—you'll have a better idea of when to rely on luck and when not to.

WEST	EAST
♣AKQ65	♣432

What are the chances that the A K Q will capture all of the opponents' cards in the suit?

You can't win every bridge trick with an ace. There are 13 tricks in bridge and only *four* aces to go around! To win tricks with cards other than aces, the knowledge of card-play technique can help a lot.

Let's say you are the declarer looking at this suit combination:

You want to take two tricks in diamonds. If you lead the ♦A, you will win two tricks only if a defender plays the ♦K under your ace. That's not likely to occur!

A better technique is to lead a diamond from dummy. You are playing for the chance that East may hold the ♦K. If East plays the ♦K, you play your ace. If East plays low, you play the ♦Q.

Half the time, East will have the ♦K and you will win tricks with both the ♦Q and the ♦A. All you have to do is *watch* what card East plays.

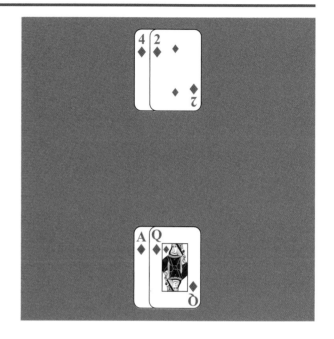

FINESSE

This very basic play in bridge technique is called a *finesse*. Finesse is not an easy word to define. Basically, it's a play that depends upon whether a certain key card has been dealt to one opponent, rather than to the other. In this example, the ♦K is the key card. As long as East has that card, South can win two tricks in diamonds.

For success, all South needs to do is to start the *first* diamond trick by leading from dummy's hand. To do that, South needs to win a trick (in another suit) in dummy, in order to have an *entry* to dummy to start diamonds from that hand.

South can then gamble on the 50-percent likelihood that East has the ♦K.

CONTINUED ON NEXT PAGE

Here's another example:

South is declarer and wants to take *one* trick in hearts. If South tries to win a heart trick by leading the ♥K from dummy, whoever has the ♥A will simply play it, and South *won't* win a heart trick at all.

Instead, South uses the technique of a finesse. The key card is the ♥A. To use this technique, South, if not already on lead, must find an *entry* to his hand, so that he can lead a low heart *toward* dummy's ♥K.

If West also plays a low heart (any heart lower than the king), declarer puts up dummy's ♥K. If West has been dealt the ♥A, then the ♥K wins the trick.

If West instead decides to play the ♥A, then declarer simply plays low from dummy. Now the ♥K is an established winner for later in the hand!

If instead East has the ♥A, then the ♥K loses. In that case, there is no way for South to win a heart trick at all, unless South can get East to lead the suit. And East probably won't. It's that simple.

TIP

Finessing: The Aftermath

While perhaps a good technique, a finesse is not always a winning play. Half the time, finesses lose! In the first example, if West had the ♦K, the diamond finesse would lose to West's king. Often enough, the chance of a finesse's success is worth the risk of its losing. After all, nothing ventured, nothing gained!

Example Hand: Technique in Finessing

Dealer: South

Both Sides Vulnerable

THE BIDDING

South	West	North	East
1NT	pass	3NT	pass
pass	pass		

Opening lead: ♠4

BIDDING EXPLANATION

With 15 HCP and a balanced hand, South, as dealer, opens 1NT. North, holding 10 HCP, knows the combined partnership count is 25, 26, or 27. That should be enough for a shot at game. Therefore, North bids 3NT. She does not see any prospect for game in a major suit, or in a minor suit.

While North can't be sure that 3NT will make, North knows her partner will have at least a reasonable chance to take nine tricks.

THE PLAY

To defeat declarer's nine-trick contract, the defenders need to win five tricks. West looks to a long suit, spades, to possibly create winners later in the hand. West selects the ♠4 for the opening lead. North places dummy on the table. South, the declarer, says "Thank you." At the same time, South begins to examine the dummy and to consider how nine tricks might be won.

Sizing things up, South can see right away that nine tricks are *not* immediately possible. Work must be done.

N

♠ Q 7 3
♥ J 9
♦ K J 10 3
♣ K 7 5 4

W

♠ A 10 8 4 2
♥ 6 5
♦ A Q 9 8
♣ Q 10

E

♠ 9 6
♥ Q 10 8 7 3
♦ 4 2
♣ J 9 6 3

S

♠ K J 5
♥ A K 4 2
♦ 7 6 5
♣ A 8 2

CONTINUED ON NEXT PAGE

At trick 1, South plays a low spade from dummy, and wins East's ♠9 with the ♠J. South can now begin to count winners. South can count on two easy winners each in clubs and hearts, one trick already taken in spades, and one more trick to take in spades, still having both the king and the queen. That makes a total of six tricks. Doing simple arithmetic, declarer determines that three more tricks must be found in order to make the contract.

$$2 + 2 + 2 + ? = 9$$

Declarer wonders about clubs for a moment; declarer might muster one extra trick in clubs. By winning with the ♣A and ♣K and playing a third round of the suit, dummy's last club might then become a winner. That would occur if East and West have three clubs each.

This time, clubs actually divide 4–2, and South's plan will not work. In fact, South will surely be *set* (defeated) taking this line of play. Clearly diamonds must provide the hope of declarer's game-going tricks. With a little bit of luck and the correct technique, the diamond suit can produce three tricks. The luck involves the location of two key cards, the ♦A and the ♦Q. The technique involves leading diamonds from the South hand toward the dummy's better diamonds.

Right away, at trick 2, declarer leads the ♦5 towards dummy. West plays the ♦8 and South plays the ♦10 from dummy. Because West has both key cards, the *finesse* of the ♦10 wins the trick. This is good news, although South must still continue to use good technique. South returns to his hand by leading a low club to the ace. Again in hand, South leads another diamond. This time, West decides to get a little tricky and plays the ♦Q. South calls for dummy's ♦K, and this card wins the trick.

Once more, South wants to use good technique, and again leads diamonds *toward* dummy. This time, South uses hearts as a hand entry, and plays the ♥9 to the ♥A.

This is now the position:

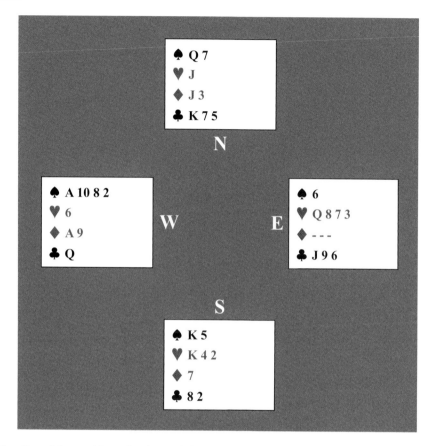

South has taken the first five tricks, and is on lead. South leads the last diamond, the ♦7, and, on this trick at last, West plays the ♦A. South plays ♦3 from dummy. Having noticed and remembered the cards already played in diamonds, declarer knows that dummy's ♦J is the high card in the suit.

South's work is nearly done, although West is on lead. If West plays ♠A and another spade, South now has one more trick in each suit, for a total of nine. The ♣K in dummy is the entry to dummy's hand so that South can play the winning ♦J.

If West plays anything else, South will lead spades to establish the final winner that is needed.

Note how the technique of finessing and using entries brings home the contract. Had declarer ever started diamonds by leading *from* the dummy, West would have won two diamond tricks.

WE	THEY	WE	THEY
✕			
100			

Playing Suit Combinations

There's no card in a suit higher than the ace. Anyone can play an ace and win a trick that way. Taking all of the tricks that you can in a suit, tricks with cards other than aces, requires a study of suit combinations. It's one of the essentials of bridge.

The diamond suit in the previous hand is a good example of a *suit combination* to be studied for its technique. It's the type of suit combination that will occur often in actual play.

Suit Combination A

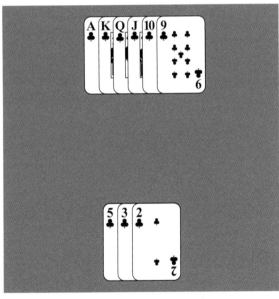

Technique NOT required.

Suit Combination B

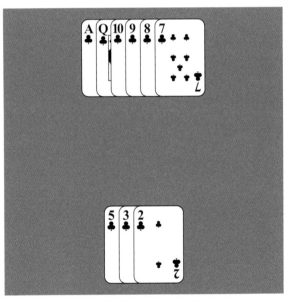

Technique required.

Some suits require no technique at all in play. In Suit Combination A, anyone can play clubs for six winners. Suit Combination B requires a little bit of skillful play.

Consider the four suit combinations below. You've seen them before. How can each be played to take the greatest number of tricks?

A	♥AJ1087	♥KQ9
B	♥AJ1087	♥Q93
C	♥AJ1087	♥K93
D	♥AQ1064	♥987

How do you best play each of the East–West heart suit combinations at the bottom of the opposite page for five tricks?

A This one should not be too difficult, but there could be a trap! If you play the ♥A first from the West hand and play the ♥9 from the East hand, then the East hand must win the next tricks with the ♥K and ♥Q. You will then need a *re-entry* to the West hand for the fourth and fifth hearts. There's no law that says you have to start a suit by leading its ace!

B The key card to think about here is the ♥K. In this case, use the technique of *finessing*. Finesse South for the ♥K by leading the ♥Q. Play low—unless, of course, South plays the ♥K. If the finesse wins, lead ♥9 to repeat the finesse. Let the ♥9 win, unless South plays the ♥K. If South has ♥K 6 5 2, East can finesse once more for the ♥K by leading the ♥3!

If the North hand has the ♥K, of course your finesse will lose, but that's the only trick you will lose in the suit. You have done the best you could, and you will win the remaining tricks in hearts.

C This time the key card missing is the ♥Q. There are actually a few different possible ways to play this suit combination. Technique-wise, the best play to take five tricks with this suit-combination is to the play the king from the East hand. If the queen does not appear, then lead through South, *finessing* South for the key card, the ♥Q.

Whenever the South hand has the ♥Q, this play will succeed, and it will also succeed whenever North has a *singleton* ♥Q. Otherwise, this play will lose a trick to the ♥Q in the North hand, after which your remaining hearts will all be winners.

D Here, *two* key cards are missing, the ♥K and ♥J. Fortunately, you can finesse for two cards at once! To win five tricks, lead the ♥9 and play low from the West hand if South plays low. If the ♥9 wins, repeat the play by leading ♥8 or ♥7. Whenever South plays a card higher than the one you lead, cover it with the card just higher than it from dummy. If South was dealt both key cards, you will win five cards in the suit. If North has one of the key cards, you will not be able to take five tricks, and if North has both ♥K and ♥J, you will probably lose to both of those cards.

Note that the same plays will work just as well in a different suit than hearts!

What are the chances that a finesse will win? Well, if you know math and probability, that can only be good news for your bridge game—especially for your declarer play!

There are levels of probability that apply to bridge that border on higher mathematics. For now, let's look at just a few basic examples of bridge odds.

What are the odds in this situation that a finesse will work?

Consider the simple suit combination shown here. When you lead a diamond from dummy and East plays low, what are the odds that the queen will win the trick?

This is a pretty easy one; the chances are 50 percent. Either East has the ♦K or West has it. Because each player has 13 cards, half the time the king is in one hand, and half the time it's in the other. (Of course, West might have the ♦K and not be paying attention, and will fail to win the trick. That's an extra chance that your ♦Q could win!)

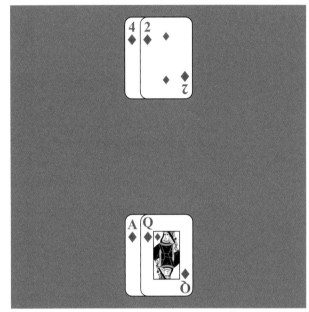

Here's another basic situation:

North–South have a 7-card spade fit, and the opponents have 6. If declarer takes three tricks with the ♠A, ♠K, and ♠Q, what are the odds that South's ♠5 will be the last remaining spade, giving South a fourth trick in the suit?

For this to occur, South needs the 6 outstanding spades to split 3–3. If West has 3, and East has 3, South's ♠5, the *thirteenth* spade, becomes a winning card. You might think the odds are about even that the 6 outstanding cards in the suit split 3–3. Actually, a 3–3 split occurs only 36 percent of the time!

With 6 cards out, a 4–2 split is the most likely division, occurring about 48 percent of the time. A 5–1 split happens about 15 percent of the time, and about 1 percent of the time, the cards will be divided 6–0.

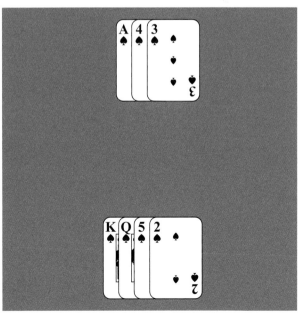

A SMALL ODDS CHART

Here's a small chart of card-division probabilities with 5, 4, and 3 cards missing in a suit.

You have 8; they have 5:	*You have 9; they have 4:*	*You have 10; they have 3:*
3-2 = 68%	2-2 = 40%	2-1 = 78%
4-1 = 28%	3-1 = 50%	3-0 = 22%
5-0 = 4%	4-0 = 10%	

PLAYING THE ODDS

Knowing a little bit about odds and percentages can guide you to making the best play as declarer. Let's say you are South at a notrump contract, and you are on lead in your own hand.

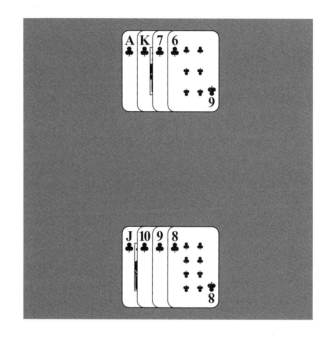

You'd like to make four tricks in clubs. You see that you have every top club except the ♣Q. The ♣Q is the key card that is missing.

You have a choice of plays. If West has the key card, the ♣Q, then you can finesse against West for that card. To do so, play the ♣J (or you could play any of your clubs; they are all *equals*). If West follows with a low club, you should also play low from dummy.

Fifty percent of the time, West will have that key card, and your finesse will win. When it wins, simply repeat the finesse by leading again from your hand, and play low from dummy unless West produces the ♣Q. This continues your good technique, because there are times when West will have been dealt ♣Q543.

An alternative method of not letting the ♣Q win is to just play the ♣A and then the ♣K—hoping those two club leads will *drop* the ♣Q. However, this play will succeed only about a third of the time. The first play, the *finesse*, is the better play.

However, as long as South has a further *entry* to his hand, South can make an even better sequence of plays.

Before finessing, South should first play *one* high club from dummy. Then, if the ♣Q doesn't fall, South should return to hand with an entry and lead the ♣J for a finesse.

This play sequence wins a bit more than 50 percent of the time. It wins every time West has the ♣Q (50 percent) and every time East has the singleton ♣Q (2.8 percent). This series of plays gives a 52.8 percent chance of success for four tricks, and is the best technique for that suit combination.

Competing in the Auction

In bridge, both pairs can take active part in the auction. Even when the other side has opened the bidding, your side can still be the one to make the *final* bid.

This chapter shows you useful and sensible ways to enter an auction that is begun by your opponents. You'll also learn when to simply pass and stay *out* of these auctions.

Ways to Enter the Bidding

Because the auction is open to every player, when the opponent at your right opens the bidding, you must decide whether to enter the auction for your side.

Or, for example, what if both opponents have bid ahead of you? Should you even think about competing in such an auction?

Pretend for a moment that as South you hold:

♠Q432
♥AK
♦K10762
♣85

You must decide whether to compete in auctions such as these:

East	South	West	North
1♣	?		

East	South	West	North
1NT	?		

West	North	East	South
1♥	pass	1NT	?

North	East	South	West
pass	1♦	?	

West	North	East	South
1♣	pass	1♥	?

West	North	East	South
1NT	pass	2♥	?

West	North	East	South
pass	pass	1♥	?

West	North	East	South
1♠	pass	2♠	?

West	North	East	South
1♦	pass	pass	?

YOUR LIMITED BIDDING VOCABULARY

Remember: A bridge auction permits a vocabulary of just 15 different words.

- one
- two
- three
- four
- five
- six
- seven
- club(s)
- diamond(s)
- heart(s)
- spade(s)
- notrump
- pass
- double
- redouble

In bridge, you pass almost as often as you bid. When the player on your right opens the bidding, you will *pass* even more often, probably about 70 percent of the time.

When you *don't* pass, there are two basic ways to enter the auction: by *overcalling* or by *doubling*. In deciding whether to compete, you must carefully consider the shape of your hand, your high card points (HCP), and the vulnerability. You can overcall with a bid in a suit or in notrump. You can enter the auction by saying the word "double." The auctions below illustrate these choices.

OVERCALL IN NOTRUMP

After the opponent opens, you may overcall in notrump at any permitted level. For the time being, we will consider only the simple overcall of 1NT, after the opponent has opened one of a suit.

East	South	West	North
1♥	1NT		

OVERCALL IN A SUIT

After the opponent opens, you may bid any new suit at any higher level.

East	South	West	North
1♣	1♥		

A simple overcall.

East	South	West	North
1♣	2♥		

A jump overcall (see Chapter 11).

For the moment, we will consider simple suit overcalls. Those are overcalls made only at the *cheapest* bidding level available. To find out more about *jump* overcalls in a suit—overcalls that skip one or more bidding levels—turn to Chapter 11.

MAKING A TAKEOUT DOUBLE

One of the few words allowed in the auction is *double*. Saying the word *double* at your side's first turn in the auction requires very special consideration.

East	South	West	North
1♠	Dbl.		

Whenever the opponent has opened a *suit* bid, the function of an early *double* is to request that partner take part in the auction. This early double in the bidding is called a *takeout double*.

In effect, the takeout double really issues your partner an order to join in the auction—assuming that the next player simply passes. You are asking your partner to bid something, and thereby *take* the partnership *out* of the doubled contract!

Note to the Kibitzer: *This use of the double for takeout is a shocking surprise to most new bridge players. They have only just learned how the double inflates the point scores that are written in one column or the other. Suddenly—and also in a most contrary way—the double of the opponent's opening suit bid is intended for quite a different purpose.*

The 1NT Overcall

Starting with the 1NT overcall, let's look at the guidelines for each method of entering an auction that was begun by the opposition.

Guidelines for Overcalling 1NT

The 1NT overcall is a straightforward bid. It indicates that you have the same sort of hand with which you would have opened 1NT.

To overcall 1NT, your hand should meet these three main criteria:

- 15–17 HCP.
- Balanced distribution, with no singletons or voids.
- Stopper(s) in the opponents' suit. If you end up being declarer, you can expect that the suit the opponents bid will also be the suit they lead. *Stoppers* are cards that are likely to win tricks in a suit that the opponents might lead.

COMPETING IN 1NT: EXAMPLES

In these examples, you are South, the next hand.

East opens 1♥. You should bid 1NT.

East opens 1♣. You should pass. You would have *opened* the bidding, but your hand is too weak to *overcall* 1NT.

East opens 1♠. You should bid 1NT.

East opens 1♦. You should bid 1NT.

How to Respond to a 1NT Overcall

Let's briefly consider what to do when you are the *partner* of the 1NT overcaller. Basically, you can respond to an overcall of 1NT almost as you would respond to an opening bid of 1NT, because both 1NT calls describe more or less the same hand.

In an auction like this, North may want to continue bidding.

East	South	West	North
1♠	1NT	pass	?

North may be seeking to reach a better part-score contract than 1NT, or North might even be thinking of game. Although East and South likely already account for 28 or so HCP, there's also just enough room for North to be holding some good cards. If North–South have a game, then West probably has a very weak hand!

You can do pretty well responding to a 1NT overcall with the calls you learned for responding to a 1NT opening bid (see Chapter 6). You can play both the Stayman and Jacoby conventions, although the situation is slightly different with the opponents having made a natural bid in one of the 4 suits. A raise to 2NT is invitational. A jump to the 3 level in a new suit is forcing, exploring for the best game contract, and requires another bid from the 1NT overcaller.

USING THE STAYMAN CONVENTION

You can even use the Stayman 2♣ bid to check out the possibility of a 4-4 major suit fit.

East	South	West	North
1♠	1NT	pass	2♣

In this example, 2♣ can also be used as a Stayman bid. In this case, North–South would be interested in hearts only, because East, the opponent, has the spades.

Note to the Advanced Kibitzer: *Some partnerships prefer to play 2♣ as a natural bid in this auction! In that case, for the purpose of the Stayman call, they would bid the opponent's suit. The bid of a suit already bid by an opponent is known as a cue bid. Here's an example where the North–South pair has decided on using the cue-bid as Stayman when partner overcalls 1NT.*

♠109 ♥QJ63 ♦AQJ82 ♣103.

East	South	West	North
1♠	1NT	pass	2♠

Realizing that her partner has 15–17 HCP, North knows that her side has at least 26 HCP. North wants to bid, and hopefully make, game at 3NT or at 4♥.

In this auction, North bids 2♠! By agreement with her partner, North uses the bid of the enemy suit—in this case, spades—as a version of the Stayman convention.

If South, who overcalled 1NT, has a 4-card heart suit, South will bid 3♥. Otherwise, South will probably just bid 2NT. North will then raise either bid to game.

TIP

Be sure that you and your partner agree as to your bids opposite a 1NT overcall. You can play both Stayman and Jacoby conventions, or you can instead decide to play suit bids as natural bids, with length in the suit called. In that case, a new suit opposite partner's 1NT overcall would be a sign-off bid, asking partner to pass. Whatever choices you make, be sure you and your partner are on the same wavelength. Every partnership is free to choose its favorite bidding methods.

To overcall in a suit, your hand should include these two essential ingredients:

① **A good suit.** This is a suit at least 5 cards long, which contains some of the highest cards of the suit. AQJ954 is an excellent suit for an overcall.

② **Good HCP values.** An overcall at the 2 level (a bid for eight tricks) should be at least the same strength of an opening bid.

An overcall at the 1 level can be a lesser hand. However, when **vulnerable,** the hand for a 1-level overcall should have near the values of an opening bid—or better! However, if *not vulnerable*, a 1-level overcall can be slightly under opening-bid values.

Bidding Level	Suit Length	HCP
1-level NON-VUL	(4) 5+	8–18 HCP+
1-level VUL	5+	12–18 HCP+
2-level NON-VUL	(5) 6+	11–19 HCP
2-level VUL	(5) 6+	13–19 HCP

GUIDELINES FOR SIMPLE OVERCALLS

Example Hands

♠1042
♥73
♦AKJ97
♣K65

East	South	West	North
1♣	?		

South should bid 1♦. South might not have opened 1♦ with only 11 HCP. However, it's okay to *overcall* 1♦. If North–South end up on defense, South wants North to lead diamonds.

> **TIP**
>
> **Bridge Lingo: "Table Talk"**
> Table talk refers to chatter by the players at the table, usually about the hand being played. While bridge laws bar this from tournament play, at home a table of players usually finds a comfortable level of talking during a bridge game, about whatever. It's good form to keep talk about the current hand down to a minimum!

♠1042
♥73
♦AKJ97
♣K65

East	South	West	North
1♠	?		

South should pass. Note that this is the same hand as in the previous example. South is allowed to overcall 2♦, but an eight-trick contract is a risky one. South needs several useful cards in partner's hand just to make 2♦. If North–South are vulnerable, the risk becomes even greater, because the penalty for being set is larger.

♠K2
♥A3
♦AKJ987
♣65

East	South	West	North
1♠	?		

In this example, South should certainly overcall 2♦, vulnerable or not. South needs very little from partner to make 2♦, and if by chance partner has good cards and continues the bidding, then North–South could bid and make a game contract, even though East–West opened the bidding. For example, North–South might be able to make 3NT.

SUIT QUALITY WHEN OPENING AND OVERCALLING

Opening one of a major suit—1♥ or 1♠—promises any 5-card suit, even one as bad as ♠65432. A minor-suit opener—1♣ or 1♦—doesn't require either strength or length in the suit bid! By contrast, a suit in which you overcall should be at least a 5-card suit, and it should also be a suit of some *quality*—headed by a few of the higher cards in the suit.

You could open the bidding 1♣ with a suit as bad as ♣765 (or worse), or with a suit as good as ♣AKQ1098 (or better!). In overcalling, it's not a very good idea to bid a suit such as ♣765.

Note to Kibitzer: *There are more reasons to enter an auction than simply trying to win the final bid. Even when the opponents gain the final contract, your overcall or double can help you and your partner in the play. For example, it may help your partner to make a good opening lead!*

CONTINUED ON NEXT PAGE

Suit Overcalls
(continued)

RESPONSES TO SUIT OVERCALLS

Another big difference between making the opening bid and overcalling is partner's role in each case. With as few as 6 HCP, the partner of an opening bidder is expected to make a bid of some sort. By contrast, the overcaller's partner does *not* have the same obligation.

To begin with, the overcaller should have a good suit. Therefore, *if no better contract seems likely*, then the overcaller's partner ought to pass with moderate values, say about 8 to 11 HCP.

♠32
♥632
♦KJ74
♣AQ85

Let's say the bidding has begun as follows,

East	South	West	North
1♥	1♠	pass	?

North should pass. North should bid in reply to partner's overcall *only* when further bidding offers a better chance to get a better score.

♠Q632
♥32
♦J7
♣K9853

East	South	West	North
1♥	1♠	pass	2♠

For example, in the same auction, North should raise partner's 1♠ over-call to 2♠, even though North has only 6 HCP.

North's 4-card trump support justifies this raise. Perhaps South will bid a game and make it. It certainly makes it more difficult for East to compete again, than if North were to pass with this hand.

Even if South does not carry on to game, North's raise to 2♠ may prevent East–West from bidding further!

Here are a few examples of completed auctions following an overcall.

South	West	North	East
1♥	2♦	pass	2NT
pass	3NT	pass	pass
pass			

WEST	EAST
♠AQ9	♠103
♥K7	♥Q1094
♦AJ10952	♦Q7
♣63	♣AK98

West has a solid 2♦ overcall and while East considers bidding 3NT right away, East decides to settle for an invitational bid of 2NT. West decides to bid the 3NT game, based on having help in hearts, the enemy suit (king doubleton), plus a respectable 6-card suit, as well as nice spade cards. East, as declarer at 3NT, will have no trouble making that contract, especially if part of South's opening bid is the ♦K. That is the key missing card in diamonds, and East should be able to use the technique of *finessing* South for that card. As soon as possible, East will lead the ♦Q to start the finesse, expecting to win 6 diamond tricks if the ♦K is indeed with South. Looks like East will be taking at least 10 tricks at notrump!

South	West	North	East
1♠	2♥	pass	4♥
pass	pass	pass	

WEST	EAST
♠K62	♠7
♥AQJ32	♥K975
♦K104	♦QJ2
♣J3	♣AK1084

West overcalls South's 1♠ opener with 2♥. Although West has only a 5-card heart suit, West's kings should be good cards, and West does not fear a spade lead—West can win the second round of that suit. East, holding a hand of opening strength with 4-card support for partner's suit, bids right to game, 4♥. East's singleton spade won't hurt either! In the play, the declarer West is not likely to lose more than the two aces held by the opponents.

East	South	West	North
pass	1♥	1♠	pass
2♣	pass	pass	pass

WEST	EAST
♠J9875	♠6
♥AK92	♥87
♦Q6	♦J1083
♣J9	♣AK10876

West, not vulnerable, decides to risk a 1♠ bid on a poor suit over South's 1♥ opener. East, with just a singleton spade but a very nice club suit responds 2♣. East–West have agreed that a new suit bid by the partner of an overcaller's is *not* a forcing bid. West, the overcaller, does not have to bid again, and so West passes. At 2♣, East will quite likely win 9 tricks (at least): 5 or 6 tricks in clubs, 2 top hearts, and probably 2 tricks in diamonds. Meanwhile, West is quite happy not to be playing in spades!

FAQ

What should I do when an opponent opens the bidding in my suit?

As West, you are looking at

♠AK1076 ♥KQ ♦J32 ♣J86

and are ready to open 1♠ when South, ahead of you, makes that bid! Now you should simply pass, and let North–South keep bidding. They may well be headed for a contract they can't make. And, don't spend any extra time mulling things over. Instead, pass quickly so that the opponents won't suspect anything. Your side will have no future declaring at spades since South has length in that suit too!

The rules of bidding in bridge always allow you to double the previous bid by the opponents.

East	South	West	North
1♠	Dbl.		

West	North	East	South
1♣	pass	1♥	Dbl.

When your opponents start the bidding with 1-of-a-suit, an early double by your side should *not* be intended as a "penalty" double, designed to earn you a big score for setting their modest 1-level contract. South's early doubles in these two auctions are *not* for penalties. Instead, these doubles carry an *opposite* purpose and meaning. In each of the auctions, South's mission is to get North to bid an *unbid* suit. Consequently, South's doubles are intended for *takeout.*

In the first auction, South is asking North to choose among all three remaining unbid suits—hearts, diamonds, and clubs. In the second auction, South is asking North to choose between the two suits that are still not bid—spades and diamonds. In each case, South has a hand of better-than-average strength, and one that will also supply North with good cards in whichever suit North picks.

Why Not a Penalty Double?

You may be puzzled about why the early double is not used as a penalty double—as it was originally intended. Basically, this is because it is very rare that your best result would actually arise from beating the opponents at the 1 level, doubled.

To begin with, just to defeat their 1-level bid (a seven-trick contract), your side would need to win seven tricks—and that's just to get a *one-trick* set. Rarely will you be dealt a hand that is *sure* to take seven tricks against the suit that is bid on your right.

Also, even if you held such a hand, how sure can you be that the auction would end at 1♣ doubled?

To clarify the dilemma, let's imagine a very extreme example.

Your right-hand opponent opens 1♣ and you have the hand shown. This is not a hand that you will see often, but it is possible! Against a club contract, you are, of course, able to take the first seven tricks just by leading top club cards.

Even if you could double 1♣ for the extra penalty score, the final contract might not be 1♣ doubled. Either opponent is free to continue the bidding, and make a call in another suit. And if any suit other than clubs were trumps, then your hand might not take any tricks at all!

Yes, it's possible to pick up this hand and hear your right-hand opponent open 1♣.

Dealer: South
No One Vulnerable

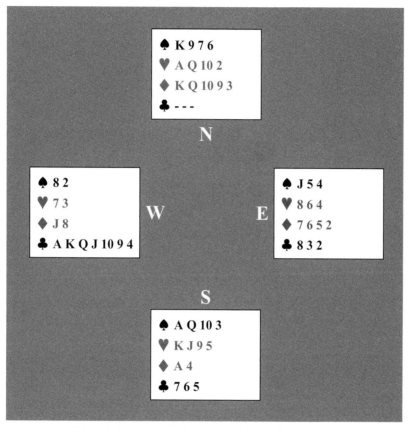

Although West can defeat a 1♣ bid, North–South can make a grand slam in any other suit.

THE BIDDING

South	West	North	East
1♣	?		

CONTINUED ON NEXT PAGE

The Takeout Double: Handy and Useful

Because low-level penalty doubles of suit-bids are both rare and impractical, a double made early in the auction has taken on a different purpose: it is for "takeout"—designed to bring partner in the auction. In fact, using the double for takeout is a rather common method of competing in the auction; it is a very handy and practical device.

THE TAKEOUT DOUBLE: INGREDIENTS AND EXAMPLES

You need these essential ingredients for a takeout double:

- **Enough HCP strength to compete in the auction.** This can be as few as 10 or 11 HCP when not vulnerable—or as many as 21 or 22 HCP, if that's how many you have been dealt!
- **Support for all other suits.** Because partner's longest suit might only be a 4-card suit, you would like to have at least 4 cards in each unbid suit.
- **Shortness in the opponent's suit, when they have bid only one suit.**

The ideal shape for an immediate takeout double is 4-4-4-1, with the singleton in the only suit the opponent has bid. This is also okay with a doubleton, although a bit riskier.

You can also sometimes use a takeout double to show an extra-strong hand with one very strong suit, which you intend to bid at your next turn.

In the following example auctions, West's double is for takeout.

South	West	North	East
1♥	Dbl.		

West has:

    ♠10952
    ♥A
    ♦AJ92
    ♣A1063

East	South	West	North
pass	1♦	Dbl.	

West has:

    ♠QJ103
    ♥AKQ102
    ♦J
    ♣AQ9

North	East	South	West
1♣	pass	1♠	Dbl.

West has:

♠32
♥A1085
♦QJ832
♣AK

West	North	East	South
pass	pass	pass	1♥
Dbl.			

West has:

♠Q1042
♥----
♦A1094
♣KJ985

North	East	South	West
1♠	pass	2♠	Dbl.

West has:

♠---
♥QJ93
♦AKQ3
♣K10742

South	West	North	East
1♣	Dbl.		

West has:

♠AJ87
♥KQ10
♦J6532
♣Q

CONTINUED ON NEXT PAGE

RESPONDING TO THE TAKEOUT DOUBLE

South	West	North	East
1♥	Dbl.	pass	?

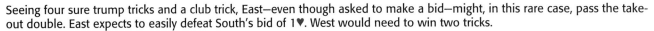

South has opened 1♥, West has doubled for takeout, and North has passed. What should East do in response to West's takeout double?

Once in a while, East will have a hand like:

♠32
♥QJ10987
♦432
♣A2

Seeing four sure trump tricks and a club trick, East—even though asked to make a bid—might, in this rare case, pass the take-out double. East expects to easily defeat South's bid of 1♥. West would need to win two tricks.

That's a very rare case. More than 99 percent of the time, East will not have a suitable hand to pass. East will not want to let the opponents play 1♥ doubled as a final contract, as East knows that each doubled *overtrick* made by declarer is worth 100 points when not vulnerable, and 200 points when vulnerable! Those overtrick points can add up.

The pressure is on for East to remove West's takeout double. Therefore, whatever *minimum* bid East makes might not promise any HCP at all!

Here's a brief set of guidelines for various responses to partner's takeout double, *assuming that the next hand passes*:

- **A new suit, bid at next minimum level:** 0–7 HCP, usually 4 or more cards in the suit bid.
- **A new suit, bid jumping a level:** 8–12 HCP, at least 4, but often 5 or more cards in the suit bid.
- **Game bid:** the equivalent of an opening hand, and at least 4 cards in the suit bid.
- **1NT:** 7–10 HCP, no 4-card major suit.
- **2NT:** 11–12 HCP, inviting partner to bid 3NT.
- **3NT:** expecting to take nine tricks with the opponent leading the suit bid.

In the following examples you are East after West has doubled South's 1♥ opener, as in the auction shown at top.

♠82
♥K432
♦10643
♣QJ4

Bid 2♦. This is better than bidding 1NT.

♠643
♥10874
♦J54
♣J32

Bid 1♠. The hand is awful, but you can't pass the double!

♠A1032
♥643
♦10972
♣KQ

Bid 2♠. Jump a level to show partner that you have at least four spades and 8 to 11 HCP. It's very likely partner also has at least four spades, to make a takeout double.

♠K9873
♥9653
♦AJ
♣A6

Bid 4♠. This looks like a good contract, so just bid it.

♠643
♥Q1094
♦K98
♣Q102
Bid 1NT.

Competing Over Opponent's 1NT Opener

When your opponent opens 1NT, any overcall you make must be at the 2 level. You cannot bid at the 1 level anymore. Furthermore, because opener promises 15 to 17 HCP, your partner's share of the HCP is likely to be low. You should proceed with caution.

GUIDELINES FOR COMPETING OVER 1NT

Usually you would like to have a 6-card suit to make any overcall at the 2 level. If you have two 5-card suits, and some strength, you may need a little luck in picking which suit to bid.

Warning: Every once in a while, you will bid over the opponent's 1NT, and find your partner to be broke—that is, with virtually no points. Be prepared to pay the price by getting set, and possibly doubled.

Here, the privilege of doubling will be used as a weapon to exert penalties against you. If you bid over 1NT with too weak a hand, the price can be high. The next hand might have most of the remaining strength, and double your bid.

With

♠Q6
♥J9732
♦AK3
♣KJ5

pass the opponent's 1NT opening bid. Your hand and your hearts are both too weak to try a 2♥ bid.

With

♠Q6
♥AJ9832
♦AK3
♣K5

your hand and your hearts are both better, and it is okay to bid 2♥.

THE DOUBLE OF A 1NT OPENING BID

An immediate double of the opponent's 1NT bid is actually a double for penalties—it is *not* meant for takeout purposes. This is very important to remember.

West	North	East	South
pass	pass	1NT	Dbl.

South doubles in expectation of defeating the 1NT bid. South should have a hand of at least the same strength as the opener, and should have a good opening lead to make, if everybody passes the double of 1NT, making *1NT doubled* the final contract.

If South has doubled with a hand like

♠J4 ♥A108 ♦AQ ♣KQJ98

then South would lead the ♣K, with a good chance of defeating the contract by one or more tricks.

Note that in doubling, South is taking a calculated risk, as South does not have seven absolutely sure tricks on hand.

Occasionally, the player to your left opens the bidding, and then the next two players each pass.

For example, it's up to South in a situation like this:

West	North	East	South
1♦	pass	pass	?

South is in what is called the *balancing* position or seat. In terms of competing, South has already gathered some useful information. In addition to learning of West's opening bid, South knows that North could only pass over 1♦, and that East doesn't have much of a hand.

South can pass, ending the auction at 1♦, or South can enter the auction, not knowing how high it may go. South can use good judgment in deciding to compete—and if so, how. South bases that decision on HCP, hand shape, and the part-score and vulnerability situations. Often South will *pass* holding three or more cards in the suit bid by the opener, unless the rest of the hand suggests a strong and solid reason for bidding. However, with two or fewer cards in the opponent's suit, South should probably take an action in the balancing position. (Another term for balancing is *re-opening*.)

GUIDELINES FOR ACTIONS IN THE BALANCING SEAT

In the balancing seat, all of your actions can be based on slightly lower values than you might have for a direct call.

1NT	About 11–14 HCP, balanced, and usually with the opponent's suit stopped.
Suit bids	You can shave a couple of HCP off the lower range on the overcall chart.
Double	9+ HCP, with appropriate shape (support for the unbid suits).

Overcall versus Balance

West	North	East	South
pass	pass	1♦	1♠

South overcalls 1♠.

West	North	East	South
1♦	pass	pass	1♠

South balances 1♠.

TIP

Bridge Lingo: "What's Trump(s)?"
Trump or trumps are often both used in the singular and plural! People say "What is trump?", "What's trumps?," or "What are trumps?"; also "Hearts are trump," or "Hearts are trumps," etc. They also say "notrumps" as well as "notrump."

What to Do When Opponents Compete

Let's briefly look at competitive auctions from the viewpoint of the pair that originally opened the bidding. What sensible calls can you make in an auction that your side has opened, and that your opponents have entered?

The following sample auctions are among the many hundreds of basic competitive auctions that could occur in just one or two rounds of bidding.

East	South	West	North
pass	1♣	1♦	?

West overcalls 1♦.

South	West	North	East
1♠	1NT	?	

West overcalls 1NT.

East	South	West	North
pass	1♥	2♦	?

West overcalls 2♦.

West	North	East	South
pass	pass	pass	1♥
Dbl.	?		

West makes a takeout double.

A FEW USEFUL OBSERVATIONS

When your *right-hand opponent* (RHO) overcalls, sometimes the call you would have made may not be available anymore—had your RHO passed. Whether it's an overcall or a double, an opponent's entrance into the auction changes your obligation to your partner. Hands at a minimum level for making a response (6 to 9 HCP), can now pass after the opponent's interference in the auction.

Opener, who may have extra values beyond the minimum for opening, will still have a chance to bid further. Your act of passing advises your partner not to expect a lot of help from your hand. Conversely, If you do have something positive to contribute to the auction, this is a very good time to do it!

As usual, let your HCP, hand shape, and the score situation be your guides in competing for your side. You can pass, raise your partner's suit, repeat a bid of your suit, bid a new suit, bid NT, or even bid the opponent's suit! You have many choices!

Here is a brief summary that covers just a few basic situations.

WHEN THEY OVERCALL 1NT

Here's what you can do:

- **Double.** Doubling is for penalties. Double when your side has more than half of the 40 HCP in the deck, and when you have a good lead to make.
- **Raise partner's suit.** This indicates a light hand, usually seven or fewer points, but with good trump support and good shape. You have no interest in letting the opponent declare 1NT.
- **Bid a new suit.** This usually indicates a 6- or 7-card suit in a hand of good shape, but with 8 or fewer HCP. This shows a good suit, but not a good hand, and requests that partner pass.
- **Pass.** You are not required to bid, and if your hand is weak, the opponents may own the balance of strength.

WHEN THEY OVERCALL IN A SUIT

Here's what you can do:

- **Double.** Doubling is for takeout purposes; this is called a *negative* double. See Chapter 13.
- **Simple (non-jump) raise of partner's suit.** You have the same kind of hand for this call as if there had been no bidding by the opponent.
- **Bid a new suit.** This requires 6+ HCP at the 1 level and 10+ HCP at the 2 level. In both cases, partner (opener) is to bid again, if the next player passes.
- **Bid 1NT, if available.** This indicates a desire to play that contract.
- **Bid 2NT.** This is an invitation for partner (opener) to pass, raise to 3NT, or make another bid.
- **Bid 3NT.** This indicates a desire to play 3NT.
- **Bid their suit.** This is a *cue-bid* to show a very strong hand, usually in support of partner's suit.
- **Pass.** This is always possible when there's no useful alternative.

WHEN THEY MAKE A TAKEOUT DOUBLE

Here's what you can do:

- **Redouble.** This requires 10+ HCP. This can be any hand, and often does not have support for partner's suit. Recall that when the opponent doubles your side's bid, you or your partner may "redouble" by saying that word in the auction. This is your first encounter with a redouble, the rarest word spoken during bridge auctions.
- **New suit at 1 level.** This requires 6 HCP, and opener is expected to bid if the next hand passes. This is the same as a new suit over 1NT overcall; partner should pass.
- **New suit at 2 level.** This usually requires a 6-card+ suit, with 9 or fewer HCP.
- **Simple raise of opener's suit.** This requires a hand similar to one that would raise if there had been no interference.
- **Jump raise of opener's suit.** This is not a strong bid. See Chapter 11.
- **Pass.** With no useful call, pass is a word partner will understand!

Note: These are basic guidelines for a few frequently occurring competitive auctions.

Note to Kibitzer: Developing keen bidding judgment in competitive auctions is one of bridge's finer arts!

CONTINUED ON NEXT PAGE

Example Hand: Competitive Bidding

Dealer: East

East–West Vulnerable

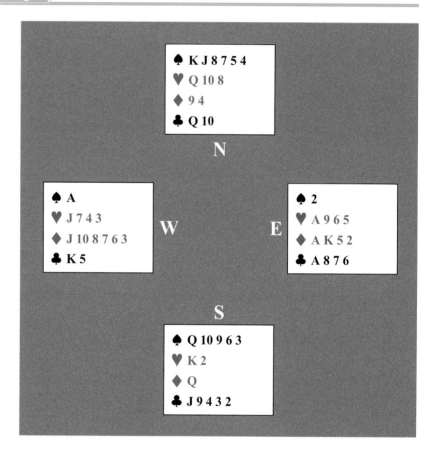

♠ K J 8 7 5 4
♥ Q 10 8
♦ 9 4
♣ Q 10

N

♠ A
♥ J 7 4 3
♦ J 10 8 7 6 3
♣ K 5

W E

♠ 2
♥ A 9 6 5
♦ A K 5 2
♣ A 8 7 6

S

♠ Q 10 9 6 3
♥ K 2
♦ Q
♣ J 9 4 3 2

THE BIDDING

East	South	West	North
1♦	1♠	2♠	4♠
Dbl.	pass	pass	pass

Opening lead: ♦J

BIDDING EXPLANATION

With a nice 15-point hand, East opens 1♦, the proper bid with 4 cards in each minor suit. South makes a light non-vulnerable overcall of 1♠, based on distributional rather than high-card strength. South also hopes that bidding may now make it harder for East–West to find their best contract. South fears the opponents may bid a game and win the rubber, as the opponents already have recorded one game.

West *cue-bids* 2♠, a bid of the enemy's suit. East–West use this bid to show a strong hand in support of the suit that partner has bid. Indeed, West has 6-card diamond support, excellent distribution, and a couple of helpful high cards.

North, also with 6-card support for her partner's suit, jumps to 4♠. North also fears that East–West can make a game contract. North is not really expecting that 4♠ will succeed, but wants to give East–West a difficult bidding decision to make.

East doubles, feeling more sure of defeating 4♠ than in bidding 5♦, a game contract. All pass, with West wondering whether game at 5♦, ending the rubber, might not be better.

The final contract is 4♠ doubled.

THE PLAY

West leads the ♦J. There's really not much to say about the play of this hand. The defense will be getting five top winners, with South, the declarer, winning the rest.

Thanking dummy, South loses the first trick to the ♦K, and then ruffs the ♦A continuation. South leads a trump and loses to West's ace. East–West also take the ♥A and the two top clubs—either now or later. South wins all of the other tricks with trumps or with high cards.

East–West's five tricks defeat the contract by two tricks, doubled, for a score of 300 points above the line.

In looking back over their hands, East–West realize that they have missed a game in diamonds, and have scored just a 300-point penalty. Playing 5♦, East would lose tricks only to the ♥K and ♥Q. Had East–West bid 5♦, they would have scored 100 points below the line, plus the 700-point bonus for winning the rubber by two games to none.

Although West feels that East really should have bid 5♦, West makes sure not to show anger or great disappointment. West wants East's mind to stay clear for the next hand. That 700-point bonus is still there to aim for.

Meanwhile, North–South are happy to lose only 300 points, when the cost could have been 800. With the rubber still alive for both sides, South hands East the cards to cut for the next deal.

WE	THEY	WE	THEY
✕			
	300		
	120		

chapter

9

Opener's Rebid and Beyond

Some bridge auctions end quickly. Others take several rounds of bidding before the final contract is reached. The first bid may or may not be the only bid for you and your partner. Maybe each of you would be happy to pass next. On the other hand, either or both of you may want to continue to bid, or be required to bid (by your bidding methods), in order to get to the best contract.

This chapter will help you continue bidding sensibly after the first round of bidding.

Let's assume the following:

1 You've opened 1NT;

2 Partner has responded; and

3 Both opponents pass.

It's now back to you, the opener. The auction may look like one of these four situations:

A

South	West	North	East
1NT	pass	2♣	pass
?			

C

South	West	North	East
1NT	pass	4♠	pass
?			

B

South	West	North	East
1NT	pass	2♥	pass
?			

D

South	West	North	East
1NT	pass	2NT	pass
?			

In each case, you must know, or else decide, what to do next. Do you pass, or do you continue bidding? And if you continue bidding, what will your next bid be?

As a 1NT opener, what you do on your second bid is determined almost entirely by what your partner, the responder, does. It's the responder to 1NT who will be guiding you in the auction, even though you may be the one with the stronger hand! It's your partner who is actually in the better position to steer the bidding to your side's best contract. The main key to reaching the best contract in an auction that begins with 1NT is knowing your partnership agreements, and bidding accordingly.

You have already met, in Chapter 6, the set of tools responder uses. Recalling that chapter, you know that lots of things can happen in auction: in the first auction North uses the Stayman convention, the second auction shows a Jacoby transfer bid, the third has partner signing off at game, and the fourth sends the decision back to you, to pass or bid 3NT!

As a 1NT opener, your rebid decision will be based on these three factors:

- Is responder's bid *limited* (not forcing) or *unlimited* (forcing, meaning you must make another bid)?
- Has your partner's reply asked for specific information?
- Does your side already have a *part-score* toward game?

Having read Chapter 6, you know that responder's bids of *game* or *slam*, while obviously indicating a good hand of some sort, are also limited. They are not at all forcing, and request (that is, demand) that you—the 1NT opener—pass. As opener you also know (via Chapter 6) that responder's 3-level suit bids are *forcing*.

Opener knows that responder's raises to 2NT, 4NT, and 5NT ask for opener to evaluate the 15–17 HCP as a *minimum* (15–16 HCP) or *maximum* (16–17 HCP). These calls are all *invitational*.

Opener knows that responder's 2♣ bid is the Stayman convention (see Chapter 6), requesting opener to bid a major suit of 4-card length or greater.

Opener knows that responder's 2♦ and 2♥ bids each are "transfer bids," requesting opener to bid the next higher ranking suit (see Chapter 6, "2♦ and 2♥ Responses: Jacoby Transfer Bids").

Let's look at a few typical situations that you might face after opening 1NT. In each case, you are South. What do you do?

EXAMPLE 1

♠QJ73 ♥A107 ♦AJ62 ♣K32.

South	West	North	East
1NT	pass	2NT	pass
?			

What do you do?

Answer: Pass. All you have is a minimum 15 HCP hand. You should pass partner's *invitational* 2NT bid.

♠KQ10 ♥A107 ♦AQJ92 ♣32

Answer: This time, you accept partner's invitation and bid 3NT. You have 16 HCP, plus two 10s and a 9! You also have a healthy 5-card diamond suit, which is likely to be the source of quite a few tricks toward your nine-trick notrump game.

EXAMPLE 2

South	West	North	East
1NT	pass	3NT	pass
?			

You have *any hand* that opens 1NT. What do you do?

Answer: South must pass in this sequence with any opening 1NT bid. When partner raises to 3NT, that's it! Any higher contract would be up to your partner, and with this bid, your partner has *signed off* at game.

CONTINUED ON NEXT PAGE

EXAMPLE 3

South	West	North	East
1NT	pass	2♣	pass
?			

You have ♠AK4 ♥AQ9 ♦KJ102 ♣965. What do you do?

Answer: Bid 2♦. Partner's 2♣ bid is the Stayman convention, and asks you to bid a 4-card major. Because you don't have one, just say 2♦, the bid that carries that message.

Note: *Do not bid 2NT. Even though you have 17 HCP, the maximum for your bid, partner is not asking about your HCP. That isn't your partner's interest—yet. Following your artificial 2♦ bid, your partner can still invite you to bid further.*

What if you have ♠10873 ♥KQJ9 ♦AQ ♣KJ7 instead?

Answer: Bid 2♠. This time you have both major suits. Although your hearts are better, respond first in spades. If responder next bids 3NT, you can then bid 4♥, with assurance that partner has four cards in that suit!

Note: *If you and your partner prefer to respond 2♥ with both majors, that's certainly okay.*

EXAMPLE 4

South	West	North	East
1NT	pass	2♦	pass
2♥	pass	2NT	pass
?			

You have ♠Q82 ♥42 ♦AQ63 ♣AK92. What do you do?

Answer: Pass. You have obediently bid 2♥ after partner's 2♦ Jacoby transfer bid. You recognize that partner's 2NT follow-up bid is only an invitation to bid on, no more. Since you have a minimum (15 HCP) and only a doubleton heart, there's no reason to bid on. With a minimum hand but 3 cards in hearts (partner's suit) you would most likely bid 3♥ rather than pass 2NT.

What if you have ♠A7 ♥AK98 ♦J75 ♣KQ86 instead?

Answer: Bid 4♥. With a maximum 17 HCP and 4 cards in partner's suit, it's easy to take partner's invitational bid of 2NT on to the major suit game. It should have a very good chance to succeed.

EXAMPLE 5

South	West	North	East
1NT	pass	2♥	pass
2♠	pass	3NT	pass
?			

You have ♠Q4 ♥AJ4 ♦KQJ ♣K8732. What do you do?

Answer: Pass. North shows at least five spades and asks South's help in deciding the best contract. With only 2-card spade support, South passes, settling for the notrump game.

What if you have ♠QJ73 ♥K10 ♦K2 ♣AK1087 instead?

Answer: Bid 4♠. This is an easy choice.

EXAMPLE 6

South	West	North	East
1NT	pass	4NT	pass
?			

You have ♠KQ86 ♥AKQJ ♦Q85 ♣97. What do you do?

Answer: Bid 6NT. With a maximum 1NT opener (17 HCP), accept partner's 4NT *invitation* and bid slam.

What if you have ♠A732 ♥Q103 ♦A54 ♣AQ2, instead?

Answer: Pass. With 16 HCP and a "flat" 4-3-3-3 shape, 6NT would likely be a struggle. You hope it won't be too hard to take ten tricks at 4NT!

When you open 1-of-a-suit, you face a different set of responses from partner than when you open 1NT.

Again, you are South. You've opened 1-of-a-suit (see the four examples below) and partner has responded. Both opponents have passed.

South	West	North	East
1♥	pass	2♥	pass
?			

South	West	North	East
1♣	pass	1♠	pass
?			

South	West	North	East
1♠	pass	1NT	pass
?			

South	West	North	East
1♠	pass	2♦	pass
?			

Two Main Factors Apply

It's your turn again in any of these auctions. You must make a decision. Do you pass, or do you continue bidding? And if you continue bidding, what is your next call?

As opener, you should select your second call based on two main factors:

1 Does partner's response require a further bid from you?

2 Does your hand feature extra strength or shape?

Regarding the first factor, there are two sorts of bids by responder that certainly require you to make a further call:

- Bids that have a very wide HCP range require another bid from you, because they offer the possibility that your side has enough combined strength for game.
- Bids by responder that are instantly forcing to game require you to continue bidding until game is reached.

By contrast, a number of partner's replies have a limited top HCP count. In those cases, a further bid from you is not required. You may pass, or you may choose to bid ahead on your own.

Now consider the second factor: Does your hand feature extra strength or shape? If your opening bid has strength or distribution beyond the minimum requirements, you may want to bid further in the auction, *even when partner has given a limited reply*.

An opening 1-of-a-suit bid covers a wide array of bridge hands. To start with such a bid has a *wide* HCP range—unlike an opening bid of 1NT, which has a narrow 15–17 HCP range.

Opening 1-of-a-suit, you might have as few as 11 HCP—if you really like your distribution. On the other hand, you might have half or more of the deck's 40 HCP. In effect, when you open 1-of-a-suit, you have anywhere from 11–21 HCP.

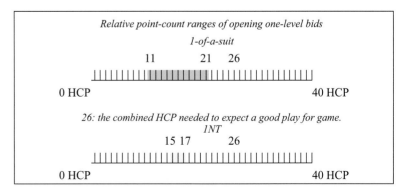

Relative point-count ranges of opening one-level bids

1-of-a-suit

11   21   26

0 HCP   40 HCP

26: the combined HCP needed to expect a good play for game.

1NT

15 17   26

0 HCP   40 HCP

You have already learned (in Chapter 4) that opening bids of 1-of-a-suit cover a "wide" HCP range, 13-21 HCP.

In addition, your holding in the suit that you bid can also vary a lot. Your suit may be at the *minimum* length needed to open in that suit, or you may have *extra* length. Moreover, your suit may or may not be headed by high cards. Here are some example hands; each is a 1♠ opener.

Weak suit, minimum length.

Another suit in the hand as good as the first suit bid, each 5 cards long.

Strong suit, extra length.

Another suit in the hand as good as the first suit bid, each 6 cards long.

On top of that, the shape of your hand can indicate further bidding from you. For example, if you have two long suits in your hand, you may want to bid the other suit next. You might have 5-5-2-1 or 6-6-1-0 distribution.

CONTINUED ON NEXT PAGE

Importance of Your Second Bid

Because you have so many possibilities for an opening bid, your second call will clarify your hand greatly. Luckily for you, there are many calls to choose from. Naturally, picking the right call is another essential step to finding the best contract. Will you:

- Raise your partner's bid?
- Rebid your first suit, at a higher level?
- Bid a new suit?
- Bid NT?
- Pass?

Your second call should reflect whether your hand rates as:

Minimum *(15 or fewer HCP).*

Better-than-minimum *(16–18 HCP, we can call this better, or "mid").*

Strong *(19+ HCP).*

Each of these three hands would be opened 1♣. Opener's next call can clarify whether the hand is of minimum, medium, or top strength.

After You Open 1-of-a-Suit, and Partner Responds: A General Guide

Look at the following chart for a very rough guide to your second call as opener:

	Your Hand		
Partner's Response	**Minimum**	**Better than Minimum**	**Strong**
1NT	bid again *only* with extra shape	bid again	jump
2NT	bid again*	bid again	bid again
Single raise of your suit	pass	bid again	bid again
Jump raise of your suit	bid again	bid again	bid again
New suit at 1 level	bid again	bid again	jump
New suit at 2 level	bid again	bid again	bid again

*2NT isn't forcing opposite a 1-of-a-minor opening, so with a minimum it's okay to pass.

As you can see in the chart, you will bid again many times. However, the chart does not tell you *what* to bid next. For that, your hand will be your main guide.

Note: *As the bidding progresses, thousands of different auctions could occur. Bridge books are filled with detailed analysis of bidding situations. They cover many bidding sequences and types of hands along the way.*

TIP

Remember, if your side has a part-score, your bidding tactics should take that into account.

For example, you are South and your side has a 60 part-score.

South	West	North	East
1♥	pass	2♣	pass
?			

Normally, North's 2♣ bid is an *unlimited* bid, and South would certainly bid again. But with North–South's 60 part-score, a 2♣ contract, worth 40 points in trick-score, is already enough to give you *game*. South can pass 2♣, with 60 on toward game, and the bidding needn't go any higher this time.

CONTINUED ON NEXT PAGE

Typical Rebid Situations

Let's look briefly at bidding examples that illustrate a few of the common bidding situations you'll face at your second turn to bid. Assume that your side hasn't any part-score. You are, yet again, South. What do you do in the following situations?

EXAMPLE 1

South	West	North	East
1♥	pass	2♥	pass
?			

You have:

♠KQJ2
♥Q10842
♦A3
♣Q3

What do you do?

Answer: Pass. North may have as few as 6 points, and so your side's total might be only about half of the HCP in the deck. Your eight-trick 2♥ contract may already be a risky venture!

What if, instead, you have:

♠KQJ2
♥K10842
♦A3
♣K3

Answer: Bid 3♥. Here, as opener, you are inviting partner to bid 4♥ with a maximum 2♥ raise, about 8–10 HCP, but to pass with a minimum (6–7 HCP).

Or you have:

♠KQJ2
♥K10842
♦A3
♣AQ

Answer: Bid 4♥. With 19 HCP, plus decent shape, go directly to game. Chances are quite good that you will take ten tricks.

EXAMPLE 2

South	West	North	East
1♠	pass	1NT	pass
?			

You have:

♠AKQ42
♥J65
♦1094
♣A6

What do you do?

Answer: Pass. With a minimum hand, you can pass partner's limited response of 1NT. Your spades should provide useful tricks at this contract. Don't bid 2♠! For that bid, you should have a 6-card suit (or longer).

What if, instead, you have:

♠Q9832
♥AKQJ3
♦J4
♣8

Answer: Bid 2♥. You show an unbalanced hand with at least five spades and at least four hearts. You would like to play in hearts, so that your side can record the 100-point bonus for *honors* held in the suit.

Or, what if you have:

♠AJ1098
♥AK6
♦AK97
♣4

Answer: Bid 3♦. With 19 HCP, South jumps one bidding level to 3♦, showing a strong hand, with 19–21 HCP. This is a game-forcing bid, and North must make another call. South's bid, skipping a level and into a new suit, is called a *jump shift*.

CONTINUED ON NEXT PAGE

EXAMPLE 3

South	West	North	East
1♣	pass	1♥	pass
?			

You have:

♠3
♥A32
♦A653
♣KQ932

What do you do?

Answer: Bid 2♥. While you have only 3-card heart support (4-card support is preferred for this raise, because partner might have only a 4-card suit), this is probably the best bid. You should avoid 1NT due to your very weak holding in spades.

What if you have:

♠A4
♥5
♦A1065
♣KQJ765

Answer: Bid 3♣. Jump to 3♣ to show a *better-than-minimum* hand, and a 6-card suit. Responder can pass, or carry on with further bidding.

Or you have:

♠AJ6
♥432
♦AKQ
♣AJ95

Answer: Bid 2NT. This also shows a hand of 18–19 HCP, too strong to open 1NT. Partner will bid again with anything but an utter minimum response.

EXAMPLE 4

South	West	North	East
1♠	pass	2♦	pass
?			

You have:

♠AK97652
♥K96
♦4
♣K3

What do you do?

Answer: Bid 2♠. Partner's 2-level new-suit reply requires another bid from you. You were going to bid again anyway. Your rebid shows a minimum-range hand, with six or more spades. If partner makes another bid, you may even wish to then bid 3♠, promising a 7-card suit.

Instead, what if you have:

♠K6543
♥62
♦KJ3
♣AQ8

Answer: Bid 3♦. Your raise of partner's 2-level suit response can be based on as little as 3-card support.

Or you have:

♠KQ852
♥743
♦A
♣KQ72?

Answer: Bid 3♣. You do not know where the bidding will end up. This bid promises a 4-card suit, and should help your partnership reach its best contract. Without a heart stopper in your hand, you should not bid notrump.

Having heard two bids from partner, responder may have a good idea of what partner's hand is like. Often responder will recognize when opener's second call shows a minimum, better-than-minimum, or strong hand.

This time you are North (responder). Let's look at three of the many typical bidding situations that responder faces on the second round of bidding.

EXAMPLE 1

South	West	North	East
1♣	pass	1♦	pass
1♥	pass	?	

Your (North's) 1♦ response can cover a lot of different hands. Luckily, you also have many possible follow-up bids at your second turn. Let's go through the main possibilities:

2♥	4-card heart support	6–10 HCP	Gives opener a chance to pass.
3♥	4-card heart support	11–12 HCP	Invites opener to bid game.
4♥	4-card heart support	13+ HCP	Short of slam-going strength.
1♠	Four spades (could be five, but *only* when responder also has at least a 6-card diamond suit)	6+ HCP	Because this bid could still have a very high upper limit, South, the opener, is expected to bid again.
1NT	Fewer than four hearts (you would raise), fewer than four spades (you would have bid them), a balanced hand, and a presumed stopper in spades, the unbid suit	6–10 HCP	This call easily allows opener to pass with a *minimum*.
2NT	Again, no 4-card major	11–12 HCP	Invites opener to bid game with just a little stronger than a minimum opener. Should have a stopper in the unbid suit, spades.
3NT	A balanced hand, and very likely with a stopper in spades, the unbid suit	13+ HCP	Short of obvious slam-going strength. Opener with a *minimum* hand will almost surely pass. With a *better* hand, opener may invite a slam, and with a *strong* hand, opener will likely bid a slam.
2♣	Likely 4-card or 5-card club support	6–10 HCP	South with a minimum can easily pass.
3♣	4-card, or more likely 5-card, support for clubs; forcing to game	(usually 11+ HCP unless very distributional)	This hand has about the strength of an opening bid, or more.
2♦	6-card suit	6–10 HCP	Allows opener to easily pass with a minimum. Because North hasn't bid a major suit, South can assume that North has fewer than four hearts and also fewer than four spades.
3♦	6-card suit	11–12 HCP	Not forcing, but highly inviting for opener to bid again.

EXAMPLE 2

Here's another example:

East	South	West	North
pass	1♣	pass	1♠
pass	2♠	pass	?

South's 2♠ bid shows a *limited* opener (13–15 HCP), usually with 4-card spade support, although sometimes South will have only 3-card support. If you pass 2♠ and make the contract (you will be declarer), then you score 60 below the line—a good *part-score* to have. Therefore, if you bid beyond 2♠, it is to look for *game*, or maybe even *slam*.

As North, these are your main options and what they mean:

Pass	6–10 HCP, with no special distributional strength.
3♠	11–12 HCP, likely 4- or 5-card spade suit, and inviting partner to bid on to game with a "good" minimum, and pass otherwise.
4♠	You have about the values of an opening hand, or your hand has very good shape, to justify a try for game. You deny interest in bidding slam. Your bid should end the auction.
2NT	11–12 HCP, not quite enough to bid 3NT.
3NT	13–16 HCP, with a feeling that nine tricks at notrump might be easier than ten tricks at spades. However, opener may decide to go to 4♠.
3♣	Probably at least four clubs, and because spades have already been "agreed to" by the partnership, the bid is at least inviting to game. You may even be looking for slam.
3♦	A forcing bid. Because spades have already been "agreed to" by the partnership, the bid is at least inviting to game. You may even be looking for slam.
3♥	A forcing bid. Because spades have already been "agreed to" by the partnership, the bid is at least inviting to game. You may even be looking for slam.

TIP

Note to Kibitzer

At any point in the bidding, the best bid is not merely a matter of counting HCP and applying certain "rules." In reality, judgment counts as much as HCP—and maybe more! For example, favorable shape raises a hand's value. However, when your distribution does *not* go well with your partner's, then your hand value declines.

CONTINUED ON NEXT PAGE

EXAMPLE 3

Try this sequence, where South is showing a *better* hand (about 16–18 HCP) with a 6-card club suit (or longer).

South	West	North	East
1♣	pass	1♥	pass
3♣	pass	?	

South's bid reveals extra values, but not quite enough strength for game if North's response is as low as 6 HCP. Note also that if South had a 4-card spade suit, South would bid 1♠ before bidding 3♣.

South is allowing North a chance to pass, and to let 3♣ become the final contract. That would give North–South a 60 part-score, if the 3♣ contract makes. Therefore, North should continue to bid only with care, if giving up the chance to tally 60 points below the line.

Here are North's main choices, and what they mean:

Pass	6–7 HCP, possibly 8 HCP without helpful shape. North might easily have just one or two clubs in her hand—she needn't worry, as partner is supposed to have six!
3♦	Should be a 4-card suit. North accepts South's try for game. North almost surely has at least a 5-card heart suit, because North responded in hearts first.
3♥	At least six, and maybe seven good hearts, and no interest in playing clubs. This call need not be considered a forcing bid.
3♠	Might or might not be a 4-card suit. Because South has already denied a 4-card spade suit, North is not really looking for a 4♠ contract. North may be showing a spade stopper, looking for South to bid 3NT if South has a diamond stopper. Perhaps North is driving to slam. In any case, North's call is forcing, and South will continue to bid on.
3NT	Suggesting this as a final contract. North should have about 8–12 HCP (a little more than a minimum response), and stoppers or length in the two unbid suits, diamonds and spades.
4♣	Inviting partner to bid 5♣.
4♥	Requesting that this be the final contract. This indicates a very good 6- or 7-card suit, with about 9–12 HCP.
5♣	3-card club support or more. This indicates a distributional hand, in the 8–11 HCP range. This bid shows no interest in a 3NT game. North's immediate 5♣ bid also shows no slam interest. (A fine point: if North had slam interest, North would *not* bid 5♣ right away. Instead, North would first make a forcing bid, such as 3♦ or 3♠, and then bid 5♣ next!)

By the time responder makes a second call, your side has made four calls in the auction. Often, either you or your partner are by now already aware of the combined HCP strength that your side has.

There remain a few auctions where neither player has had a chance to indicate either hand's limits:

South	West	North	East
1♣	pass	1♦	pass
1♥	pass	1♠	

North's 1♠ call can still indicate a very strong hand, and South's bidding has also not suggested any top limit. While each player has given some information on suit-lengths, the picture of each hand is still sketchy.

Although the bidding sequences discussed in this chapter are just a few among many, they should give your partnership useful guidance. They contain a number of general principles that you can apply to other bidding sequences that may arise. If you and your partner have time, you should discuss as many bidding sequences as you can. It's all part of the game.

FREQUENTLY ASKED QUESTIONS

What's the main difference between auctions that start 1NT and auctions that start 1-of-a-suit?

The main difference is the *role of responder*. Because the 1NT opening hand has a limited and narrow 15–17 HCP range, responder can immediately start steering the bidding towards the best contract. By comparison, as responder to a *suit* bid, you cannot measure your side's full potential.

When is opener's jump bid *forcing* and when is it *invitational*?

Opener's jump bid in a *new suit* is forcing to game. Opener's jump re-bid in the opening suit, jump raise of responder's suit, or jump to 2NT all promise better-than-minimum hands, and are invitational to game.

Do all bridge players use the same bidding methods?

No. Many different bidding systems have been developed.

chapter 10

Defensive Play

In every facet, bridge is an ongoing test of talents. To play good defense has often been called the game's toughest art of all.

When your mission is to set the opponents' contract, you and your partner join together in strategic battle against a single player, the declarer. Normally, two heads are better than one. But when those two heads are defending a bridge hand, it ain't necessarily so!

This chapter will introduce you to the basic skills that you and your partner will need to become good defenders. To succeed, you'll both want to be following the same strategies as much as possible!

After the auction ends, the defender to declarer's left makes the opening lead. Dummy's cards then go down on the table.

A single player, the declarer, oversees the play of two hands—his own hand and dummy's. That player controls the play of both hands in an effort to win tricks and bring home the contract. By contrast, each defender sees only his or her own cards, plus the dummy's cards.

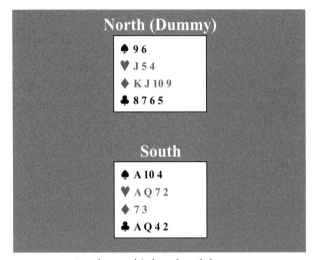

South sees his hand and dummy.

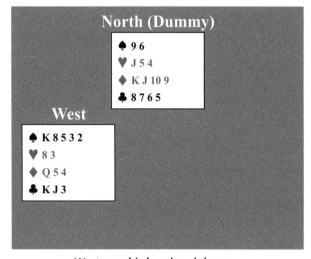

West sees his hand and dummy.

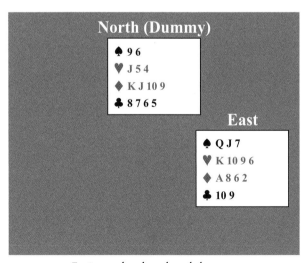

East sees her hand and dummy.

Defenders' Goal

You and your partner—two individuals—will try to "act as one" in a joint effort to *set* (defeat) declarer's contract. That is, your side's goal is simply to take enough tricks to defeat the bid.

One of the first things to do is to calculate that number of tricks. For example, let's say that your opponents bid 3NT. Declarer needs to win nine of 13 tricks, and will be happy to let your side take four tricks. That's because you'll need *five* tricks to set them.

The biggest challenge to the defenders is that they can't view their cards together (like declarer views his and dummy's hands both)—and they can't hold a discussion, either.

Defenders' Chances

While your side may need a lot fewer tricks than declarer does, you are likely outnumbered in HCP. If it's a trump contract, your side is also probably outnumbered in trumps.

Occasionally—very occasionally—your side can take enough tricks at the start of the hand to set the contract. For example, as defenders against 4♥, your side might be able to take the first four tricks.

But that isn't the usual case. Usually, the defenders find that their winning tricks come later in the hand. Winning the 13th and final trick can be every bit as important as winning the first trick.

The defense doesn't care which tricks it wins to set the contract as long as it sets the contract!

TIP

Bridge Lingo: Defeating a Contract
There are a few different ways to describe defeating the opponent's contract. You can *set, beat, sink, stop,* or even *scuttle* them. You can *put* the contract down, or *shoot* it down.

How the Defense Can Win

There are a number of ways in which the defense can prevail. This can depend on many things, including how well the defenders play their cards.

- Sometimes the opponents just bid too high, and you can set them, no matter what you do.
- Sometimes declarer just plays poorly, giving you the chance to win enough tricks to set the contract.
- Sometimes declarer simply has bad luck. A few finesses may lose, or one or more suits may divide badly. As a result, you can set the contract. For example, in the hand shown, North–South bid to a grand slam that will make 90 percent of the time, but this time they are unlucky. Here's an example of that:

Dealer: East

Both Sides Vulnerable

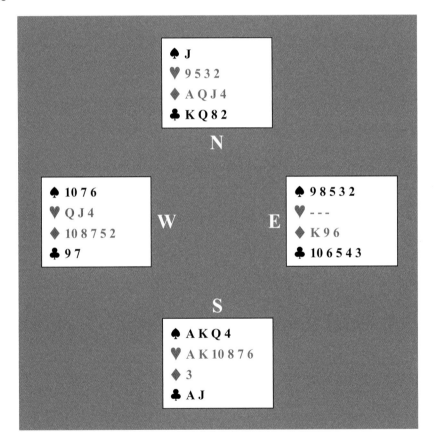

THE BIDDING

East	South	West	North
pass	1♥	pass	3♥
pass	4♣	pass	4♦
pass	7♥	pass	pass
pass			

BIDDING EXPLANATION

South, with 21 HCP, has a very strong hand. North's 3♥ raise shows 4-card support and strength enough for game. South bids 4♣ to see if North will bid 4♦. South is confident that North's 4♦ bid indicates the ♦A. South decides to go for the big bonus of a *grand slam*, and bids 7♥.

Alas! The unlucky 3-0 *break* in trumps dooms South's contract: West, with ♥QJ4, will win a trick. In fact, West is so happy to be earning a positive score on this deal that West doesn't even bother to double 7♥ for the slightly bigger penalty score.

More Ways the Defense Can Win

- Sometimes the defenders just need to let declarer take some tricks, and wait until the middle or end of the hand to gather the tricks that they will need to defeat the contract.
- Sometimes the defenders need to promote some lower-ranked cards to high rank, by attacking declarer in one suit or another.
- Sometimes the defenders need to lead a suit that declarer must trump.
- Sometimes the defenders need to lead trumps.
- Sometimes the defenders need to take their tricks right away.

Basic Defensive Skills

To make the right defensive plays—and to avoid making bad ones—you and your partner need to learn a number of basic defensive skills.

SKILLS ALL PLAYERS USE

Whether defender or declarer, be sure to use the fundamental skills of *pausing* and *looking*.

After the bidding ends, the player at declarer's left selects a card to play for the opening lead. Dummy's cards go down on the table, as declarer utters words of thanks.

Most declarers now take a moment or two to survey the situation. For you as a defender, this should be the time to do the same thing declarer is doing—*pause* and *look*. As the tricks are played, dummy's cards will be disappearing. You won't be seeing the full dummy again, and so you had better look now.

It's a good idea to review the bidding in your mind as you are inspecting the dummy. The bidding can give you clues to figuring out which player has certain cards that you *can't* see.

This is also a time for the defenders to think about the entire hand. Taking the bidding, the dummy, and your hand into account, you can also now begin to make a count of the remaining cards in one or more important suits. Your abilities here will grow with experience.

SPECIAL SKILLS FOR DEFENDERS

You and your partner, as defenders, need to remember and cultivate these special skills:

- Good defense begins with making a good opening lead. It continues with watching and remembering the cards as they are played.

- As tricks are played, try to keep count of how many cards are played in each suit. This will also tell you how many unplayed cards remain in each suit. Be sure to get a good look at each trick that is played. If a completed trick is turned over too quickly, ask to look at it again!

- When you can't follow suit, and must discard, it is important to discard intelligently. Be sure to make note each time your partner or declarer *shows out* in a suit—that is, when they fail to follow to the suit led. If you've been watching all the tricks, you know for sure how many cards that player originally held in a suit.

- You also need to know the right card to play in suit combinations that occur again and again at the bridge table. And, as the art of defense becomes more comfortable, you can learn to choose cards to play as signals to give extra information to your partner.

Before looking more deeply into these skills, let's take a look at the defense in action.

Example Hand: The Defense in Action

Dealer: North

Neither Side Vulnerable

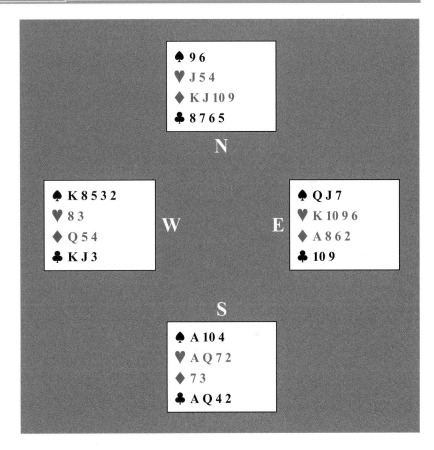

♠ 9 6
♥ J 5 4
♦ K J 10 9
♣ 8 7 6 5

N

♠ K 8 5 3 2
♥ 8 3
♦ Q 5 4
♣ K J 3

W   E

♠ Q J 7
♥ K 10 9 6
♦ A 8 6 2
♣ 10 9

S

♠ A 10 4
♥ A Q 7 2
♦ 7 3
♣ A Q 4 2

THE BIDDING

North	East	South	West
pass	pass	1NT	pass
pass	pass		

Opening lead: ♠3

BIDDING EXPLANATION

On this deal, only South in third seat has a hand worth opening. South bids 1NT, and that becomes the final contract.

THE PLAY

West chooses her longest suit, spades, to lead against South's 1NT contract. West selects the ♠3 as the card to lead to the first trick.

Dummy's hand is placed on the table, with declarer's thanks. West and East pause to inspect the dummy, and notice that it has 5 HCP. Added to South's expected 15-17 HCP, each defender knows that the 40 HCP are about evenly split between the two sides. It may be close as to which side will take seven tricks and earn a score for the deal.

After South plays a low spade from dummy, East inserts the ♠J and South *ducks* the trick, withholding the ♠A and letting East win. East continues with the ♠Q and South ducks again. East continues with the ♠7 and South must win this trick. South discards the ♣5 from dummy. West has seen 11 spades on the first three tricks. West's two remaining spades are now winners!

CONTINUED ON NEXT PAGE

Looking to establish some winners, South leads ♦7 and finesses dummy's ♦J after West plays low. East sees that if he takes the ♦A on this trick, South will later be able to easily win tricks with all three of dummy's remaining diamonds. East therefore decides to duck.

Now in dummy, South tries another finesse, leading the ♥4 and winning with the ♥Q after East plays low. South leads his remaining diamond, and after West plays low, South plays dummy's ♦9. Again, East elects to duck.

This is the position after the first six tricks:

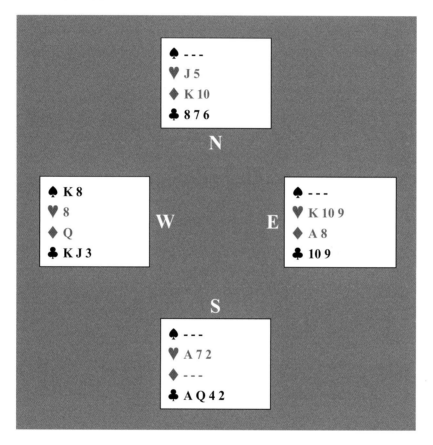

South has taken four tricks and still has two aces left. The defense has taken only the first two tricks. South sees that a winning club finesse will provide the final trick needed for the contract, and so South leads ♣6 from dummy to his queen. However, West wins with the ♣K and cashes her ♠K and ♠8 as dummy throws clubs, East throws a heart and a diamond, and South discards a heart and a club on these two tricks.

The defense now has five tricks in. West plays the ♦Q in this ending:

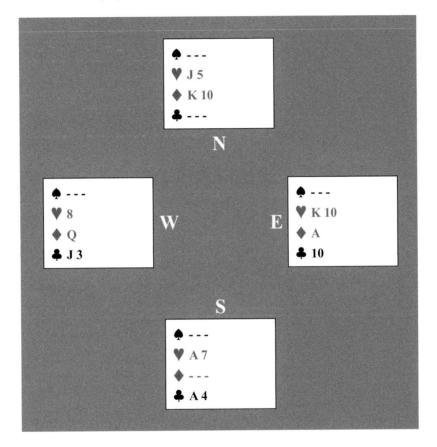

South can only win with his two aces and is down one. East–West tally a hard-earned 50 points above the line for taking seven tricks and setting South's 1NT contract.

WE	THEY	WE	THEY	WE	THEY
✕		✕		✕	
	50				

TIP

Note to the Kibitzer

A mere 1NT contract often can be very challenging to both the defending and the declaring sides. When both sides have strength, the play could go many different ways.

Making the Opening Lead

After the bidding ends, the defense begins the play of the tricks. Whoever is to the left of declarer has 13 cards to pick from for the *opening lead*. If it's you, the card you choose can have a big impact on the final result.

Sensible Leads

Every 13-card hand is new, and so there is no complete guide to making the best opening lead every time. What matters most is to consider the bidding, use common sense, and have clear lead agreements with your partner. Whether you are defending against a suit contract or against a notrump contract is also important.

When your partner has bid a suit, leading that suit can make good sense. But if your partner hasn't bid, then you are on your own.

Sometimes you will have enough good cards in a suit to make an *attacking* lead. For example, if you hold ♣KQJ9, the ♣K would likely be a good lead. After the ♣K *drives out* the ♣A, you will then have winners with the ♣Q, ♣J—and maybe even the ♣9.

On the other hand, leading the ♣K from ♣K94 would be risky. Your opponents are quite likely to capture your ♣K with the ace, and since your ♣9 is far from a winner. It would really be up to your partner to take club tricks.

Lacking an attacking lead, you might choose a *passive* lead rather than make a risky or foolish one. For example, ♦7653 is a suit with low risk. If you lead the ♦7, you are not really figuring on taking the first trick. However, by not taking a risk, you protect cards in other suits that could win tricks later.

Occasionally you may have a singleton in a suit when another suit is trump. Leading that singleton may make sense: the next time the suit is led, you can capture that trick with a small trump.

TIP

It's normal at first to feel a little lost on opening lead. After a while, you'll become comfortable and confident making the opening lead.

Choosing Which Card to Lead

You and your partner are allowed to have agreements as to what card you lead from various suit combinations. Since certain suit holdings and types of holding come along over and over again, it is good to have agreements.

The following chart indicates in *red* the preferred card to lead from a variety of holdings. In some cases, a second choice is given in *blue*.

Note: *The symbol x refers to any low card. This helps to focus interest on the more significant higher cards in a suit. Often the exact rank of a low card can be very meaningful, and so this shorthand is only for times when that number rank doesn't matter. The use of x's is a very common and useful bridge notation.*

Top of a Sequence

Note: *Consecutive cards in a suit are called a sequence, and are also called touching cards. Lead the highest card from a sequence of touching high cards.*

A K x x
K Q J x x
Q J 10 x x
A K J x x
Q J x x
J 10 9 x x
J 10 x x
10 9 x x

Note: *The suit may be any length. Also, K is preferred to A, from an AKJ combination.*

"Fourth Best" from a 4-Card or Longer Suit Headed by an Honor

K x x x x
Q x x x x
J x x x x
10 x x x x

5-card example: From K9532, lead the 3, the fourth highest card you have in that suit.

K x x x
Q x x x
J x x x
10 x x x

4-Card Example: From J876, lead the 6, the fourth highest card you have in that suit.

Low from a Tripleton

K x x
Q x x
J x x
10 x x
x x x

Examples:

From 1082, lead the 2, the lowest card you have in that suit.

From 543, lead the 3, the lowest card you have in the suit.

High from a Doubleton

A x
K x
Q x
J x
10 x
x x

Top Card of Four or More Low Cards

x x x x x
x x x x

Note: *This lead is often called top of nothing. Some partnerships prefer leading second highest from such holdings.*

Knowing these lead agreements helps your partner *read* the card that you lead. Your partnership can also use the above charts as a guide for leads later in the hand.

Playing the Right Card

When playing to a trick when someone else leads, a defender can play right cards and wrong cards. Let's look at a few common situations. In each case, you are East.

EXAMPLE 1

West leads a low club. Dummy plays low. Your correct play is the ♣J, not the ♣Q.

Here's why. When declarer wins the ♣A, West (your partner) knows that the ♣Q is in your hand. If declarer had the ♣Q, then declarer would have certainly used that card to beat East's jack, saving the ♣A.

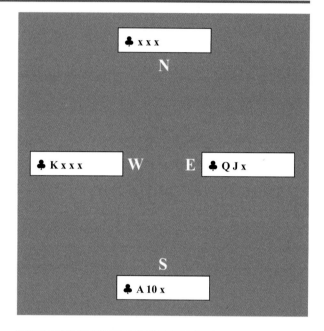

EXAMPLE 2

West leads her fourth-best diamond. South plays low from dummy, and you as East must play the ♦J, not the ♦A. When you win with the ♦J, it is as if the defense has made a successful finesse. In this case, the key card you are finessing for, the ♦Q, is visible in the dummy.

When you win with the ♦J (the right card), the defense can now also win tricks with the ♦A and ♦K. If you were to play the wrong card—the ♦A—on the first lead of the suit, dummy's ♦Q could later win a trick.

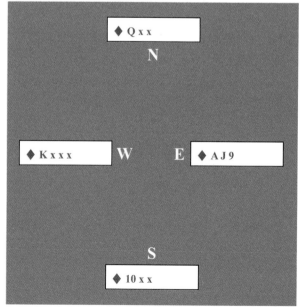

EXAMPLE 3

South leads a low heart from dummy. You as East must also play a low heart, the right card. You must let South win the trick with the ♥K. If instead you play the ♥A—the wrong card—you win that trick, but South will then win tricks with both the ♥K and the ♥Q. However, if you play low on the first heart, South can only win with the ♥K.

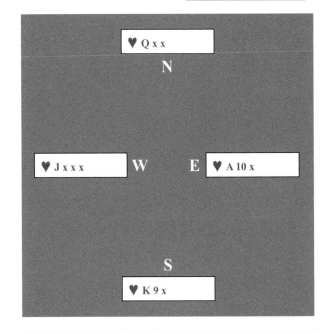

EXAMPLE 4

South leads dummy's ♠J. You must cover with the ♠K (correct). If instead you play a low spade (wrong), South will play ♠9 and let dummy's ♠J hold the trick. South will next lead another spade from dummy and will successfully finesse you for the ♠K, thus taking three tricks in spades.

However, if you cover the ♠J with the ♠K, South can win only the ♠A and ♠Q. West's ♠10 can then capture South's ♠9.

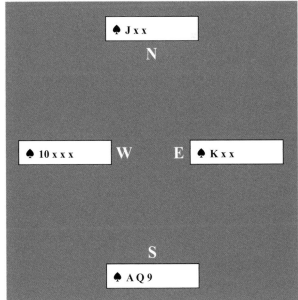

Defensive Signals

Defenders may agree that the cards they choose to play can carry extra information. Information conveyed by choice of play is referred to as *defensive carding* or *defensive signals*. For example, partners often agree to lead the highest of sequential cards.

This section describes a few more basic signals that defenders use.

SIGNALING INTEREST IN A SUIT

Interest in a suit can be signaled by playing an unnecessarily high card in that suit. Lack of interest in a suit can be shown by playing your very lowest card of that suit.

Example: West leads ♣Q and dummy plays ♣A.

The trick is already won by dummy, but East, holding ♣K982, should follow with the ♣9, to signal interest or encouragement in the suit. West should be able to read this signal. Had East instead played ♣2, West would have read this as a discouraging signal, since the deuce is clearly the lowest card East can have.

SIGNALING SUIT LENGTH

Suit length information can also be signaled by simple carding agreements. When following suit, playing your *lowest* card in a suit can signal an *odd* number of cards in that suit (1, 3, 5, or 7).

When you play a high card first—to be followed by a lower card the next time that suit is led—you are showing an *even* number of cards in the suit (2, 4, 6, or 8). This play of a higher card followed by a lower card is called a *high-low*, or an *echo*.

Example

Defending South's 5♣ contract, West leads ♥K. East follows with ♥10. West reads the ♥10 as an encouraging card, probably showing a doubleton. West cashes the ♥A and notices East's echo with the ♥6. West leads another heart, and East ruffs with a club to set the contract.

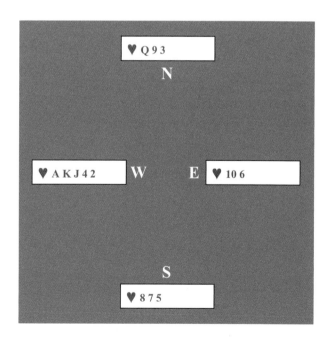

Returning Partner's Suit

It's easy and helpful to signal your suit length when you return the suit of partner's opening lead. When you are returning a suit your partner has led, return your fourth best with an original holding of four or more. Otherwise, return your highest remaining card.

EXAMPLE 1

West leads ♠5, and you, as East, win with the ace. With only three cards in the suit, you return your highest remaining card, the ♠8. South covers with the ♠10, and West wins the ♠J.

Reading your ♠8 as showing an original holding of ♠A83 or ♠A8, West knows (by counting) that South still has the ♠Q with at least one more spade. West therefore does *not* now try to cash the ♠K, but instead leads another suit. West will wait for the ♠K9 to take *two more* tricks sitting over South's ♠Q6.

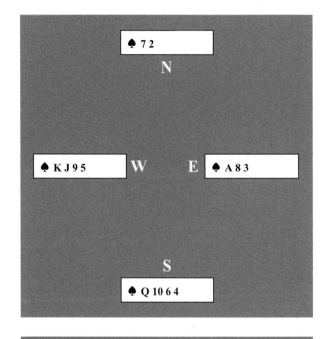

EXAMPLE 2

West makes the same ♠5 lead, and you (East) win the ace. Having four cards in the suit, you return the ♠3, your original fourth-best card. West takes South's ♠10 with the ♠J and, reading your ♠3 as showing four spades, knows that South's ♠Q will fall under the ♠K. West cashes the ♠K and ♠9 now and doesn't have to wait for later.

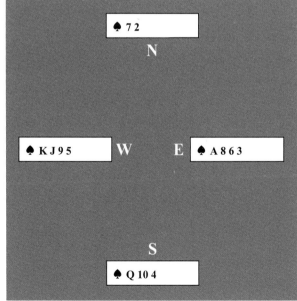

FACT

Such carding agreements—or others—are perfectly legal, although your opponents are entitled to know the understandings you have. Of course, you can defend at bridge without carding signals at all, but it makes the game more difficult.

Tips and Strategies for Defenders

Defensive play is a large topic, and numerous books have been devoted entirely to the subject. Here are a few good tips to strengthen your defense.

PREVENTING REVOKES

When partner *shows out* on the lead of a suit, bridge rules permit you to ask out loud if partner truly has no cards of the suit. "No spades, partner?" you say when partner fails to follow to a spade lead. Asking the question actually helps you count out the distribution of the entire suit. And when partner really does have a spade, your question can prevent the penalty of a revoke. Each defender thus has the same right dummy has in checking whether partner really is unable to follow suit (see Chapter 7).

SPOT CARD LEADS

When you lead a *low* spot card, this indicates that you have higher cards in the suit, and when partner wins a trick, you probably want partner to *return* the suit (lead it again). By contrast, when you lead a *high* spot card (such as an 8 or a 9), it indicates no interest in partner's return of that suit.

RISK IN LEADING AN ACE

Try not to lead an ace, especially on opening lead—unless you also have the king. Granted, your ace will usually be a winner for your side. However, when you lead an ace and you don't have the king, you've instantly promoted the king to top rank. It can be a winner when the suit is led the next time.

Your opponents are twice as likely to have that king as your partner—simply because there are *two* of them, and you have only *one* partner. If they also hold the queen—that's another winner for them. If you or your partner have the queen, it may now be much tougher for that card to take a trick! Leading an ace will sometimes work out okay, but usually you are doing your opponents a big favor.

Neither side wants to lead a suit arranged like this!

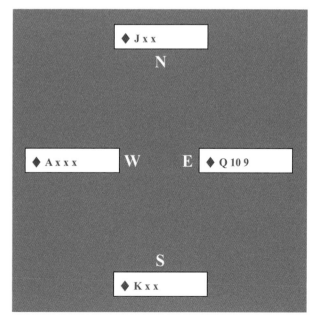

THE RULE OF ELEVEN

If your partnership leads fourth best, there's a very handy trick called the *Rule of Eleven* that will help you figure out declarer's cards in the suit.

Take the number of the card partner has led and subtract it from 11. The result is the number of cards in the suit that are higher than the card led, and that are *not* in your partner's hand.

West leads the ♣7 against 3NT, and South plays low from dummy. You, East, use the Rule of Eleven (11 minus 7 equals 4), meaning that outside of West's hand, there are four cards higher than the ♣7.

You can see all four of them! You have two, and dummy has two. You can therefore conclude that declarer has no clubs higher than the ♣7. As a result, you can play low, and partner's ♣7 will win the trick. Now partner leads another club, and dummy's ♣Q will not take a trick.

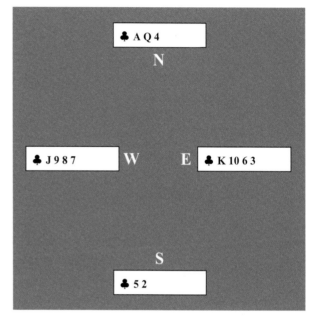

TAKE ADVANTAGE OF DUMMY'S WEAKNESS

As defenders, you can see where dummy has good cards and where it has weak cards. If a dummy like this one appears, when East gains the lead, East may well want to play hearts, dummy's weakest suit. West now has a great advantage, because she is playing after South and is able to see that dummy has only low cards in hearts.

LEAD TRUMPS!

If you listen to the bidding, it may tell you that dummy and declarer have short suits (singletons and voids) and that declarer may want to take many ruffs in each hand. When this is the situation, the defense does well by leading trumps. This makes declarer play two trumps on each trump lead—so those two trumps cannot be used to win two separate tricks!

YOU DON'T *ALWAYS* HAVE TO SIGNAL

Declarer—as well as partner—is looking at the cards you play, and sometimes your signal of suit interest or length will be more helpful to declarer than to your partner. In such cases, you *don't* need to signal special information.

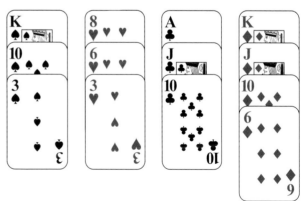

Preemptive Bids

You might think that the more you bid, the more high card points (HCP) you should have. After all, the higher the bid level, the more tricks you'll need! While big hands and big bids often do go together, it isn't always so. At times, bids made at an unnecessarily high level denote a relatively weak hand in HCP. Experience has shown that if your hand has the right shape, such bids are good tactics.

This chapter explores *preempts*—jumps made during the auction based chiefly on distributional values. Everyone in the auction can preempt—including the opening bidder, the responder, and the overcaller.

The Philosophy of Preempting

It may seem foolish to bid for more tricks than you really expect to make, but the scoring of bridge is set up to encourage just these actions. If you bid high when low on HCP, you are willing to give your opponents a small score for setting your contract. You prefer that your opponents get 50, 100, or even 300 points above the line rather than have them score a game.

WHY MAKE A PREEMPTIVE BID?

The purpose of a preemptive bid is to take away comfortable bidding space from the enemy. For instance, when an opponent opens 3♥, any bid your side could have made at a lower level is now impossible.

3♥ 3♠ 3NT
4♣ 4♦ 4♥ 4♠ 4NT
5♣ 5♦ 5♥ 5♠ 5NT
6♣ 6♦ 6♥ 6♠ 6NT
7♣ 7♦ 7♥ 7♠ 7NT

If you want to compete for the final contract, you and your partner now have to launch your bidding at 3♠ or higher, as shown in the chart above. Compared to being able to start out at the 1 level, there's now much more risk in entering the auction, as well as a much lower chance for bidding accuracy.

REQUIREMENTS FOR PREEMPTIVE OPENING BIDS

The two basic ingredients for opening preempts are a long suit and a hand with fewer than 13 HCP. Here are some hands with suits that qualify.

A 6-card suit, and too weak for an opening 1 bid.

A 7-card suit, and too weak for an opening 1 bid.

An 8-card suit, and too weak for an opening 1 bid.

PREEMPTIVE OVERCALLS AND RESPONSES

When your opponents open the bidding, a simple overcall (that is, one at the lowest available level for the suit to be bid, see Chapter 8) is one way to compete in the auction.

North	East	South	West
pass	pass	1♥	2♣

Simple Overcall (Made at the Next Possible Bidding Level)

You can also overcall by *jumping*, or skipping, one or more levels of bidding. (It's quite okay to stay seated while you do this!)

North	East	South	West
pass	pass	1♥	3♣

Jump Overcall (Skips One or More Bidding Levels)

There are even a few times when the *responder* is the one to preempt, to jump on distributional values, rather than high-card strength.

South	West	North	East
1♥	pass	4♥	

Here, North's raise to game is based on a hand with distributional values (see Chapter 5), such as this:

♠1072
♥K9654
♦---
♣KJ832

Preemptive jump raise by responder.

Opening 2-Level Preempts

In the first 3-4 decades of contract bridge, opening 2-level bids were made only on what players at the time judged to be *very strong* hands (that is, hands of about 22 or more HCP.) In that era, just about everyone played *strong* 2 bids. However, such hands being quite infrequent, strong opening 2-level bids did not occur very often.

Instead, a few players decided to try out a new treatment. They looked for and found a strategic advantage opening at the 2 level with a much more common sort of hand, a hand of merely average strength but with one long suit. Since up till then *strong* 2 bids had been the norm, the new style became known as *weak 2 bids*.

A few partnerships still go for those old-time *strong* 2-level opening bids. However, nowadays most partnerships prefer that their 2♦, 2♥, and 2♠ opening bids be *weak* 2 bids. Note carefully that the 2♣ opening bid is not included in this group. That opening bid is reserved for very strong hands (see Chapter 12).

INGREDIENTS FOR A WEAK 2 BID

All you need to open 2♦, 2♥, or 2♠ is a good 6-card suit and a hand in the 7–12 HCP range. It's okay to have another 4-card suit, but with 6-5-1-1, 6-5-2-0 or 6-6-1-0 distribution, you should avoid starting the auction with a weak 2 bid.

Many partnerships prefer to open 1♥ on a hand with 12 HCP and a 6-card heart suit, and you are free to do so if you wish. However, the preemptive value of a 2-level bid often outweighs the opportunity to tell your partner that you have (almost) 13 HCP!

Here are a few possible opening weak 2 bids:

♠K109865
♥K43
♦J2
♣A3

Open 2♠. With 11 HCP you are just about at the top range for a weak 2 bid. Your spades are not fabulous but they've got some substance.

♠84
♥AK8764
♦Q109
♣86

With 9 HCP, open 2♥.

♠52
♥Q952
♦KQJ1093
♣Q

Open 2♦. And if you play a contract in diamonds, don't forget to claim your 100 honors for holding ♦KQJ10.

♠KQJ975
♥832
♦AQ108
♣---

Open 1♠. Although your HCP total is less than 13, your distribution and good suits suggest a 1-level bid.

WHAT'S A GOOD SUIT?

Not all bridge players agree on what a *good* 6-card suit is. Some partnerships insist that the 6-card suit for a weak 2 bid be headed by the AK, AQ, or KQ (that is, by two of the top three honors). You needn't be that selective, but you should be wary of opening a weak 2 bid on a poor suit, especially when your side is vulnerable. For example, with ♠Q75432 ♥J98 ♦J5 ♣K10, it may be safer just to pass, even though you do have 7 HCP.

Note to Kibitzer: *Some partnerships prefer a range lower than 7–12 HCP for their weak 2 bids. If you want, you may use a range of 6–11 HCP, or even 5–10 HCP, for your weak 2 bids. The advantage of the 7–12 HCP range is that it covers the greatest number of hands.*

 FACT

> Howard Schenken was one of the first to embrace the weak 2 bid. Both he and his wife Bee were avid bridge players. His book, *The Education of a Bridge Player* (Simon & Schuster, 1973), is highly regarded.

Responding to a Weak 2 Bid

In responding to a weak 2 bid, the most useful tool is common sense. Just because you have a hand that might have opened with a 1-level bid does not mean that you should bid now, at a higher level, after your partner preempts. In fact, you should usually pass. Bid only when you can improve the contract!

Definitely consider bidding further in any of these situations:

- You have 3-card or more support for your partner.
- You have a suit of your own and want to play in that suit rather than your partner's.
- You have 15+ HCP.

You can respond by raising partner's suit, bidding a new suit, or bidding notrump.

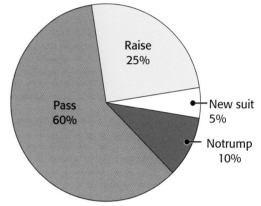

Possible Percentages of Responses to a Weak 2 Bid.

PASSING

When you have 14 or fewer HCP and no clear bid, you should probably just pass partner's bid. Partner may make this contract, while any higher contract likely would be at greater risk. In case your opponents decide to bid, you may earn points by setting their contract.

RAISING

A raise of partner's suit *short* of game is designed to increase the effect of partner's preempt. A raise to game, on the other hand, may be either preemptive (based on many trumps), or quite strong, based on the expectation of taking enough tricks to make game.

Single Raise

A single raise is usually based on 3-card support, with too few HCP to expect game to have much of a chance.

For example, if your partner bids 2♦ and you hold ♠K106 ♥Q96 ♦J65 ♣K932, then bid 3♦. This raise increases the pressure begun by partner's preempt.

Jump Raise

In the major suits, a double raise of a weak 2 bid is a *game* bid. Many different hands could suggest such a bid. For example, in response to 2♠, bid 4♠ on:

First Hand:

♠K10
♥A2
♦KQ10743
♣AQ4
(18 HCP)

Second Hand:

♠Q532
♥52
♦A108754
♣J
(7 HCP)

By contrast, a double raise of 2♦ to 4♦ is still a part-score. You should play this bid simply as a furtherance of partner's preempt, perhaps with a hand like ♠A102 ♥5 ♦K865 ♣Q10754.

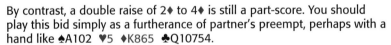

Your opponents may well have game at either major suit, but now will have to begin to sort things out at a risky bidding level.

When you raise 2♦ all the way to 5♦, you have either of two types of hand: a very preemptive raise (often as many as five trumps), or a very strong hand that expects to help take 11 tricks at diamonds.

BIDDING A NEW SUIT

A new-suit response to an opening bid of 1-of-a-suit is forcing for one round. By contrast, a new-suit response to a 2-level suit opener is *not* forcing. It is simply designed to reach a better part-score contract than partner's opening bid would be.

For example, if your partner opens 2♥ and you hold ♠KJ10 ♥--- ♦K54 ♣KQJ10873, then bid 3♣. You should have a very good chance to make 3♣, while partner may have a real struggle at 2♥. You will also score 100 honors at clubs, no matter what.

CONTINUED ON NEXT PAGE

BIDDING NOTRUMP

The 3NT Response

A 3NT response to a weak 2 bid is based on a strong hand. Usually you've got 15 or more HCP, and you also expect to have a play for nine tricks. This either means that you are counting on opener's long suit to be a source of many of those tricks, or else you have a lot of tricks available in your own hand.

It's important to have stoppers in all three unbid suits, because your opponents will have their choice of which suit to begin their attack in.

In response to partner's 2♦, bid 3NT with this hand.

In response to partner's 2♥, bid 3NT with this hand.

The 2NT Response

A 2NT response to a weak 2 bid has little merit as a *natural* bid. If your sights are limited to a part-score contract, why not just pass and let partner play in a long trump suit? Therefore it makes sense to use 2NT as a kind of all-purpose *forcing* bid.

The 2NT response to a weak 2 bid is a signal back to partner that you have a hand with interest in game, but one that is not yet ready to pick the final game contract. Opener's best move is to bid a new suit where opener may have a high card, usually an ace or a king. This information should be the most help to responder.

East	South	West	North
pass	2♥	pass	2NT
pass	3♣	pass	

South has

    ♠Q9
    ♥KQ9832
    ♦86
    ♣A109

Note: *Some partnerships prefer to play a new-suit response to weak two bids as forcing. As with many other bidding areas, discuss this with your partner ahead of time. A new suit not forcing is recommended because it gives responder more flexibility. Responder can always bid 2NT to suggest a strong hand, and follow up from there.*

Example Hand: A Weak 2 Bid in Action

Dealer: North

North–South Vulnerable

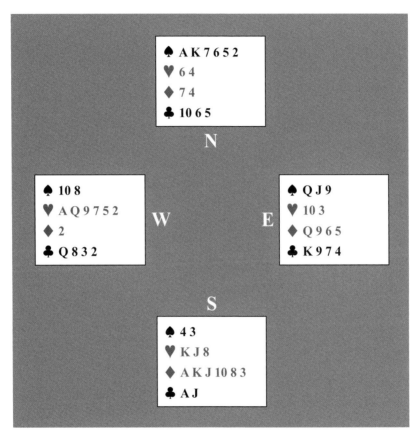

♠ A K 7 6 5 2
♥ 6 4
♦ 7 4
♣ 10 6 5

N

♠ 10 8
♥ A Q 9 7 5 2
♦ 2
♣ Q 8 3 2

W

E

♠ Q J 9
♥ 10 3
♦ Q 9 6 5
♣ K 9 7 4

S

♠ 4 3
♥ K J 8
♦ A K J 10 8 3
♣ A J

THE BIDDING

North	East	South	West
2♠	pass	3NT	pass
pass	pass		

Opening lead: ♥7

CONTINUED ON NEXT PAGE

BIDDING EXPLANATION

Vulnerable, North takes aggressive action by opening 2♠ with a bare-minimum 7 HCP count. South, with 17 HCP and a diamond suit that should take a lot of tricks, promptly bids 3NT, a game that ought to have a chance to make, opposite a typical weak 2♠ opener.

THE PLAY

West leads the ♥7. Declarer thanks North, and sees that the dummy is on the lightweight side—but has a few useful cards.

East plays the ♥10 and South wins with the jack. South sees that if East wins a trick early in the play, another heart lead will sink the contract. South finds a simple plan for success.

South plays a spade to dummy's ace, in order to lead a diamond for a finesse. When East follows with a low diamond, South wins the ♦J. South now uses dummy's final entry, the ♠K, to lead dummy's other diamond. East, of course, plays low again, and this time South wins with the ♦10.

South can now take four more diamond tricks (because the ♦A and ♦K now bring down the ♦Q), plus the ♣A. South ends up winning the first ten tricks: taking one heart trick, six diamond tricks, two in spades, and one in clubs. South concedes the last three tricks to the defense. North–South score game with an overtrick, plus a 700-point rubber bonus.

Note that South prevailed despite the annoying diamond *break*, with four to the queen in the East hand. Crucial for declarer was to lead diamonds twice from dummy, in order to finesse East for the ♦Q each time. If South had taken the diamond finesse one time only, or not at all, South would have to let East win a trick with the ♦Q or—later—with the ♣K. East would lead his remaining heart, and set the contract by two or three tricks!

Also notice that declarer would be happy losing a diamond trick to the West hand (if West has the ♦Q), because if West wins and leads hearts, declarer's ♥K will become a winner.

WE	THEY	WE	THEY
✗			
700			
30			
120			
100			

Opening at the 3 level can put plenty of pressure on opponents who may have good cards but no easy bids. At the 3 level, every suit-opening is preemptive. It is nearly always based on a 7-card suit in a hand that is too weak for a 1-level opener.

SUIT QUALITY

Usually you'd like a suit with quite a few high cards, just in case you end up as declarer, and partner has no help for you in trumps. When your suit is ◆KQJ10984, you have only *one* trump loser, the ace, even if partner is void in diamonds. By contrast, when your suit is ◆J865432, you can expect to lose four (or more) trump tricks if partner has a void!

The standard of suit quality that you adopt is up to you, and tastes will vary. Some players preempt only with a very good suit. Others preempt on any 7-card suit, or even with only 6 cards when they want to "create some action" at the table. (Do this at your own risk.) Of course, your opponents are entitled to know any agreements that your partnership may have made as to preemptive style. Here are some examples:

Open 3♠ with this hand.

Open 3♥ with this hand.

Open 3♦ with this hand.

Open 3♣ with this hand.

As usual, take into account the factors of vulnerability and part-score in your decision to open at the 3 level or not.

CONTINUED ON NEXT PAGE

Responding to 3-Level Preempts

Most of the time, you'll pass partner's 3-level preemptive openers. You'll often do this even with a hand that would have opened the bidding at the 1 level. Keep bidding opposite partner's 3-level preempt only when you can improve the contract. Again, experience and common sense are your best guides for handling preemptive auctions.

- With 3-card support or more for partner, a raise is a good possibility. This can be in expectation of making the contract, or for the strategic purpose of increasing the pressure on the opponents that has already been started with partner's opening preemptive call.

- Sometimes 3NT will be an appropriate bid, even when you have as many as three of partner's suit, especially if partner has bid a minor suit. To bid 3NT, you'll want to have stoppers in all three unbid suits, plus an expectation of taking nine tricks either with high cards in your hand, or else with dummy's expected 7-card suit.

- A new suit in response to a 3-level preempt is forcing to game.

Let's consider a few examples with a 3-level preempt. In each case, partner opens and the next hand passes:

Partner opens 3♣. You hold

    ♠AJ73
    ♥KQ9
    ♦KJ10
    ♣K102

What should you bid?

Answer: Bid 3NT. You expect to win six or seven tricks in clubs plus enough tricks in the other suits to make game.

Partner opens 3♥. You hold

    ♠A1085
    ♥8
    ♦KQ97
    ♣AJ87

What should you bid?

Answer: Pass. Don't bid 3NT. If you play at NT with only a singleton heart in your hand, you may not win many tricks in partner's long suit, and the rest of your cards will produce only about half the tricks you need.

Partner opens 3♠. You hold

    ♠Q
    ♥AK2
    ♦AKQ
    ♣1087652

What should you bid?

Answer: Bid 4♠. Your ♠Q will be helpful to partner's suit, even though a singleton, and your five red-suit winners should come in very handy!

Partner opens 3♦. You hold

    ♠4
    ♥A98
    ♦10632
    ♣K10965

What should you bid?

Answer: Bid 4♦ if vulnerable, or 5♦ if not vulnerable. You are likely to take nine tricks at diamonds, and will accept a small penalty (for getting set) in return for making it hard for your opponents to bid game.

Example Hand: Upsetting Their Apple Cart

Here's a hand where a preempt had an unexpected and unsettling effect!

Dealer: West

Neither Side Vulnerable

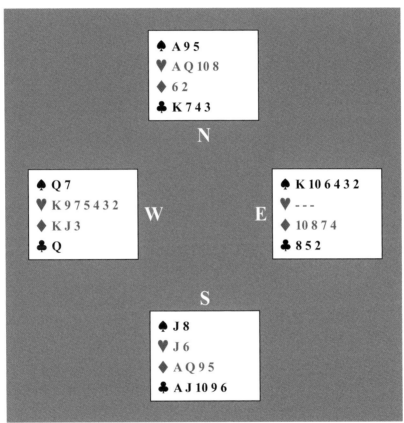

♠ A 9 5
♥ A Q 10 8
♦ 6 2
♣ K 7 4 3

N

♠ Q 7
♥ K 9 7 5 4 3 2
♦ K J 3
♣ Q

W

♠ K 10 6 4 3 2
♥ - - -
♦ 10 8 7 4
♣ 8 5 2

E

S

♠ J 8
♥ J 6
♦ A Q 9 5
♣ A J 10 9 6

THE BIDDING

West	North	East	South
3♥	pass	pass	4♣
pass	5♣	pass	pass
pass			

Opening lead: ♥5

BIDDING EXPLANATION

This bidding is not recommended all around, but it did actually occur at a bridge club tournament game. West might have liked a better suit for a preemptive opening bid, but with seven hearts and a bit less than the values for an opening one bid, West chose to exert pressure on the opponents with a 3♥ bid.

North passed, expecting at the very least to score a few points for defeating West's bid. East calmly passed, although inwardly cringing at the thought of a final 3♥ contract—possibly doubled!

CONTINUED ON NEXT PAGE

South, who did not want to "sell out" to 3♥, had a problem. South did not want to make a takeout double with only 2 cards in support of spades. South also did not want to bid 3NT without a heart stopper. South should probably have passed. However, South bid a risky 4♣. North, with very good values, raised to 5♣, and that became the final contract.

THE PLAY

The 5♣ final bid was a good contract, and South should have made it, but didn't! West led the ♥5, which East ruffed. (Please refer to the full diagram on the prior page). Looking for an *entry* back to West's hand to receive a second heart ruff, East returned the ♦8.

Declarer could have actually made the contract by winning this trick with the ♦A. However, declarer was upset over not playing 3NT, which would have been easy, or 3♥ doubled, which would have earned at least an 800-point penalty score! South chose to finesse the ♦Q, and lost to West's ♦K. West then played another heart for East to ruff and defeat South's contract by one trick.

The result was 50 points above the line for East–West.

South should have made the contract easily, simply by winning the ♦A at trick 2. South would then win tricks with the ♣K and ♣A, drawing the three remaining East–West trumps.

Now South leads the ♥J to finesse for West's known ♥K. Assuming West plays low, South overtakes with dummy's ♥Q and cashes the ♥A, discarding the ♠8. The position would now be as follows (see diagram on this page):

```
                         N
                    ♠ A 9 5
                    ♥ 10
                    ♦ 6
                    ♣ 7 4

   W                                      E
♠ Q 7                               ♠ K 10 6 4
♥ K 9 7                             ♥ - - -
♦ K J                               ♦ 10 7 4
♣ - - -                             ♣ - - -

                         S
                    ♠ J
                    ♥ - - -
                    ♦ Q 9 5
                    ♣ J 10 9
```

South is in dummy, and has lost only one trick so far: East's heart ruff on the opening lead. South cashes dummy's ♠A, and then ruffs a spade in hand. South gives up a diamond trick to West. South then takes the last four tricks with an easy cross-ruff, each remaining trump winning a separate trick.

WE	THEY	WE	THEY
	50		

Preempts at the 4 level are most often based on an 8-card suit. Using mathematical calculations, a player is dealt an 8-card hand about once every 200 deals. This means that every 50 hands or so, someone should receive an 8-card suit.

Also, preemptive openers of 4♣ or higher use up even more bidding room than lower-level preempts do. For starters, they stop the opponents from bidding 3NT. The bidding is not allowed to go backwards!

OPENING 4♣ AND 4♦ BIDS

Both 4♣ and 4♦ preemptive openers are *part-score* bids. In general, you'll have an 8-card suit in a hand that doesn't quite meet the standards for a 1-level opener.

OPENING 4♥ AND 4♠ BIDS

Both 4♥ and 4♠ preemptive openers are *game* bids. You'll usually have an 8-card suit and a hand that doesn't quite meet the standards for a 1-level opener. Sometimes you will have opening-level strength, especially in last seat.

West	North	East	South
pass	pass	pass	4♥

North	East	South	West
pass	pass	4♠	

OPENING 5♣ AND 5♦ BIDS

Both 5♣ and 5♦ preemptive openers are *game* bids. Ideally, you'll want to have a hand of quite dynamic shape, such as 8-4-1-0. Your hand can be primarily preemptive, especially when non-vulnerable against vulnerable. Vulnerable, you should have a pretty good hand, for at this level, it is usually a lot easier for your opponents to make a penalty double if you open with too light a hand.

Here are some example hands of high-level preempts:

You have ♠--- ♥K2 ♦1076 ♣AJ1087542. What should you bid?

Answer: Open 4♣. If vulnerable, it's a bit risky, and players of a more timid nature might bid only 3♣.

You hold ♠AK ♥QJ1098763 ♦J2 ♣9. What should you bid?

Answer: Open 4♥. At hearts, your hand has eight tricks (six hearts and two spades) and partner may have a useful card or two. On defense, two likely spade tricks are about all you can count on. It's best to apply bidding pressure on the opponents right at the outset.

You hold ♠A ♥--- ♦AK1065432 ♣J652. What should you bid?

Answer: Open 5♦. The hand is too good for 4♦, and opening just 1♦ invites your opponents in at a safe level for them. Nevertheless, some players may prefer to open 1♦ on a hand like this.

You hold ♠QJ109875 ♥KQJ ♦--- ♣AQ5. What should you bid?

Answer: With just a 7-card suit, in first or second seat, it's probably wisest to open 1♠. But if you're in fourth seat, open 4♠ after three passes. This will probably be the final bid, and partner is likely to have a couple of cards that will help.

RESPONDING TO HIGH-LEVEL PREEMPTS

Bids of 4♣ and 4♦ can be raised to game. Responder raises 4♦ to 5♦ (or 4♣ to 5♣) either to increase the pressure of opener's high-level preempt, or because responder has a powerful trick-taking hand (that is, aces) and expects the contract to have a chance for success. All higher-level opening preempts are already game bids, and so any bids by responder should be moves towards slam.

Preemptive Jump Overcalls

The same philosophy behind making opening preempts lies behind *overcalling* preemptively.

A Little History

In the early days of contract bridge, jump overcalls showed very powerful hands, perhaps 17 or more HCP—much better than a simple overcall showed. Today a few partnerships still hold onto using the old-time strong jump overcalls. You are also free to do so. The main drawback is that you don't often get super-strong hands to overcall on, and so the bid doesn't get very much use. On the other hand, you'll see long suits in hands of about average strength much more often.

In all of the following auctions, West's jump overcall is *preemptive*.

South	West	North	East
1♥	3♣		

North	East	South	West
pass	pass	1NT	3♦

East	South	West	North
pass	1♣	4♥	

North	East	South	West
pass	pass	1♦	2♠

INGREDIENTS FOR A JUMP OVERCALL

In general, the same guidelines for an opening preempt apply to a preemptive jump overcall.

Auction A				Auction B				Auction C			
West	North	East	South	West	North	East	South	West	North	East	South
pass	1♦	2♥		pass	1♦	3♥		pass	1♦	4♥	

In Auction A, East should have a 6-card suit and about average strength—the sort of a hand that would open 2♥. In Auction B, East should have a 7-card suit and about the same strength as a hand that would open 3♥. In Auction C, East likely has an 8-card suit.

We've already seen a few cases where you can raise partner's suit preemptively. North's raise in each of these auctions is based not on high-card power, but on distributional features.

South	West	North	East
1♥	pass	4♥	

South	West	North	East
2♦	pass	4♦	

These jump raises can discourage your opponents from bidding, by forcing them to face a risky situation. They may also just decide to guess what to bid, and may guess wrong!

JUMP RAISES IN COMPETITION

Responder's immediate double-raise of a 1-of-a-suit opening bid is strong and is forcing to game (see Chapter 5). However, in a competitive auction, responder's jump raises can be *preemptive*, rather than strong.

Auction A			
South	West	North	East
1♥	pass	3♥	

Auction B			
South	West	North	East
1♥	1♠	3♥	

Auction C			
South	West	North	East
1♥	2♣	3♥	

Auction D			
South	West	North	East
1♥	Dbl.	3♥	

In Auction A, North's raise is forcing to game. In the three other auctions, where West has competed, North's jump raise to 3♥ is *preemptive*.

North has

♠J95
♥Q1032
♦K9843
♣8

If North wants to show a heart raise with game-going interest, North should do the following: in Auction B, *cue bid* 2♠; in Auction C, *cue bid* 3♣; and in Auction D, *redouble* and then raise hearts on the following bidding round. By discussion with partner, South will understand that these show hands that fit the opener's suit well, and that have value at least to invite South to bid a game on his own.

When partner has *overcalled*, the jump raise is also a valuable preemptive call that can exert pressure on the other side. In these two auctions, East's jump raises are preemptive.

Auction E			
South	West	North	East
1♥	1♠	pass	3♠

Auction F			
South	West	North	East
1♥	2♣	2♥	4♣

If East wants to show a strong raise, East could *cue bid* 2♥ in Auction E, and 3♥ in Auction F.

Tips for Preemptive Bidding

PREEMPT, AND THEN STAY OUT

As a preempter, once you've done your preempting, it's wise to leave it up to your partner to do any further competing for your side. It's a losing policy for a preempter to continue competing.

Here's a case in point. No one was vulnerable and East held ♠J8 ♥3 ♦K76 ♣AK87642. East opened 3♣ and the bidding proceeded this way:

East	South	West	North
3♣	pass	pass	Dbl.
pass	3♥	pass	pass
?			

East should have "sold out" to South's 3♥ bid, but instead, East now committed a mortal bridge sin by bidding again. East bid 4♣, South doubled, and East took only six tricks. North–South scored 800 points, and it was later realized that West, with five hearts, would have defeated South's 3♥ contract.

PAY ATTENTION TO VULNERABILITY

Take vulnerability into account when preempting. If your hand is too weak for the bid you make, you may end up paying the price for your risk in *doubled* undertricks. All that has to happen is for one opponent to double, and the other to pass as in either of these auctions.

East	South	West	North		East	South	West	North
3♦	pass	pass	Dbl.		3♦	Dbl.	pass	pass
pass	pass	pass			pass			

RESPONDING TO PREEMPTIVE JUMP OVERCALLS

Generally, bidding a new suit opposite a simple overcall is not considered forcing, but bidding a new suit opposite a preemptive jump overcall is considered a forcing call.

South	West	North	East
1♦	2♥	pass	2♠
pass	?		

East probably has a strong distributional hand and is looking for the best game contract. For example, he may have ♠AQJ872 ♥65 ♦--- ♣AK1053.

What do you do if your opponents preempt? Maybe you will have no problem and it will be easy. You might have a pretty awful hand, and be happy to pass. Or maybe you will have a great hand, with support for your partner's suit, and the preempt won't trouble you at all. You can still bid your game.

However, more often than not, you'll be caught with an in-between sort of hand. If you pass, your side may miss bidding to a good contract. However, if you strain to bid, your side may bid too high, and go down. Also, what about the possibility of *doubling* the preempter's bid to gain a nice penalty score?

There are thousands of possible auctions where someone at the table makes a preemptive call. You and your partner will never be able to discuss them all individually, but you still both need to have some agreement on how to deal with opponents' preempts.

Here are a few typical examples that will illustrate the logic behind the appropriate response to a preempt. In each case, you are South, and the bidding goes as shown:

East	South	West	North
3♥	?		

♠K854
♥---
♦AQ109
♣AK874

Double. This is a *takeout double*. No matter which suit partner picks, you will put down an excellent dummy.

♠102
♥Q9854
♦KQ7
♣QJ5

You should pass quickly and happily, and hope that West also passes and that North, your partner, will balance with a double for takeout. If North doubles, you will *pass* the double, expecting a likely three-trick set.

This time, the bidding goes:

East	South	West	North
2♦	?		

♠AJ8
♥K4
♦KQ4
♣QJ1097

Bid 2NT. This shows about the equivalent of a 1NT opening bid, and a hand prepared for a diamond lead.

♠Q987
♥KQ654
♦10
♣AJ4

Double. Although you have only 12 HCP, and might not have opened the bidding, the weak 2 bid has made it easy for you to show your ability to play in any of three suits. It's a little risky to do this when vulnerable, but your short diamond suit still makes it very tempting.

12

2♣ and 2NT Opening Bids

Every now and then, you're dealt a really fabulous hand. It has so many high card points that you run out of fingers and toes trying to count them all! You're quite certain that your side should bid a game. In fact, you may need only a little help from partner's hand for a slam to succeed. One opening bid, 2♣, tells your partner that you have such a splendid hand.

Besides 2♣, there's one other *strong* opening bid on the 2 level: 2NT. This chapter will guide you through auctions starting with 2♣ and with 2NT.

Opening bids of 2♦, 2♥, or 2♠—the so-called *weak* 2 bids (Chapter 11)—each show a limited hand of 7–12 HCP. You'll notice that 2♣ is not part of that group. Instead, 2♣ opening bids are reserved for a very special purpose—to show extremely strong hands. You open 2♣ on hands where you need little or perhaps no help from partner's cards to make a *game* contract.

ANOTHER ARTIFICIAL BID

The 2♣ opening is another one of bridge's *artificial* bids, because the clubs you hold are irrelevant to the fact that clubs are what you bid. You can hold *any* clubs to begin the auction at 2♣; for example, you could have a few clubs or more, or you might even be *void* in clubs.

THE PHILOSOPHY IF THE 2♣ BID

If you were to open an extremely strong hand at the 1 level, you run the risk of partner passing with fewer than 6 HCP. However, you might have been happy finding only 2, 3, or 4 HCP in partner's hand! To solve this problem, the artificial 2♣ opening requires partner to bid in response to it—even with *zero* HCP! Your following bids will then indicate where your strength really is, and how truly powerful your hand is.

THE ROLE OF RESPONDER TO 2♣ (A QUICK PEEK!)

East	South	West	North
pass	2♣	pass	?

When South opens a strong and artificial 2♣, North must bid, even with the most awful hand imaginable! If North bids 2♦, then South will understand that this could, by agreement, show a very bad hand.

East	South	West	North
pass	2♣	pass	2♦

North's 2♦ response to South's artificial and forcing opening bid is, of course, also an artificial bid. It indicates nothing about diamonds. North may have one diamond, many diamonds, or perhaps none at all. North–South have agreed to use this 2♦ response so that South can make an easy rebid. Any response by North other than 2♦ is a natural bid.

GUIDELINES FOR OPENING 2♣

Balanced distribution (22 or more HCP)
With 22–24 HCP, you'll open 2♣ and rebid 2NT
With 25–27 HCP, you'll open 2♣ and rebid 3NT
With 28–30 HCP, you'll open 2♣ and rebid 4NT

Unbalanced distribution
21 or more HCP if your longest suit is 7 cards long
23 or more HCP if your longest suit is 6 cards long
25 or more HCP if your longest suit is 5 cards long

Note: *With very dynamic distribution, the HCP requirements for unbalanced hands can be shaded (reduced) by another point or two.*

Let's consider some likely prospects.

♠AKJ
♥AQJ643
♦A
♣KQ3

Open 2♣, intending to bid hearts next.

♠KQ102
♥AQ7
♦AQJ4
♣AJ

Open 2♣, intending to bid 2NT next.

♠A
♥QJ108
♦KQJ
♣AKQ87

Open 1♣. Although you have 22 HCP, the hand falls just short of the requirements for a forcing 2♣ bid. Unfortunately, your shape is unsuitable for bidding notrump right away. However, you intend to make the strongest bids possible after opening just 1♣.

CONTINUED ON NEXT PAGE

♠AK76542
♥AK
♦AKQ3
♣---

Open 2♣, intending to bid 2♠ next, and explore the chances of small slam—or grand slam—in spades or perhaps possibly in diamonds.

♠AKQ10753
♥AQJ10
♦---
♣K3

Open 2♣, planning to bid 4♠ quickly. Even though you have only 19 HCP, you will have ten tricks at spades, even with no help from partner—except perhaps if one opponent has ♠Jxxx or more. And even then, maybe the opening lead will be a club to make your ♣K good!

♠J
♥AKQ98764
♦KQJ
♣7

Open 4♥. Other choices include 1♥ (as you have 16 HCP), or even 2♣, since it looks like you'll win 10 tricks (8 in hearts and 2 in diamonds); game in your own hand. It's better to save the 2♣ opener for hands with more all-around strength than this hand has. Opinions may vary, but the 4♥ opening has the 2-way appeal of getting your side to game, while making it awkward for the opponents to learn if they have good spades together or not.

When opener bids 2♣, it's a virtual force to game. Bids at the 1 level are now out. Fortunately, after 2♣, there's a fair amount of "bidding room" before the first game-level contract, 3NT, is reached.

~~1♣~~	~~1♦~~	~~1♥~~	~~1♠~~	~~1NT~~
2♣	2♦	2♥	2♠	2NT
3♣	3♦	3♥	3♠	3NT
4♣	4♦	4♥	4♠	4NT
5♣	5♦	5♥	5♠	5NT
6♣	6♦	6♥	6♠	6NT
7♣	7♦	7♥	7♠	7NT

NEGATIVE AND POSITIVE RESPONSES

When responder bids 2♦, the partnership still should have enough bid choices to discover its best game or slam contract. Responder should be very comfortable making a 2♦ response, because it promises no HCP at all. This 2♦ call can be used as a *negative* response or just as more of a *waiting* response. It simply gives the 2♣ opener a chance to start probing for the best contract.

Instead of bidding 2♦, responder can make a *positive* response to the strong and forcing 2♣ opener. For a positive response in a suit, responder needs 7+ HCP, as well as a 5-card or longer suit. For a positive response of 2NT, responder should have a minimum of 8 HCP and a very balanced hand, and probably with little interest in a major-suit contract (hearts or spades).

You are North and your partner South has opened 2♣.

♠Q93
♥QJ4
♦Q106
♣Q864

Bid 2NT. Partner can count on you for 8 or more HCP, with values especially suitable for a notrump contract.

♠832
♥J8652
♦42
♣1096

Bid 2♦. This bid warns partner that you may have no high card points at all. If you next bid hearts, partner will play you to hold at least five hearts, but can assume nothing else.

CONTINUED ON NEXT PAGE

♠965
♥AQ632
♦Q32
♣97

Bid 2♥. With 8 HCP and a nice 5-card heart suit to the AQ, you know the partnership's combined holdings should make game a comfortable venture. You should show partner these good values right away.

♠4
♥K2
♦KQJ987
♣10876

Bid 3♦. Because 2♦ is artificial and could show a very poor hand, a jump to 3♦ is a natural and *positive* response.

♠J2
♥986
♦A105
♣KJ1032

Bid 3♣. You have a good 5-card suit and want to indicate that game is assured and that slam may be within range.

♠KJ32
♥3
♦75432
♣QJ7

Bid 2♦. Although you have 7 HCP, you have no clear positive bid. Your diamond suit is too weak for a 3♦ bid. By keeping the bidding low, your side will reach its best spot.

THE 2♣ OPENER'S SECOND CALL

When you open 2♣, you already have in mind what your next bid will be. You assume partner will make a 2♦ response (*negative* or *waiting*), although partner may surprise you with a *positive* response.

After partner's artificial 2♦ call, bid your best suit—or bid 2NT or 3NT—as planned. If you bid a suit, partner **must** take another bid. If partner instead makes a positive response, you both know game is a virtual certainty, and the partnership will keep bidding until game is reached.

2-OF-A-SUIT REBID AND RESPONSES

In general, once your partnership knows it is bidding to a game contract, the more bids you squeeze into the auction on the way to that contract, the more values are being shown. These extra bids may indicate an interest in a slam contract. On the other hand, if either player bids game directly, it tends to show no further interest in a slam contract.

In auctions beginning 2♣, this applies whether or not responder has made the negative 2♦ reply. Compare these two auctions:

North	East	South	West
pass	pass	2♣	pass
2♦	pass	2♠	pass
4♠			

North	East	South	West
pass	pass	2♣	pass
2♦	pass	2♠	pass
3♠			

Both auctions show that North is willing to play in spades. The immediate bid of game shows a very limited hand. The second auction suggests that North has a card or two that may help South, and gives South another chance to show additional values.

SECOND NEGATIVE RESPONSE

After responder's initial 2♦ reply and opener's rebid of 2♥ or 2♠, you and your partner may want to play 2NT as a bid to show a very weak hand. Alternatively, you can let 2NT show a few points, and play a further *artificial negative* response. That artificial call would be the **cheapest** suit-bid available at the 3 level.

North makes an *artificial* call of 3♣, the cheapest suit at the 3 level, to show a very poor hand. What North holds in clubs doesn't matter at all.

North	East	South	West
pass	pass	2♣	pass
2♦	pass	2♠	pass
3♣			

CONTINUED ON NEXT PAGE

2NT REBID AND RESPONSES

In the auction shown, South's sequence shows a balanced hand with 22–24 HCP.

What will North's second call be?

North	East	South	West
pass	pass	2♣	pass
2♦	pass	2NT	pass
?			

RESPONDER'S SECOND CALL AFTER 2♣ - 2♦ - 2NT

The North hand needs to provide only 2 or 3 useful HCPs for a likely game at 3NT or 4 of a major suit.

Here are the main choices for North:

- **Pass** with 0-1 HCP, or even 2 HCP if the hand is very flat (balanced).
- **3♣** is the Stayman convention (see Chapter 6) a level higher, at the 3 level.
- **3♦** and **3♥** are *Jacoby transfer* bids (see Chapter 6) a level higher, at the 3 level.
- **4♥** and **4♠** are limited hands, seeking to make ten tricks at either contract, with about 2–5 HCP, and at least a 6-card suit.
- **3NT** shows about 3–7 HCP and fixes the final contract.
- If your 2♦ bid was really a waiting bid, then with a good hand of 7 HCP or more, you may have merely bid **2♦** to see what opener might do. If so, over partner's 2NT, you may now bid the following over partner's 2NT rebid:

  4NT with 9–10 HCP. This is a raise in notrump that invites opener to pass or bid slam. Opener passes with a minimum hand and bids 6NT with a maximum.
  5NT with 13–14 HCP. This is a raise in NT, forcing to 6NT. Opener bids 6NT with a minimum, and bids 7NT with a maximum.
  6NT with 11–12 HCP. This is a raise to small slam in notrump, and opener must pass.
  7NT with 15+ HCP.

Length Meets Strength

Dealer: East

Neither Side Vulnerable

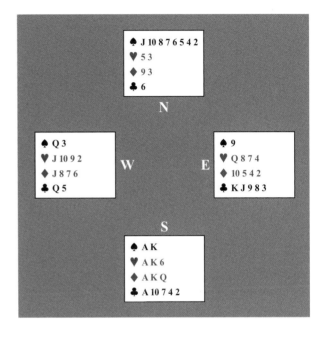

THE BIDDING

East	South	West	North
pass	2♣	pass	2♦
pass	3NT	pass	4♠

Opening lead: ♦2

BIDDING EXPLANATION

With 27 points in a balanced hand, South opens 2♣, planning to jump next to 3NT over North's likely 2♦ negative reply. Even though holding an 8-card spade suit, North does not bid spades right away. First, North bids 2♦ to indicate a hand possibly very low in HCP.

At his second round, South bids 3NT as planned. Despite holding only 1 HCP, North now takes charge and runs from South's 3NT bid to 4♠. South has shown a balanced hand, and therefore will have at least a doubleton in spades. As a result, North knows that the partnership combined has at least ten spades.

While North's very long spade suit might be of no use to South at 3NT, it will surely win many tricks should spades be trump. North therefore takes South out of the questionable 3NT contract, and selects a safer one, 4♠. South passes with reluctance, giving up the chance to score the 150 bonus above the line for holding all four aces at notrump.

There's not much to the play. In fact, North very easily takes all 13 tricks: eight spade tricks plus five high-card winners in the South hand.

Together, North–South discuss how they might have bid a slam that was so easy to make. Things could have been worse, though. If North with 1 HCP had passed South's 3NT rebid, South would not very likely make that contract! At notrump, South has eight top winners, but there doesn't seem to be a ninth trick anywhere. The sad part would be that after South's ♠AK are taken, North's remaining spades would all be winners, but the North hand has no entry to cash those good tricks.

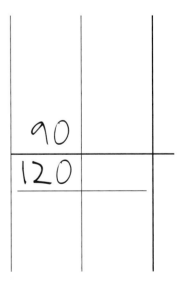

Opening 2NT Bid

Whereas 2♣ is an *artificial* strong opening bid, 2NT is a *natural* strong opening bid. When you open 2NT, you indicate a balanced hand with 20 or 21 HCP—possibly 22.

Open these hands with a bid of 2NT:

The 2NT opening bid completes your coverage of opening bids on balanced hands. See the following chart for more information.

HCP Ranges for Balanced Opening Bids	
HCP	**Action**
12–14	Open 1-of-a-suit, rebid NT at minimum level
15–17	Open 1NT
18–19	Open 1-of-a-suit, expecting to jump a level in NT
20–21	Open 2NT
22–24	Open 2♣, rebid 2NT
25–27	Open 2♣, rebid 3NT
28–30	Open 2♣, rebid 4NT

Once opener has shown 20–21 HCP, a hand of narrow point-count range, responder is the one who can better add up the point count and distributional assets of the two hands combined. Again, responder is the one who will steer the contract to its best destination, even though opener is the one who has all the points! It's like a lightweight jockey riding a big thoroughbred to the finish line.

RESPONDER'S CHOICES

Your responses to an opening 2NT bid are akin to those when partner opens 2♣ and rebids 2NT, which shows an even stronger hand of 22-24 HCP. Here are some possibilities:

- **3♣** is the Stayman convention (see Chapter 6) a level higher, at the 3 level.
- **3♦** and **3♥** are Jacoby Transfer bids (see Chapter 6) a level higher, at the 3 level. Responder can follow up the transfer next by bidding 3NT with a 5-card major (allowing opener to choose between that contract and 4 of the major), by raising to game in the major with a 6-card suit, or by bidding a new suit at the 4 level, forcing if in a minor suit. With an awful hand, responder can even pass the transfer, and play in a part-score.
- **3NT** shows about 5–10 HCP and fixes the final contract.
- **4♥** and **4♠** are limited hands, seeking to make ten tricks at either contract.
- **4NT** shows 11–12 HCP. This is a raise in notrump that invites opener to pass or bid slam. Opener passes with a minimum hand and bids 6NT with a maximum.
- **5NT** shows 15–16 HCP. This is a NT raise, forcing to 6NT. Opener bids 6NT with a minimum, and bids 7NT with a maximum.
- **6NT** shows 13–14 HCP. This is a raise to small slam in notrump, and opener must pass.
- **7NT.** You have 17+ HCP.

TIP

Note to the Kibitzer
Because the partnership has a forcing 2♣ opening bid, this makes it sensible and easy for responder to pass opening **1 bids** with 5 or fewer HCP.

CONTINUED ON NEXT PAGE

Example Deal: The King Rules

In this example, we won't even need to look at the East–West hands!

Dealer: West

North–South Vulnerable

THE BIDDING

West	North	East	South
pass	pass	pass	2♣
pass	2♦	pass	2NT
pass	3♣	pass	3♠
pass	3NT	pass	pass
pass			

Opening lead: ♥J

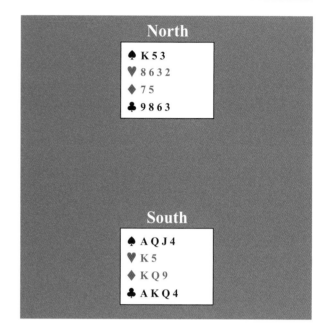

North
♠ K 5 3
♥ 8 6 3 2
♦ 7 5
♣ 9 8 6 3

South
♠ A Q J 4
♥ K 5
♦ K Q 9
♣ A K Q 4

BIDDING EXPLANATION

South's 2NT rebid promises 22–24 HCP. North, with 3 HCP, knows that her side's total is about 26 HCP, just right to try for a game. As a result, North bids 3♣, the Stayman convention, looking for a possible 4–4 fit in hearts. When South shows a 4-card spade suit, North "signs off" at 3NT.

THE PLAY

South will have a pretty easy time at this contract, and we don't even need to see the East–West cards.

West's ♥J opening lead will give South a sure trick with the ♥K. South also has four top spades, as well as three top clubs. If the clubs divide 3-2 (with three in one defender's hand and two in the other's), then the fourth round of clubs will be South's ninth trick.

As soon as South gains the lead, South will test clubs. If they divide 4-1 or 5-0, South will stop after two rounds and lead the ♦K to establish one trick in that suit. South will have to be *very* unlucky not to win nine tricks!

WHAT TO DO WHEN YOUR OPPONENTS INTERFERE

Occasionally, your opponents will step into an auction that you have begun with a 2♣ bid. The opponent should know the risk in competing against a hand that contains more than half the deck's HCP. However, as in the auction shown, West may be feeling jealous, or pesky, and end up making a foolish bid. Your side needs to be in position to extract the maximum penalty.

West may simply be offering you the chance to double at a low level (the 2 level), and take the points you can earn there. East–West will give you that penalty score rather than have you bid a game, or possibly even a slam.

East	South	West	North
pass	2♣	2♠	?

Your partnership must be in position to double the opponents and defeat them if that's where your best score is! The best way to handle this is for North to *double* with a terrible hand, and to *pass* with a slightly better hand, in order to give South the chance to double. If, instead, North would much rather simply turn to the business of bidding a game, or more, North should just make a natural bid reflecting the values of her hand. Make sure you and your partner follow the same strategy in this situation.

OPENING 2NT WITH A "BAD" 22 HCP

With a balanced 22 HCP, you can actually choose between opening 2♣ and 2NT. If your hand is very balanced (4-3-3-3 or 4-4-3-2) and is low on aces, 10s, and 9s, then you have a "bad" 22-count. Treat it as 20–21 HCP and open an immediate 2NT bid. You'll probably need about 4+ HCP from partner for game. However, if your 22 HCP includes a 5-card suit, or has plenty of aces, 10s, and 9s, first bid 2♣ and then bid 2NT, to show a hand in the 22–24 HCP range.

STRETCHING TO OPEN 2♣ WITH A PART-SCORE

If your side has a part-score, you might open 2♣ on a hand of slightly lesser strength than the initial guidelines stated. If your side has a 40 part-score, any contract of 2♥ or higher is enough for game. You can start at 2♣ and not worry about bidding much higher. This may also discourage your opponents from getting into the auction. Of course, you should still have very good defensive cards in case your opponents do bid. Then your side can double them in confidence.

ALTERNATIVE METHODS FOR RESPONDING TO 2♣

Using 2♦ as a weak or all-purpose response is a simple and popular way to bid after the strong artificial opener. You can try other methods, including one where a 2♥ reply to 2♣ is used as an immediate way of showing an utterly weak responsive hand with no more than a jack or two, such as in the hand shown here. Just be sure you and your partner have adopted the same methods, in this and other auctions.

The Unusual Notrump

A colorful convention that has been around for many decades is the *unusual notrump*. It's the creation of Alvin Roth (1924–2007), a superb player and author whose bidding ideas have been embraced by many players.

Al Roth. Photo courtesy of the American Contract Bridge League.

The unusual notrump is an overcall in notrump that is made after the opponents have opened at the 1 level. Most often, it's a 2NT bid, because a simple 1NT overcall is a natural bid. Usually, a bid in notrump suggests a balanced hand pattern; however one clear and **unusual** feature of the unusual notrump is that it actually indicates an unbalanced, 2-suited hand. It also shows a hand with two specific long suits—the two lowest-ranking, unbid suits. For example, if a major suit has been bid, the unusual notrump bid shows length in both minor suits.

An unusual notrump bid uses up bidding space, which often can make the auction tougher for your opponents. Their next bid must at least be at the 3 level. With a jump to 2NT, you preempt in two suits at once!

In these auctions, West's NT bid is the unusual notrump, showing at least 5 cards in each of the two lowest unbid suits.

East	South	West	North
pass	1♠	2NT	

West has clubs and diamonds:

♠AQ
♥7
♦KJ632
♣QJ1084

North	East	South	West
1♥	pass	3♥	3NT

West has clubs and diamonds:

♠---
♥K84
♦AKQ97
♣109874

(Notice that in all of these auctions, West has little need for a natural 2NT bid!)

South	West	North	East
1♣	2NT		

West has diamonds and hearts:

♠10
♥AKJ93
♦AQ987
♣K4

West	North	East	South
pass	1♠	pass	2♠
2NT			

West has clubs and diamonds:

♠A
♥4
♦J9876
♣J108632

South	West	North	East
1NT	2NT		

West has clubs and diamonds:

♠6
♥Q
♦QJ10984
♣AK983

North	East	South	West
1♦	pass	2♦	2NT

West has clubs and hearts:

♠Q10
♥KQJ54
♦8
♣KQJ106

CONTINUED ON NEXT PAGE

Guidelines for Using the Unusual Notrump

With three suits not yet bid, you should be absolutely sure that your two long suits are the two lowest-ranking unbid suits. Remember—spades rank highest, followed by hearts, diamonds, and clubs. Thus the unusual notrump bid never shows spades! Also, you should almost always have at least 5 cards in each suit promised.

Highest

Lowest

HCP STRENGTH

An unusual notrump bid covers a wide HCP range, and so your HCP strength can vary. You must keep in mind that the enemy will be in a good position to double your side for penalties. If your hand is too weak, you might suffer a very large defeat!

VULNERABILITY

At *favorable* vulnerability (when they are vulnerable and you are not vulnerable), your hand can be quite light. When vulnerable, you need a better hand, with a minimum HCP of not much below opening-bid strength.

At any vulnerability, an unusual notrump bid could actually be a very strong hand. By making a further call later in the auction, you show extra values. However, if your hand contains a minimum HCP, you should leave all further bidding up to partner.

Replying to the Unusual Notrump

Because partner has bid notrump, but really has the two lowest unbid suits, it's up to you to choose a suit for your side. Because you have been commanded to bid, partner understands that your bid does not promise meaningful length in that suit, nor any HCP at all.

Usually, you will have at least 2 or 3 cards in at least one of partner's suits. Simply bid the suit that you have more of. If you have the same length in each suit, it's usually a better strategy to bid the higher ranking suit. (That's because if you feel the need to make a bid later in the auction, you can bid the lower-ranking one next, giving your partner a fuller picture of your hand.)

FAQ

When is 2NT a natural overcall?

When your opponents open with a weak 2 bid, 2NT is a natural overcall; it shows about the same sort of hand that would have opened 1NT, and which can handle the lead of the opponents' bid suit. Similarly, 3NT over a preemptive 3-level opening bid is most valuable as a *natural* bid to suggest 3NT as a final contract.

In the following auctions, you are East, and West's 2NT unusual notrump bid asks you to choose between the two lowest unbid suits.

♠AQ62
♥Q1O52
♦A5
♣J92

South	West	North	East
1♦	2NT	pass	?

Bid 4♥. You have much more strength than partner could expect, and you should have a very good play for ten tricks.

♠K84
♥Q9632
♦83
♣J32

South	West	North	East
1♥	2NT	Dbl.	?

Bid 3♣. Your hand isn't good, but you have a preference for clubs over diamonds.

♠KQ84
♥Q963
♦J32
♣83

South	West	North	East
1♥	2NT	3♥	?

Pass. If North had passed, you would have bid 3♦. Your hand is not strong enough to bid 4♦ now, even at favorable vulnerability.

CONTINUED ON NEXT PAGE

♠QJ109873
♥8
♦94
♣AJ2

South	West	North	East
1♣	2NT	pass	?

Bid 3♠. Even though partner has asked for hearts or diamonds, you want to play in spades.

♠J5
♥74
♦QJ32
♣AKJ92

East	South	West	North
pass	pass	pass	1♥
1NT			

Note: *This example shows that a passed hand can make an unusual notrump call at the 1 level! In this auction, East's 1NT bid is unusual, seeking to compete in the minors at the 2 level. Because East has already passed, East cannot have 15–17 HCP!*

TIP

"Reviewing" the Bidding

If you need to have the calls of the auction repeated for you, either during the auction or very shortly after it ends, you can get a "review" of it. You must wait until it's your turn, and then ask your opponents to repeat the auction, including passes. They must tell you. If they don't remember it, your partner can try. If no one remembers, try your best together, and be sure to all sign up for memory lessons!

Your right to a bidding review *ends* when you play a card on the first trick (whether declarer or defender).

UNUSUAL NOTRUMP: EXAMPLE HAND

Dealer: West

Neither Side Vulnerable

THE BIDDING

West	North	East	South
1♥	2NT	3♥	5♣
pass	pass	pass	

Opening lead: ♠K

BIDDING EXPLANATION

North makes a typical 2NT unusual notrump call. East stretches to raise partner's suit, bidding 3♥. South decides to take a chance on an 11-trick game, and bids 5♣, having lengthy trumps and a few key aces and kings.

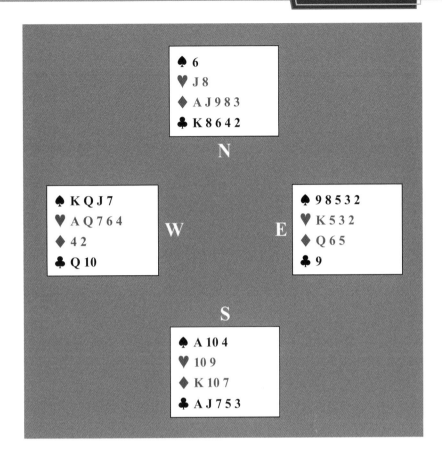

THE PLAY

West leads the ♠K. South, the declarer, thanks the dummy and surveys the situation. If trumps are 2–1, then South has no loser in that suit. It looks like South will lose two hearts, and that all will hinge on not losing a trick to the ♦Q. The North–South diamond holdings give the opportunity to finesse either opponent for the ♦Q.

Rather than make a guess as to how to play diamonds, South finds a much better way. South wins the spade lead with the ♠A and ruffs a spade in dummy. South now cashes dummy's ♣K, and then leads a club to the ♣A, pulling the enemy's trumps. South now trumps the last spade in dummy, which removes the last spade from either the North or South hand.

Now South exits with a heart. The defense can win this trick and take another heart trick, but then they are out of options. If either defender leads diamonds, South can easily avoid a loser in that suit. And if the defenders lead a heart or a spade, South can ruff with the last trump in dummy, and discard a diamond from his hand. Again, the diamond loser disappears.

South has executed an *end-play*, putting the defense on play at a time when their next lead has to help South. "Well done, partner," says North, as she tallies game, 100 points below the line.

WE	THEY	WE	THEY
✕			
100			

Michaels Cue Bid

Michaels cue bid is a convention named after Mike Michaels. After an opponent opens 1-of-a-suit, the Michaels cue bid is an immediate bid in that suit at the two level. It's a bid that has little natural use.

Mike Michaels (1924–1966). Photo courtesy of the American Contract Bridge League.

Like the unusual notrump, Michaels cue bid also shows a hand with two long suits (each usually 5 cards or longer). However, this time, the suits are different. Over a *minor* suit opening bid (1♣ or 1♦), a Michaels cue bid—an immediate bid of that suit—shows the two **highest**-ranking suits. A Michaels cue bid over a *major* suit opening bid (1♥ or 1♠) shows the other major suit and one minor suit.

In each of these auctions, West makes a Michaels cue bid.

South	West	North	East
1♣	2♣		

West has spades and hearts:

♠QJ875
♥109632
♦Q
♣AK

East	South	West	North
pass	1♠	2♠	

West has hearts and a minor suit:

♠K3
♥J9754
♦AKQJ8
♣5

West	North	East	South
pass	pass	pass	1♦
2♦			

West has spades and hearts:

> ♠A10987
> ♥Q10963
> ♦A
> ♣102

Because West has passed, East knows that West's hand is below opening bid strength.

North	East	South	West
pass	pass	1♥	2♥

West has spades and a minor suit:

> ♠AJ732
> ♥2
> ♦7
> ♣QJ10754

Replying to a Michaels Cue Bid

Partner has made a Michaels cue bid, bidding the opponents' suit—but really has two other suits. If the next player passes, it's up to you to determine which suit to play in, even if your hand isn't very good for any suit that partner may have. How high you bid depends upon the strength of your hand and how "big" your fit is with your partner. Of course, factors of vulnerability and part-score can figure in your decision, as in any bidding situation.

If partner's Michaels cue bid asks you to pick one of the majors, just bid your longer major suit—even if it's only a doubleton. With equal length in the majors, bid spades first. If partner's Michaels cue bid shows a major suit and a minor suit, you need-n't assume or guess which minor suit it is. To learn whether partner has diamonds or clubs, simply bid 2NT, an artificial call. This signals partner to bid the minor suit.

Note: Remember, you can use a Michaels Cue Bid only directly after the opponent opens 1-of-a-suit!

Now let's look at a few Michaels cue bid auctions. In each case, you are East.

South	West	North	East
1♦	2♦	pass	?

> ♠10832
> ♥J962
> ♦K4
> ♣Q87

Bid 2♠. Although you have 4 cards in each of partner's suits, you haven't enough strength to bid at the three level.

CONTINUED ON NEXT PAGE

East	South	West	North
pass	1♠	2♠	Dbl.
?			

♠J1076
♥Q72
♦Q93
♣Q108

If North had passed, you would have bid 3♥. Now you can pass and let partner pick the suit to escape to.

East	South	West	North
pass	1♥	2♥	pass
?			

♠65
♥A85
♦J532
♣J976

Bid 2NT. Partner now bids 3-of-a-minor suit.

East	South	West	North
pass	1♠	2♠	3♠
?			

♠10532
♥9
♦KQ109
♣KQ98

Bid 3NT, asking partner to bid 4-of-a-minor suit. Your hand is strong enough to compete at the 4 level in diamonds or clubs, whichever suit partner has.

TIP

Observation by the Kibitzer

I notice that Michaels cue bid, like the unusual notrump, has a very wide HCP range.

FACT

Did You Know?

Mike Michaels' original plan for his cue bid convention was as a light takeout double, but it evolved into a two-suited bid.

Remember: Use Michaels Cue Bid only directly after the opponent opens 1-of-a-suit!

Chapter 8 introduced you to the *takeout double*—a double early in an auction that your opponents start, to help your side find its best suit to bid. The takeout double has been used in bridge for a very long time.

As an example, in Auction A, West makes a typical takeout double, requesting East to bid an unbid suit.

Auction A			
East	*South*	*West*	*North*
pass	1♠	Dbl.	pass
?			

A takeout double.

Auction B			
East	*South*	*West*	*North*
pass	1♠	2♣	Dbl.
pass	?		

Now . . . a negative double.

Auction B also contains a double made early in the bidding, except that here partner opens and the opponent makes a suit overcall. For many decades, North's double of West's 2♣ overcall in Auction B remained a penalty double. North, judging that West won't win eight tricks at clubs, doubles 2♣ in order to increase the point score of each undertrick that North–South can achieve. South was expected to pass North's penalty double.

Today, though, the immediate penalty double of the opponent's overcall has fallen out of use. Nowadays, this double immediately following an opponent's overcall has taken on a different use—and it has a special name. It's called the *negative double*.

Using negative doubles, North's double of a suit overcall is *not* intended for penalties. Instead, it shows length (at least 4 cards) in each of the other two suits—the unbid suits. North's double in Auction B shows hearts and diamonds. North should have at least 4 cards in each of these suits, and enough strength to compete at the two level—about 7 HCP—or more. South is expected to bid.

Note: *Remember, the only word you actually say in the auction is "double." You cannot include any other word, such as "negative," "penalty," or "takeout."*

Did You Know?
The negative double's popularity took off in the late 1950s, just after the USSR launched Sputnik, the first space satellite. As a sign of its bridge novelty, the negative double was initially called the *Sputnik double*!

CONTINUED ON NEXT PAGE

The Negative Double *(continued)*

Ingredients for a Negative Double

You can make a negative double whenever partner opens the bidding 1-of-a-suit, and the next player overcalls in a suit. For your double, you usually require at least 4 cards in each unbid suit.

By agreement with your partner, your opponent's overcall must be at the 1 level, 2 level, or 3 level. Of course, the strength needed for making a negative double goes up with each level of the bidding. Roughly, for a negative double, you need 6+ HCP at the 1 level, 8+ HCP at the 2 level, and 10+ HCP at the 3 level.

In these auctions, North's double is a negative double.

Auction C			
East	*South*	*West*	*North*
pass	1♣	1♦	Dbl.

Auction D			
East	*South*	*West*	*North*
pass	1♥	2♣	Dbl.

Auction E			
North	*East*	*South*	*West*
pass	pass	1♦	2♥
Dbl.			

Auction F			
South	*West*	*North*	*East*
1♦	3♠	Dbl.	

In Auction C, North needs only about 6 HCP for a negative double, because South can still make a call at the 1 level.

Let's say you held this hand as North in Auction D.

You would have responded an easy 1♠ to partner's opening 1♥ bid, but West's 2♣ overcall stops that. You could pass, of course, except that you have some good cards and would like a say in the auction. After all, your side has the balance of strength.

The problem is that you have no natural bid. Your hand has neither the strength nor the suit length to bid 2♦ or 2♠. Nor should you raise to 2♥ with only 2-card support. It is also clear that you are too weak for a 2NT bid.

The solution is the negative double! You have 4 cards in each unbid suit, and enough general strength to compete at the 2 level. You expect your partner (South, the opener) to make a sensible call, knowing this information.

FACT

Did You Know?
The negative double is another innovation that Alvin Roth helped to develop and popularize.

Replying to the Negative Double

After the opponent overcalls and partner makes a negative double, opener must make a sensible call.

Playing negative doubles, you are South, and the auction goes this way:

East	South	West	North
pass	1♦	2♠	Dbl.
pass	?		

Because East has passed, the pressure of partner's double rests on you and requires you to make a bid. If, instead, you pass in this auction, you leave your opponents to play a final contract of 2♠ doubled.

If made, 2♠ doubled is worth 120 in trick-score (not just 60), and so it is a game contract. Because your side will need six tricks to set 2♠, you may not beat them unless you, South, yourself have very good spades.

Let's look at a few different hands and consider the calls that South should make in the auction shown.

♠K32
♥AJ104
♦KQJ104
♣A

Bid 4♥. You may not always make it, but you probably have a very good chance.

♠AJ9
♥K7
♦Q10842
♣KJ3

Bid 2NT. A 3♦ rebid is out, with only a 5-card suit, and you can't afford to pass, as you might not set their contract.

CONTINUED ON NEXT PAGE

♠A752
♥4
♦AQ83
♣K643

Bid 3♣. Your hand is not good for notrump. Once your ♠A is gone, your opponents should be ready to take a lot of tricks in that suit.

♠Q9
♥Q1053
♦KQ987
♣AJ

Bid 3♥. You have a minimum hand, and so should make a bid at the 3 level only. Your hand is not strong enough to try for 4♥.

DO YOU REALLY GIVE UP YOUR CHANCE TO PENALIZE YOUR OPPONENTS?

Any overcaller runs a risk by entering the auction. Their contract could be doubled and set a few tricks, for a poor score. You want your side always to be in position to heavily penalize an opponent who makes an unwise or unlucky overcall.

However, you have chosen to play negative doubles. As a result, you are no doubt asking yourself, "How can we do that, if our double of their overcall is *negative*?"

Here's how. Let's say partner opens 1♥, and the next hand bids 2♦. You hold

♠QJ9
♥52
♦Q10976
♣KQ3

East	South	West	North
pass	1♥	2♦	pass
pass	Dbl.	pass	?

To achieve a nice penalty score in 2♦ doubled, you as North must pass (as shown in the auction), and wait for partner (who is the opening bidder) to reopen the auction with a double. Then at your next turn (see the ? in the auction), you pass!

This is an essential tactic to include when you play negative doubles. If partner passes after an overcall, opener is expected to reopen the bidding with a double, whenever opener is *short* in the overcaller's suit. Shortness is a doubleton, singleton, or void. The double by opener in the "pass-out" seat, is a used as a "reopening" double—based again on shortness in the opponent's suit, for takeout purposes — but in the example hand, South passes and, as is said in bridge, *converts* the reopening double into a penalty double. Bridge is a complicated game!

IMMEDIATE DOUBLES THAT ARE FOR PENALTIES

Note that North's doubles in these auctions are *not* negative doubles.

East	South	West	North		East	South	West	North		East	South	West	North
pass	1♥	1NT	Dbl.		pass	1♥	2NT	Dbl.		pass	1♥	2♥	Dbl.

In the first auction, North's is an old-fashioned penalty double, looking for a good score. North does not believe that West will succeed at 1NT and wants to increase the value of the undertricks. In the next two cases, North is doubling an artificial bid, first an unusual notrump bid, and then a Michaels cue bid. In both cases, North doubles to show interest in doubling the contract that East–West retreat to.

How High to Play Negative Doubles

How high you choose to play the negative double is up to you and your partner.

Let's assume that your partnership agrees to play negative doubles up to the level of 3♠. This means that if your opponent makes any suit overcall up to and including 3♠, the next hand's double is a negative double. It shows the other two suits and is not a penalty double. However, when your side makes an immediate double of a suit overcall higher than 3♠, by agreement, that double is for penalties.

FOCUS ON THE MAJOR SUITS?

Some partnerships merely require that after a minor-suit opening and a major-suit overcall, the negative double only promises 4-card length in the other major suit, and does not make any promises with regard to the missing minor suit.

South	West	North	East
1♣	1♠	Dbl.	

You may choose to agree that North's double promises at least 4-card length in hearts, but makes no promise about diamonds.

PART-SCORE AND VULNERABILITY

Just as with any other call in the auction, be sure to consider the two factors of part-score and vulnerability when using negative doubles.

TIP

Watch the Vulnerability

It's always good to remember that bidding when vulnerable is riskier than when not vulnerable. If you go down vulnerable, especially doubled, the penalty can be quite large. Take care when straining to get into the auction vulnerable. It may be a lot wiser to pass.

14

Strong Hands and Slam Bidding

A big thrill for every bridge player is the first slam that he or she bids, a thrill that you will also experience. It will be an even bigger thrill if your slam makes!

This chapter gives you useful advice for bidding slams. You'll also learn a few bidding tools so that your first slam—and perhaps all of your slams—will succeed.

After opening the bidding, the first thing a partnership wants to learn is whether they belong merely in a part-score, or whether they should seek a higher contract—even a *slam* contract, a bid to win 12 tricks (small slam), or all 13 tricks (grand slam). To bid and make a slam, you need luck, you need to bid well, and, of course, you need to win all of those tricks that you've bid for!

The luck comes in being dealt good cards—cards that are able to capture 12 or 13 tricks. These deals don't occur often. A *small slam* (12 tricks) might happen once every 20 or 30 deals. A *grand slam* (all 13 tricks) is even rarer. However, when you do get these hands, you and your partner want to be ready to steer the auction to the right contract.

The reason to bid a small slam or a grand slam is the big bonus that it carries—up to 1500 points for a vulnerable grand slam!

500 – 750
Small Slams

1000 – 1500
Grand Slams

FIGURING OUT HOW HIGH TO BID

Occasionally, the first two bids are enough for one or both partners to realize the limit of the hand. For example, in Auction A, both players know after two bids that 3NT is as high as they wish to go.

Auction A			
South	*West*	*North*	*East*
1NT	pass	3NT	

Auction B			
South	*West*	*North*	*East*
1♣	pass	1♦	

By contrast, in Auction B, the partnership may be on the way to slam, to game, or they may end up struggling to make just a part-score. Usually it will take more than one round of bidding for the partnership to discover how high they can go.

CAN WE MAKE A SLAM?

The HCP bidding guide for slam bids applies especially to *notrump* contracts, when balanced hands face each other. With a *trump* contract, distributional strength can often make up for lack of high cards. For example, if you are void in a suit and have plenty of trumps, the opponents' HCP in that suit are worthless!

Hopefully the chart at the top of the next page looks familiar, because you've seen it earlier, in Chapter 4. It's repeated here for your convenience.

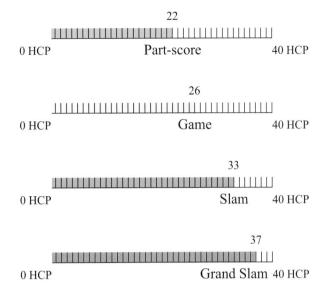

SLAM CONSIDERATIONS

If the opponents can win two tricks, your side can't make a slam. To consider slam seriously, either you or your partner—or both of you—must believe that you won't have two losing tricks.

A small slam is possible whenever:

- The opponents can't take the first two tricks, and
- Your side can take 12 tricks.

A grand slam is possible whenever:

- The opponents can't take the first trick, and
- Your side can take all 13 tricks.

CONTINUED ON NEXT PAGE

AN EXAMPLE SLAM HAND

Dealer: North

Neither Side Vulnerable

THE BIDDING

North	East	South	West
pass	pass	1♥	pass
1♠	pass	3♦	pass
5♦	pass	6♦	pass
pass	pass		

Opening lead: ♦9

BIDDING EXPLANATION

South in third seat has a powerful hand in both distribution and high-card strength. To explore for the best possible contract, South opens **1♥**. North responds **1♠**, bidding her 4-card suit first, as a bid of **2♦** would show at least 10 HCP. South now shows great strength (19+ HCP) by making a game-forcing *jump-shift* to **3♦**. (A jump-shift is a bid between partners that skips a level of bidding, and names a new suit.) North now leaps to **5♦**, because **4♦** does not tell the full story of her hand.

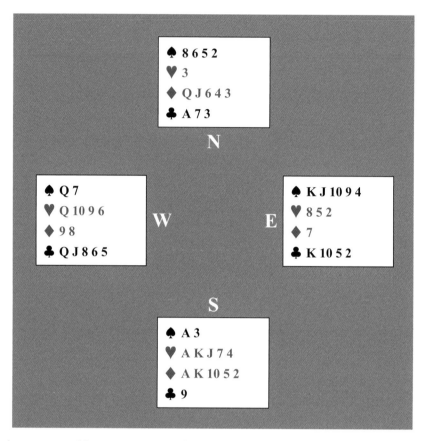

South reads this bid correctly as showing 5-card ♦ support, with one or two useful cards elsewhere. If South is correct, slam should be a successful venture! South cannot see the opponents winning the first two tricks and *can* envision winning 12 tricks.

THE PLAY

South, the declarer, has a very easy time with this contract. South wins the trump lead (it doesn't matter in which hand) and then draws the remaining trump. It's now an easy matter to play ♥A and ♥K and ruff a heart in dummy, play ♣A and ruff (trump) a club, ruff another heart, ruff another club, and so on. Along the way, or at the end, South gives up one spade trick to the opponents. Doing the arithmetic, it turns out that North–South made their diamond slam on a combined total of just 26 HCP, clearly less than the 33 HCP needed for balanced hand to bid a notrump slam.

In the previous section, one essential ingredient in North–South's success was South's ability to show *strength*. Another was the partnership's accurate auction that uncovered a 10-card *trump fit*. The final key factor for North–South was their power to *control*—that is, their ability to win a trick in any suit the defense might lead. Let strength, trumps, and controls be your cornerstones to suit-slam bidding. You can even use the acronym STAC (**S**trength, **T**rumps, **A**nd **C**ontrols) as a handy memory device!

A LOOK AT CONTROLS

Assuming your side can pick the trump suit, here's how to refer to the *controls* you have in each suit. The x's stand for any small card.

First-round control—an ace or a *void* (none of a suit)
Second-round control— Kx or a *singleton*
Third-round control—Qxx or a *doubleton*

A *singleton* ace controls all rounds of a suit, as does an ace-king *doubleton*. If you are the declarer, holding an ace and queen gives you both first- and second-round control of a suit, inasmuch as you play last on the opening lead.

In the slam just bid in the previous section, North–South had all of the *controls*, except for the second round of spades.

SLAMS AND CONTROLS

If your side lacks first-round controls in two different suits, you cannot make a slam. If your side lacks first- and second-round controls in any suit, the opponents can win the first two rounds of the suit; this is another case where you should not try to bid slam.

Of course, just because you and partner have first-round control of all four suits doesn't mean that you can make a slam. In fact, if your side has all four aces and the next-highest card you have is a 7—as shown in the E–W at right—those four aces may be the only tricks you'll win!

WEST	EAST
♠652	♠A743
♥A62	♥753
♦543	♦A62
♣A752	♣643

*East–West have first-round control in **every** suit, but they might win only four tricks!*

The Gerber 4♣ Convention

Because you can't make a slam if you lose the first two tricks, it was only a matter of time before conventions came along to address that very concern.

In 1942, John Gerber published a small booklet on his 4♣ slam convention. This convention checks the partnership's *controls*, so important for slam, after a bid in notrump. Gerber (1906–1981) was also an inspirational figure to many rising bridge stars.

Because 3NT already is a *game* contract, to bid beyond 3NT just to play a 4♣ *part-score* makes little sense. In many bidding situations, the best use for a 4♣ bid is to aim for a better score than 3NT.

Gerber came up with an *artificial* 4♣ inquiry to ask for the number of aces partner holds. Partner chooses the *artificial* bid which reflects that number. In reply to 4♣, a 4♦ bid shows either no aces or all four aces; 4♥ shows one ace; 4♠ shows two aces; and 4NT shows three aces.

In any given auction, North should have no trouble determining when a 4♦ reply by South indicates no aces, rather than all four aces.

In each auction shown below, North's 4♣ bid is the Gerber convention, which asks South to make the correct reply. The question marks signal that South is to choose the appropriate artificial bid that reflects the count of aces in South's hand.

South	West	North	East
1NT	pass	4♣	pass
?			

South	West	North	East
1♥	pass	1♠	pass
1NT	pass	4♣	pass
?			

South	West	North	East
2♣	pass	2♦	pass
2NT	pass	4♣	pass
?			

East	South	West	North
1♦	1NT	pass	4♣
pass	?		

The chart below shows the bid South is supposed to make after looking, counting, and determining whether the hand has 0, 1, 2, 3, or 4 aces. South needs to know the correct answers to Gerber by memory; at the table there's no chart to consult.

Partner's Responses to a 4♣ Gerber Bid, Asking for Aces	
Bid	*Number of Aces*
4♦	0 or 4
4♥	1
4♠	2
4NT	3

North only has very simple arithmetic to do: Add the number of aces shown by South to the number of aces in North's hand. If the total is four, then North–South have all of the aces, and they control all four suits. The opponents have no aces and can be stopped with a high card from winning the first trick. If the total is three, then the opponents have one ace. They could win at least one trick at a notrump contract. If North–South have two aces only, then so do the opponents.

When you find that your side lacks two aces, you also now have to stop the bidding at a safe level. The Gerber bidder just slams on the bidding brakes by signing off at **4NT** or at another contract. Occasionally, the artificial reply to **4♣** will itself be the desired contract to stay at, and the Gerber bidder will pass. The player asking for aces is the one who places the final contract.

ASKING FOR KINGS

When you find that your side has all four aces, you can now use the Gerber convention at the 5 level to ask about kings.

South	West	North	East
1NT	pass	4♣	pass
4♠	pass	5♣	pass
?			

In the auction shown, if North finds that the partnership has all four aces, North can then follow with a **5♣** bid to ask about kings. As you might expect, the responses are as follows: **5♦** shows either no kings or all four kings; **5♥** shows one king; **5♠** shows two kings; and **5NT** shows three kings.

Partner's Responses to 5♣ Gerber Bid, Asking for Kings	
Bid	*Number of Kings*
5♦	0 or 4
5♥	1
5♠	2
5NT	3

TIP

Note to Kibitzer

It's easiest if your partnership decides to play **4♣** as Gerber only in very clear situations: as a jump to **4♣** over a notrump bid, and with neither partner bidding clubs previously. Not every **4♣** bid is a Gerber bid!

CONTINUED ON NEXT PAGE

EXAMPLE HAND: USING GERBER

East–West hands are irrelevant.

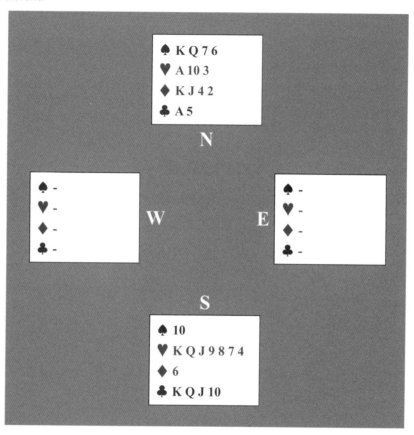

THE BIDDING

West	North	East	South
pass	1NT	pass	4♣
pass	4♠	pass	5♥
pass	pass	pass	

BIDDING EXPLANATION

When North opens 1NT, South ponders a slam. If North has 3 aces, South can make a slam in hearts. So, South simply bids 4♣, the Gerber convention, to ask for the number of aces North has. When North bids 4♠ to show 2 aces. South knows that the opponents can win two aces, and slam is not possible. South signs off at 5♥, knowing North will pass. The Gerber bidder places the final contract, knowing how many aces the partnership has.

If North had shown 3 aces with a 4NT bid, South would bid a small slam, 6♥, And if North had shown 0 or 4 aces (with a 4♦ answer), South could have bid a grand slam in NT (on this deal North can't have 15–17 HCP and *no* aces)! Without the Gerber convention, South would just be guessing how many hearts to bid.

In the mid-1940s, when Easley Blackwood (1903–1992) turned 4NT into an artificial *ace-asking* bid, could he have known that one day it would be bridge's **most** widely known convention?

To a partnership looking for game or slam in a suit, 4NT has very little practical advantage as a natural bid. However, as Blackwood demonstrated, it does lend itself well to *artificial* use for slam-related purposes.

Easley Blackwood. Photo courtesy of the American Contract Bridge League.

ASKING FOR ACES

In these auctions, North's 4NT bid is the *Blackwood* convention, which asks for the number of aces that partner holds. The question marks signal that South is to choose the appropriate artificial bid that reflects the count of aces in South's hand.

South	West	North	East
1♥	pass	2♣	pass
3♥	pass	4NT	pass
?			

South	West	North	East
2♦	pass	4NT	pass
?			

The chart below shows which bid South is supposed to make, after looking and determining whether his hand has 0, 1, 2, 3, or 4 aces. South needs to know the correct answers to Blackwood by memory; at the table there's no chart to consult.

Responses to 4NT Blackwood Bid	
Bid	**Number of Aces**
5♣	0 or 4
5♦	1
5♥	2
5♠	3

Again, the Blackwood bidder does very simple addition to see whether the partnership may be missing two aces. The Blackwood bidder must be prepared to stop the bidding at the five level, when missing two aces. Blackwood is good both for bidding slams that can make, and for not bidding slams that won't make!

Note: *Blackwood should never be used simply to show strength. Often in the bidding, partners who show strength or find a fit can reveal their slam interest by bidding new suits below the game level. Skilled partnerships can often disclose their extra strength even before they reach the game level in the bidding!*

ASKING FOR KINGS

When you find that your side has all four aces, you can now use the Blackwood convention at the 5 level to ask about kings. Do that by bidding 5NT.

CONTINUED ON NEXT PAGE

EXAMPLE HAND: USING BLACKWOOD

Dealer: North

Neither Side Vulnerable

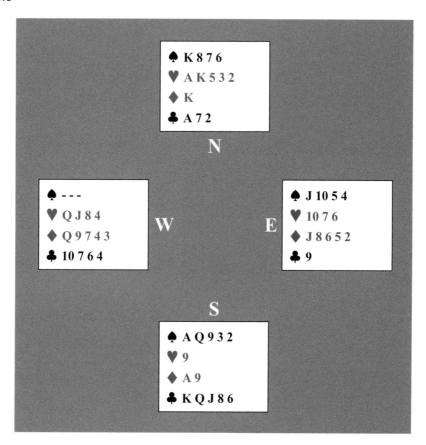

THE BIDDING

North	East	South	West
1♥	pass	1♠	pass
3♠	pass	4NT	pass
5♥	pass	5NT	pass
6♠	pass	7♠	

Opening lead: ♣4

TIP

Use Blackwood in suit auctions, and Gerber in notrump auctions. When NT has already been bid, then 4NT is often useful as a NT raise, inviting a bid of 6NT. In contrast, when suits have been bid, 3NT is the bid to make to try for game in NT. Thus 4NT in an auction when suits have been bid can be given a special use, like the one Mr. Blackwood discovered.

BIDDING EXPLANATION

North opens 1♥ and South responds 1♠, eager to hear North's next bid. When North raises to 3♠ to show a better-than-minimum hand with 4-card spade support, lights begin to flash for South. South trots out Blackwood, and learns that the partnership has all of the aces and kings. Because South also has the queen of trumps, there appear to be no losers, as well as 13 winners. South bids a *grand slam* in spades.

South thanks the dummy for having a fine hand, and wins the opening club lead in his hand. It looks like a great contract!

Eager to draw trumps and claim the contract, South lays down the ♠A and—oh no!—West shows out in spades, and South must lose a trump trick to East!

Did South really play that way? Well, actually, South didn't. Actually, South led a small spade from his hand at trick 2, and when West showed out, he won the trick with dummy's ♠K. Now South led a spade from dummy and East played the ♠10. South won in hand, and played the ♦9 to dummy's ♦K, in order to lead another spade from dummy. This sequence of plays picked up all four of East's trumps without loss, and South made his grand slam.

South must play that way to make his grand slam whenever East holds all 4 missing trumps. If West happens to be the player with all four trumps, South cannot stop West from taking a trump trick. When East has all four enemy trumps, then South can capture them by playing the hand the correct way, using proper technique.

The moral is that bidding a grand slam is half of the grand puzzle—the other half is to be sure to make your contract. Bridge is not a lazy person's game.

WE	THEY	WE	THEY
✕			
	50		

WE	THEY	WE	THEY
✕			
1500			
210			

Which one really was the score?

FACT

Did You Know?

The Blackwood convention spawned several more recent varieties, with names such as *Redwood*, *Voidwood*, and *Roman Keycard Blackwood*.

chapter 15

Play Duplicate Bridge

This chapter introduces you to the world of *duplicate bridge*. With a format and strategy all its own, duplicate bridge differs considerably from rubber bridge. In rubber bridge, picking up poor hands isn't much fun—and it will thin out your wallet, too! In duplicate bridge, the luck factor is greatly reduced. Now, picking up good hands or bad hands doesn't matter at all. It's how you bid and play them that counts.

While a game of rubber bridge needs only four people and a deck or two of cards, duplicate bridge accommodates a roomful of people, and uses many decks of cards. It's called *duplicate* because the same deal is played many times over by various pairs—all deals are *duplicated* around the room.

The object in duplicate bridge is simply to earn better scores than the other pairs get! Scores in duplicate bridge are also calculated differently than in rubber bridge, as you shall see in the section, "Duplicate Bridge Scoring," later in this chapter.

In most towns and cities, you're likely to find a duplicate bridge club hosting a regular schedule of games. Welcome to the club!

In duplicate bridge, special equipment and procedures allow the same deal to be played by many pairs at many tables. As the game moves on, you play against these pairs. At the end, your scores are matched against the scores of other pairs who held the same hands as you.

Photo courtesy of the American Contract Bridge League.

EQUIPMENT FOR DUPLICATE BRIDGE

- Each table has a numbered *table marker* on it to guide you and your partner to your assigned starting position. You also each have a *convention card*, with room to write your names and pair number at the top.

- Special *duplicate boards* (tray-like holders with four slots) hold the hands that are dealt for each deal.

- Using *bidding boxes*, the auction takes place *silently*.

- After cards are played, they are kept aside in a special way that allows each player's hand to be returned intact to its original slot in the duplicate board. This manner of keeping your played cards near you (see later in the chapter) is another distinctive feature of duplicate bridge.

- At the end of each deal, the North player enters the score on a special numbered score sheet, which when not in use is folded and kept in the North slot of the duplicate tray. Because that score sheet stays with the board and travels around the room along with the board, it is called a *traveler*.

GETTING STARTED

Each duplicate game has a director who helps arrange seating and who gets the game up and running. Play begins at all tables at the same time.

① You and partner take your assigned places by going to the table whose *table marker* matches your pair # (a). Each of you should have a copy of your *convention card* visible for your opponents to see (b). A duplicate bridge convention card covers many bidding agreements beyond Stayman, Jacoby Transfers, the Unusual NT, Michaels Cue Bid, negative doubles, Gerber, and Blackwood!

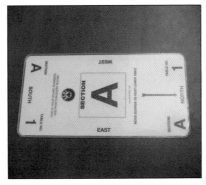

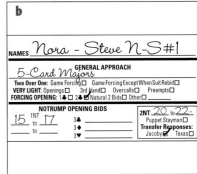

b

NAMES _Nora - Steve N-S #1_

GENERAL APPROACH
5-Card Majors

Two Over One: Game Forcing ☐ Game Forcing Except When Suit Rebid ☐
VERY LIGHT: Openings ☐   3rd Hand ☐   Overcalls ☐   Preempts ☐
FORCING OPENING: 1♣ ☐ 2♣ ☑ Natural 2 Bids ☐ Other ☐

NOTRUMP OPENING BIDS

1NT		
15 to 17	3♣	2NT 20 to 22
to	3♦	Puppet Stayman ☐
	3♥	Transfer Responses: Jacoby ☑ Texas ☐

② Before the first round of play begins, players shuffle the cards in the duplicate boards that are placed at each table. After dealing out new hands, 13 cards are returned face-down back into each slot. In some games, the hands are all pre-dealt, and no shuffling is needed.

Each duplicate board shows seat-direction, as well as each pair's vulnerability. Also indicated is the *dealer*—the player who starts the auction.

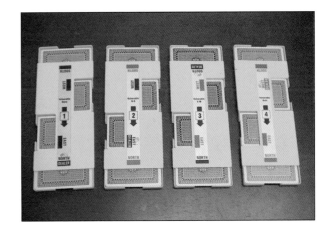

TIP

Observation by the Kibitzer
I notice both table markers and duplicate boards show the North, South, East, and West player positions!

Bidding in duplicate bridge is usually kept silent. Instead of speaking, players indicate their calls through *bidding boxes* that are supplied to each table. Using bidding boxes has two benefits: it prevents the auction from being heard at a nearby table, and it also eliminates any clues that your tone of voice might contain.

Each bidding box contains tabbed cards for each of the 35 possible bids from 1♣ to 7NT, along with green *Pass* cards, red *Double* cards (X), and blue *Redouble* cards (XX).

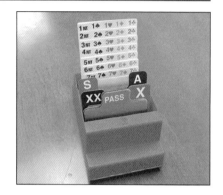

To select a call, you grip its tab between thumb and forefinger. You then place it in front of you near the table's edge, positioned so that your partner sees it right side up.

Note: *It's easiest to grab all of the bids under the one you want, and then place them as a packet on the table (see bottom photo), with your bid showing on top.*

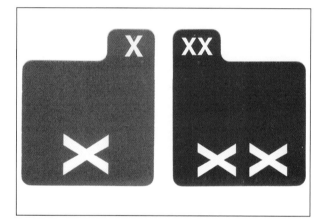

You place each subsequent call in the auction to overlap the previous call, in the order that they appear in sequence. The bidding ends, of course, after three consecutive players have put out green *Pass* cards. As a courtesy, players let the bids remain out briefly to let all players see the completed auction. Players then gather the cards back into the bidding boxes, and the play begins!

Note: *To accommodate visually handicapped players, clubs allow bidding aloud at those players' tables only. Furthermore, blind players are often accommodated in tournaments with Braille cards that all at the table use.*

In rubber bridge, you play each card to the center of the table. The side that wins a trick collects the cards in the trick, and then stacks them together and puts them aside (see Chapter 2).

In duplicate bridge, you play each card right in front of you, near the table's edge. When a trick is completed, you turn your card over, and keep it by the edge. You point it to indicate whether your side won or lost the trick.

Vertical placement indicates a trick won, and **horizontal** placement indicates a trick lost.

Note: The player who is dummy plays the cards declarer calls for, and turns each card over in the same manner as the other players. (Declarer at duplicate bridge still has the privilege to manually reach and select the card to play from dummy.)

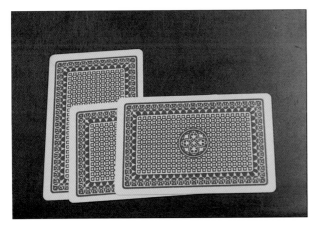

Your side has won the first trick and then lost the next two.

Your side has won nine tricks, and the opponents have won four.

After all 13 tricks are played, and both pairs agree to the result, gather up the cards. Shuffle them a bit from the order in which they were played, and then return them to the slot they were in. Record the score on the traveler (North does this) and move on to the next board for a new deal.

 TIP

Tip for Good Duplicate Bridge Bidding

At each turn, think over your call before reaching for the bidding box. Then, take from the box the card showing your call, and place it with confidence in front of you. Never let your fingers wander in the bidding box when considering your call!

Movement of Players and Boards

In duplicate bridge, each pair plays against a number of other pairs in the room. A special *movement* of players and duplicate boards makes this work smoothly.

Let's assume there are seven tables, and that each round of play consists of four boards. After the first round of four boards has been played, the Director calls the *change* for the next round of play. At this change call, the East–West (E–W) pairs depart their table and move up to the next higher-numbered table.

Thus, E–W at Table 1 go to Table 2, E–W at Table 2 advance to Table 3, and so on up to E–W at Table 6, who advance to Table 7, and E–W at Table 7, who advance to Table 1.

As this is happening, the North–South (N–S) pair pass the set of boards just played in the **opposite** direction, to the next table downwards. N–S at Table 1 pass board numbers 1, 2, 3, and 4 to Table 7. Table 7 passes board numbers 25, 26, 27, and 28 down to Table 6. Table 6's boards go down to Table 5, and so on—down to Table 2, who passes board numbers 5, 6, 7, and 8 to Table 1. As the second round begins, N–S at Table 1 are ready to play boards 5 to 8 against E–W from Table 7.

After six rounds of play, each E–W pair has played four boards against six different N–S pairs, and vice versa. All pairs have played 24 deals.

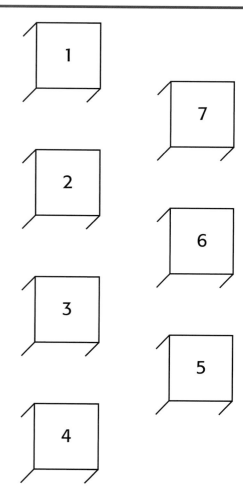

Seven-table duplicate bridge set-up. After each round, E–W pairs move up to the next higher number table, while boards go down one table.

TIP

Director!

A qualified director is on hand at every club or tournament game. The director assigns players their starting seating assignments, calls each new round, and solves any problems that arise from time to time during the course of the game. If you need help, just call out, "Director!"

After you play a hand and agree on the score, the North player records that score, usually on a folded traveling scoresheet—or *traveler*—that accompanies each board. The traveler will continue to accompany the board as it goes from table to table in later rounds.

The first time a board is played, North writes the board number at the top of the traveler, and then enters the contract, result, and score on her pair number's line. North then folds the traveler up, and again writes its board number on the outside. North puts the scored traveler back in with the cards in the *North* slot of the board.

At subsequent tables, each North player removes the traveler to start the board but keeps it folded, aside, until the last trick of the hand has been played. Then North opens the traveler to record the score information. All players should check the score North writes on the traveler before it is refolded and returned to the board.

TIP

Score-Calculating Tip

When unsure how to figure the score on a hand that is just played, you can look for the score for any result on the reverse side of the bidding box cards, table marker, or traveler!

Inside the convention card you will find a *private scorecard*, with room to record up to 36 results. Although each duplicate session usually consists of 24 played hands, up to 36 numbered boards may be needed to run the game.

OFFICIAL (Mitchell or Howell) TRAVELING SCORE

NORTH PLAYER only keeps score.

SECTION _____   ENTER PAIR NO. OF EW PAIR   Board No. _____

N.S. Pair No.	E.W. Pair No.	CON-TRACT	BY	Made	Down	SCORE North - South	SCORE East - West	MATCHPOINTS North - South	MATCHPOINTS East - West
1									
2									
3									
4									
5									
6									
7									
8									
9									
10									

BD # PAIRS	DLR AND VUL	BD # TEAMS	VS	CONTRACT & DECLARER	PLUS	MINUS	PTS EST.	PTS
1	N NONE		6	5H x W	300			
2	E N–S		6	3D W		130		
3	S E–W		6	3n S		50		
4	W BOTH		6	2n S	180			
5	N N–S							
6	E E–W							

Scores entered for boards 1–4 inside the convention card.

Duplicate Bridge Scoring

In duplicate bridge, there's no longer any line to score *below* or *above*. There's also no *rubber* for which to compete. Part-scores aren't added together to make a game, and honor scores go out the window!

Instead, each deal is scored as a single number—the sum of its trick-scores and bonuses. A game bid now receives an instant bonus, changing with vulnerability. Part-scores receive a small instant bonus, regardless of vulnerability.

Summary of Changes in Scoring in Duplicate Bridge	
Trick-Scores	SAME as rubber bridge (see Chapter 3)
Overtricks	SAME as rubber bridge
Undertricks	SAME as rubber bridge
Slam Bonuses	SAME as rubber bridge
Doubled and Redoubled Scoring	SAME as rubber bridge
Part-Score	immediate 50-pt. bonus
Game (not vulnerable)	immediate 300-pt. bonus
Game (vulnerable)	immediate 500-pt. bonus
Honors	Do NOT score at *duplicate bridge!*

Duplicate Bridge Scoring Examples

Part-Scores

1NT making 3.
40 (trick-score) + 60 (for 2 overtricks) + 50 (part-score bonus) = **150.**

2♣ making 3.
40 (trick-score) + 20 (for 1 overtrick) + 50 (part-score bonus) = **110.**

3♥ making 6.
90 (trick-score) + 90 (for 2 overtricks) + 50 (part-score bonus)= **230.**

Games

4♥ vulnerable, making 4.
120 (trick-score) + 500 (game bonus) = **620.**

4♠ not vulnerable, making 5.
120 (trick-score) + 30 + 300 = **450.**

3NT vulnerable, making 4.
100 (trick-score) + 30 + 500 = **630.**

3♥ vulnerable, doubled, making 3.
180 (trick-score, doubled) + 500 (vulnerable game bonus) + 50 (bonus for making a doubled contract) = **730.** (Remember, doubling a part-score can turn it into a game contract, if made!)

Slams

6♦ not vulnerable, making 6.
120 (trick-score) + 300 (game bonus) + 500 (small slam bonus) = **920.**

6NT doubled, vulnerable, making 7.
380 (trick-score of 190, doubled) + 200 (doubled vulnerable overtrick) + 500 (game bonus) + 750 (small slam bonus) + 50 (bonus for making a doubled contract) = **1880.**

7♠ not vulnerable, making 7.
210 (trick-score) + 300 (game bonus) + 1000 (grand slam bonus) = **1510.**

At rubber bridge, either you score or your opponent scores on each deal. At the end, if your scores add up to more than your opponents' scores, you're the winner.

In duplicate bridge, your result on a deal is viewed alongside the results of other pairs who played the **same** deal. All that matters now is how many of those scores your score beats. You get a point—called a *match point*—for every pair whose score on a board you beat. You also get one-half match point for every pair with a score equal to yours.

Let's look at the *traveler* for Board number 4, played six times in a duplicate game.

The highest North–South (N–S) score is at Table 6, where N–S Number 6 earned +620 for bidding and making 4♥. Because that score beats all five other N–S scores, N–S Number 6 wins 5 *match points* on the board.

The next best score is for N–S Number 7, who scored +180 playing 2NT and making 4. They win 4 match points. N–S Number 3 win 3 match points for being +170 at 3♥ and making 4. N–S Number 1 win 2 match points for making +140 at 3♥. N–S numbers 4 and 5 each bid 4♥ but went down a trick, for a score of -100. Although they beat no other pair's score, by tying each other's score, each wins one-half match point.

Viewing the results from the other direction, the best East–West (E–W) score is +100, achieved by E–W Numbers 2 and 7. They receive 4.5 match points each. The low score is for E–W Number 4, who scored -620. They receive no match points on the board, because they beat no other pair's score.

At the conclusion of play, the scores from all the travelers get entered into a computer. The computer instantly displays which pair has the highest score N–S and E–W, and who has finished second, third, fourth, and so on. The computer also shows how your game compares to an average score. Winners and high finishers receive *masterpoint* awards issued by the American Contract Bridge League.

In very high-tech clubs, computers have taken over both bidding and scoring. Players register their calls in the auction on hand-held devices, and the results of each deal also go immediately to the main computer. As the game moves along, everybody can see the current standings, displayed on a large screen. Many clubs also offer printed records of the hands just played, with a compact summary of the contracts both sides can make on every deal!

OFFICIAL (Mitchell or Howell) TRAVELING SCORE

NORTH PLAYER only keeps score.

Section _____ ENTER PAIR NO. OF EW PAIR Board No. _____

N.S. Pair No.	E.W. Pair No.	CON-TRACT	BY	Made	Down	SCORE North - South	SCORE East - West	MATCHPOINTS North - South	MATCHPOINTS East - West
1	1	3♥	N	3		140		2	3
2									
3	5	3♥	N	4		170		3	2
4	7	4♥	N		1		100	.5	4.5
5	2	4♥	N		1		100	.5	4.5
6	4	4♥	N	4		620		5	0
7	6	2N	S	4		180		4	1

```
Odd Pairs Monday Eve Session July 23, 2007
Scores after 28 boards  Average:   60.0                    North-South
Pair   Pct    Score  Rank
  1    57.08  68.50    1    Suzy Singleton - Naria Poynt
  2    56.67  68.00    2    Noah Lurt - Major Disaster
  3    55.00  66.00    3    I. Reed-Hubble - M. T. Chair
  6    52.50  63.00         Slam Spade - Loopy Leeds
  5    49.17  59.00         Iris Pond - Juan Oatrump
  4    41.25  49.50         Patty Preempt - Kenny Crubb
  7    38.33  46.00         Cy Kick - I. C. Goodbridge

Odd Pairs Monday Eve Session July 23, 2007
Scores after 28 boards  Average:   60.0                    East-west
Pair   Pct    Score  Rank
  5    59.17  71.00    1    Cole Topps - Hans Fitzwell
  7    58.33  70.00    2    Lucky Braikes - Watts Trumpz
  4    51.25  61.50    3    Lotta Hartz - Willie Passnow
  2    50.83  61.00         Myra Zultz - U. R. Downe II
  1    50.42  60.50         Igor Lerner - C. Lastric
  6    45.83  55.00         Howie Huddles - O. Verbidder
  3    34.17  41.00         Wanda Finesse - Izzy Voyd
```

Scores from a 7-table duplicate game.

The keenest form of bridge competition is head-to-head team play. Teams of four players square off over a fixed number of boards. Each team seats a N–S pair at one table, and an E–W pair at the other table.

Let's say Al, Amy, Ann, and Art—the A-Team—are playing a 24-board match against Bea, Ben, Beth, and Bob—the B-Team. Ann and Al sit N-S at Table 1, while Amy and Art go to Table 2 and sit E-W. For the B-Team, Beth and Bob fill the E-W chairs at Table 1, with Ben and Bea sitting N-S at Table 2.

The first half of the match begins with boards 1 to 6 at Table 1 and boards 7 to 12 at Table 2. When each six-board set is over, the sets are exchanged between tables and now boards 7 to 12 are played at Table 1 and boards 1 to 6 are played at Table 2.

When these boards are over, the teams get together and compare the scores that they achieved on the first 12 deals, board by board. The difference between the two scores on each board translates into *International Match Points*, referred to as *IMPs*. (This IMP Scale also appears inside the convention card.)

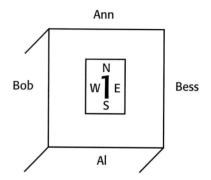

You should have more space than this between tables of a team-of-4 match!

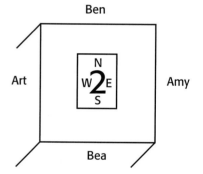

Bridge Lingo: "Making It"
At bridge, there's a lot you can *make*. You can make a bid, make a lead, make a contract, make a part-score, make a game, make a slam, make an overcall, make a preempt, make a raise, and make an overtrick. Of course, try never to make a mistake!

IMP Scale			
Point Difference	*IMPs*	*Point Difference*	*IMPs*
20–40	1	750–890	13
50–80	2	900–1090	14
90–120	3	1100–1290	15
130–160	4	1300–1490	16
170–210	5	1500–1740	17
220–260	6	1750–1990	18
270–310	7	2000–2240	19
320–360	8	2250–2490	20
370–420	9	2500–2990	21
430–490	10	3000–3490	22
500–590	11	3500–3990	23
600–740	12	4000–& up	24

The *Point Difference* refers to the two scores a team achieves on the same board, one score by the team's N–S pair, the other by the E–W pair. For example, on Board Number 1, the A-Team is +420 at Table 1, and -140 at Table 2. The point difference is +280, or +7 IMPs to the A-Team on Board Number 1. It may even be a total, rather than a difference, if both pairs have either a positive score, or a negative score. For example, on Board Number 2, the A-team is -170 at one table, and -300 at the other. The total is -470 or -10 IMPS for the A-team on Board Number 2. By adding the results of these two boards together, the A-team has -3 IMPs.

When all 12 boards have been played and scored at each table, teammates meet again to determine IMP results. Then there's a short break and the second half of the match resumes, with board numbers 13 to 18 at Table 1 and numbers 19 to 24 at Table 2. After these are played, they are switched between tables, as before. Upon completing all 24 boards, and comparing all results, the team with the larger IMP total wins the match.

Strategy for IMP scoring differs from match points. At match points, a score of +180 beats every score of +170. At IMPs, those scores are considered equal because on the scale above, no IMPs are awarded unless the score difference is at least 20 points. At match points, making an extra trick can be very important. At IMP scoring, an overtrick is not as important as making the contract!

Did You Know?

Top teams from every country compete annually for trophies in Team-of-Four play.

The American Contract Bridge League

In existence for over 70 years, the American Contract Bridge League (ACBL) does a great job organizing bridge competitions, from the club level all the way up to national championships that are held three times a year. You don't need to join the ACBL to play duplicate bridge at a club or tournament, but membership has great advantages!

The ACBL sponsors tournaments, registers masterpoint awards, and provides its nearly 160,000 members with a highly informative monthly magazine, *The Bridge Bulletin*. The ACBL also lets you know when your master-point total advances your *player ranking*.

ACBL Player Rankings	
Junior Master	5 masterpoints
Club Master	20 masterpoints
Sectional Master	50 masterpoints
Regional Master	100 masterpoints
NABC Master	200 masterpoints
Life Master	300 masterpoints
Bronze Life Master	500 masterpoints
Silver Life Master	1000 masterpoints
Gold Life Master	2500 masterpoints
Diamond Life Master	5000 masterpoints
Emerald Life Master	7500 masterpoints
Platinum Life Master	10,000 masterpoints

The ACBL's Web site is full of information for beginners, intermediates, and experts about tournament bridge from the club level to national championships. The screen shown includes links to many other navigable pages on the site.

The ACBL awards its largest masterpoint awards at sectional, regional, and national tournaments. Their Web site, www.acbl.org, contains a vast amount of information about bridge, as well as club locations and tournament schedules. You can also contact the ACBL by calling 901-332-5586, or writing to ACBL, 2990 Airways Blvd., Memphis, TN 38116-3847.

The World Bridge Federation (www.worldbridge.org) hosts championship events as well. There's no reason why a reader of this book can't win a world championship!

Paul Soloway, 65,511 MP

Mike Passell, 58,997 MP

The ACBL's top two masterpoint holders (totals as of September 2007).
Photos courtesy of the American Contract Bridge League.

FACT

ACBL members who play in online tournaments can win masterpoint awards without ever leaving home (see Chapter 16)! You can also keep an eye on your masterpoint totals at the ACBL Web site.

Duplicate Strategy and Tips

Duplicate bridge strategies and tactics are a little different from those of rubber bridge.

STRATEGIES FOR MATCHPOINT SCORING

- **Aim for notrump.** Because notrump contracts earn the highest trick-score, players should always try to consider whether a notrump contract is viable. You should avoid notrump when you have unstopped suits, unbalanced hand-patterns, and a 4-4 (or better) major suit fit.

- **Watch your vulnerability.** Respect the vulnerability, and take your risks accordingly. You'll invite bad results by making lightweight or chancy bids when vulnerable. Even if you aren't doubled, a two-trick vulnerable set of -200 might be a very poor score when the opponents can make no more than a part-score!

- **Compete quickly and fully.** In competitive auctions, bid as high as you can as early as you can. For example, if you are East with the hand shown here, raise to 2♠ right away, which immediately makes South's next call a lot riskier. If you pass, you give South the opportunity for an easier low-level rebid. While you can still bid 2♠ later, you will lose that bid's pressure impact.

♠J93
♥A1084
♦K64
♣1032

East	South	West	North
Pass	1♥	1♠	pass
?			

- **Know that down one is good bridge.** Down one in rubber bridge is rarely a very good result. The best it means is that your side has lost a little, when it could have lost more. On the other hand, in duplicate bridge, a score of -50 or -100 (for down one) can be a very good result, if at most other tables the opponents make part-score (or game) contracts worth an even higher score. However, down one is not as happy a result if you could have set their contract!

- **Don't hesitate.** Try to avoid noticeable hesitations or long pauses at your turn in the bidding, or other acts that might convey extra information, such as smiles or tears. Your partner is forbidden to take advantage of any such information, but your opponents can!!

- **Keep a poker face.** In rubber bridge, if you have poor cards, you are going to be a loser. In duplicate bridge, if you have poor cards, all you have to do is keep pace with others who have the same poor cards as you. Even if you can't take a trick, try to appear very involved.

- **Consider opportunities for "sacrifice" bids.** For example, vulnerable opponents bid 4♠, which they will make for 620 if allowed to play. If your side bids 5♦ and goes down 2 tricks doubled, *vulnerable*—or 3 tricks doubled *not vulnerable*—your score of -500 will beat other pairs' scores of -620!

- **Each trick can mean a lot.** In rubber bridge, you try for enough tricks to make your contract—or to defeat the opponents' contract. Any extra tricks just increase your score. In duplicate bridge, your goal is quite different. For example, as defenders you want to defend better than the others who hold your cards, not necessarily defeat the actual contract you are defending! If you hold opponents at 3NT to 10 tricks, for a score of -630, while every other pair allows the opponents to make 11 tricks, for -660, you get a *top*—all of the matchpoints on the board!

STRATEGY AND TACTICS AT IMPS

Matchpoint scoring and IMP scoring call for different strategies. Tactics at IMPs are quite similar to rubber bridge!

- **Bid safe contracts.** Plus scores are important at IMP scoring. Don't be the one to put your partnership, and therefore the team, at risk of a negative score.

- **Make your contract.** In matchpoint scoring, every trick can be important, including overtricks. At IMPs the most important trick is the one that fulfills your contract. An overtrick cannot affect the IMP score significantly!

- **Don't compete too hard for part-scores.** In competitive situations, don't strain to compete. With questionable values, rather than suffer a possibly expensive penalty score, it is safer to pass and let the opponents bid a contract and make a small plus score. After all, your teammates at the other table will have the same cards as your opponents, and may do just as well.

- **Double part-scores for penalties only if you forecast a two-trick set:**

  South expects to set East's bid by at least two tricks.

South	West	North	East
pass	pass	1NT	2♥
Dbl.			

TIP

The Joy of Passing

Lots of space in this book is devoted to bidding, but in bridge *passing* is just as important. You'll pass at least as often as you bid—probably more often! An important general bidding goal is to make the bids your hand-values call for, and then to comfortably pass, having shown those values.

chapter 16

The World of Online Bridge

If you can connect to the Internet, you can link to a bridge game any minute of the day. An empty seat will be waiting for you on a number of Web sites. You can also host your own table and invite friends to it, or just see who shows up. If you just want to kibitz, you are welcome at most tables.

You can win masterpoint awards in scheduled tournaments day and night. There are even places to play tournament or rubber bridge for money, the traditional stake.

This chapter will guide you to popular Web sites for online bridge play, with tips on finding a friendly partner, game, or tournament.

Features of Online Bridge Sites

Like just about everything, bridge is much quicker on a computer than it is in real life. The instant one computer deal fades from view, the next pops up—and with your hand all arranged, besides! And there are lots of further features that make online bridge fun and exciting to players of all levels.

What You May Expect

- **Viewing options.** You often get a number of viewing options for your bridge display. During a hand, you can more easily review the auction and previous tricks played than if you were in an actual game. You can also look back on an entire hand—or an archive of hands.

- **Different levels of play.** For new players, there are starter games and learning resources. For experienced players, there's competitive play, including ACBL-rated duplicate bridge tournament games.

- **Scoring options.** Most sites offer scoring, both by matchpoints and IMPs, while a few sites offer scoring using the rubber-bridge style as a standard format.

- **Money bridge.** Some sites offer the chance to play rubber bridge at moderate stakes or enter tournaments for cash prizes.

- **Fun sound effects.** Internet bridge tables also feature friendly sound effects, like the snap of each card being played. Most have a little buzzer or chime to remind you to bid or to play, in case you become distracted—or maybe doze off!

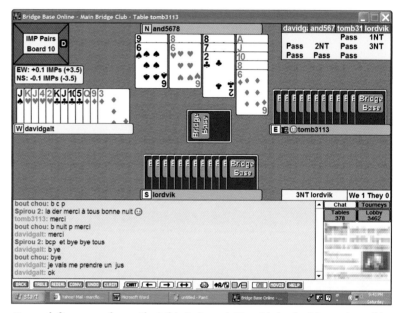

Upper left corner shows that this is Board 10, with both sides vulnerable in an IMP pairs game. The author, West, is defending 3NT, and his side has just won the first trick. The chat below the hand is partly in French.

- **Error undo.** Most online games also make it easy to undo an error that you made through a slip of the mouse, or of the mind.

- **Possible subscriber's fee.** You may have to pay. While some sites are free, others require a subscription. Most require a brief download of software. Keep in mind, also, that not all sites accommodate both PCs and Macs.

TIP

Online bidding can go at a quick pace—similar to a live table. Playing to the tricks may be quite rapid. As a courtesy to the other three players at your online table, try to make your bids and plays without delay. When in a fast-moving game, it makes sense to plan ahead. If you're going to get hungry, keep provisions handy. Only as dummy can you grab a brief break.

It's common throughout the Internet to represent yourself with made-up names and with pictures you choose. The first thing you'll need to provide when you join an Internet bridge site is a player name.

Your user name can usually be any combination of letters and numbers that nobody else has chosen. You can remain an anonymous player on any site, or use all or part of your actual name. You also will often be able to add a picture and other further information, including an e-mail address if you wish to provide one, and an approximate geographical location. At a number of sites, you can supply a real or whimsical image or choose from site-available avatars. You may also have the chance to include bridge information about yourself, such as your level of play and the conventions you prefer.

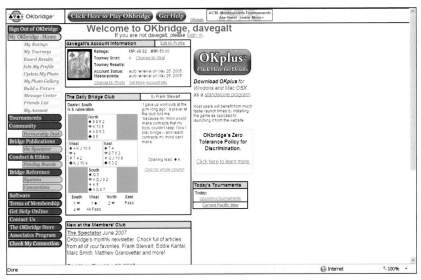

On the greeting page of OKbridge, the author has joined under his own name, and has supplied an antique ♠K as his visual avatar.

TIP

Note to the Kibitzer

Almost every site has games that you can kibitz, although some tables may choose to block kibitzers. Kibitzing is a good way to get used to how a site works.

Where to Play

A search online for "online bridge" will turn up a manageable number of leading sites. Having learned what bridge bidding, play, and scoring entail, you may deem it a miracle that a bridge game always awaits you on your desktop, laptop, or other device! Here's how to access some of these online sites.

Bridge Base Online (BBO)

Bridge Base Online (www.online .bridgebase.com) is free, easy to use, and has many smart features. A premier location for Internet bridge, it's also where the most tables are in play. A handy icon will sit on your desktop after you download its software. While you navigate the BBO site, small explanations in balloons may appear as you glide over buttons, and right-clicking often gives you added options.

Like many sites, you can play or kibitz in anonymity, or instead let others know just who you are. You can view the names of whoever's logged in at any moment, and easily look for *friends* among them, or find one of the helpful *guides* who are always on hand. Players with stars next to their names are good to kibitz.

On BBO, you can play for fun, masterpoints, or money. At peak times, 12,000 or more members may be signed in, but that doesn't slow anything down!

You can pick from eight different BBO play areas. New players should head for the very popular Main Bridge Club, where most of the tables play duplicate-style bridge with IMP scoring, although you can also find matchpoint tables and

Many (18) drop-down buttons for alternate choices; preselected default settings.

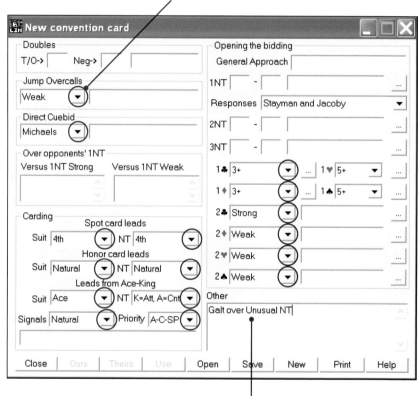

Added: Galt over Unusual NT

a few rubber bridge tables. The Tournament room is also well attended, as is the room for Team Matches. In addition to these, you can also enter the Relaxed Bridge Club, the Masters Bridge Club, Private Bridge Clubs, Public Bridge Clubs, and Money Tables. New players also may register in the Beginner's and Intermediate Lounge.

BBO gives you a great opportunity to learn, observe, and practice the game in order to develop your bridge skills. You can play duplicate or other forms of bridge continuously, and at no charge. You can also arrange with your partner to be on BBO together in order to work on your convention card. In the image, the customizable Convention Card includes blanks to fill in as well as drop-down choices (with default choices already supplied) which you can change. In the Other box, a convention called "Galt over Unusual Notrump" has been added.

A BBO fanfare welcomes you to your chosen table, and you instantly see a hand of cards. To learn more about who else is sitting at the table, just glide your cursor over each player name. Dealer and vulnerability are clearly indicated for every board number, shown at the upper left-hand corner of the hand layout. When it's your turn to bid, another window opens up showing you the available bids. To bid, click the number and suit (or notrump), and post your bid. The full auction shows in the center of the table.

When it's time to play out the hand, you double-click the card you want to play. Tricks appear in the center of the table, and once taken, they are shown in one row, in the familiar manner of duplicate bridge, with winning tricks pointed vertically. In the hand shown, marked Board 11, the author has landed in a contract of 4♠ after a 1NT opening bid and a 2♣ Stayman sequence. North has led the ♦K and the next two cards, the ♦3 and ♦4, have been played. The author is about to win the ♦A and will proceed to make 11 tricks for a very good result on the hand. Note that the dummy is visible, but, of course, not the defenders' cards.

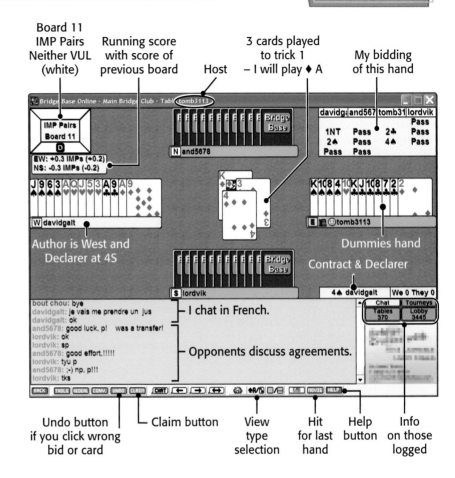

Board 11
IMP Pairs
Neither VUL
(white)

Running score
with score of
previous board

Host

3 cards played
to trick 1
– I will play ♦ A

My bidding
of this hand

Author is West and
Declarer at 4S

Dummies hand

Contract & Declarer

— I chat in French.

— Opponents discuss agreements.

Undo button
if you click wrong
bid or card

Claim button

View
type
selection

Hit
for last
hand

Help
button

Info
on those
logged

On BBO, as soon as a deal is over, you receive your score and can see how it compares to other pairs that also played the hand. Your IMP or matchpoint result will appear on the next screen, as you begin the next new hand.

CONTINUED ON NEXT PAGE

Using the *bridge movie* feature, you can view the hand just played. Just click the button marked MOVIE at the screen bottom, to examine it in detail. You can see the contracts, results, and IMP or matchpoint scores for the deal as played at every other table. You can compare your result to all those other scores. You also can click further to see who is playing at those tables, and see how the play of the tricks went at each.

In the screen shown, the author is beginning Board 14 but has clicked on the MOVIE button to review Board 13, just played. All 4 hands are shown at once, as well as the bidding. In addition, the author's result on the board, +500 at 4♣ doubled (in a yellow band), wins 7.8 IMPs and is tied for third best result on the board. In the corner of Board 14 can be seen the running IMP total, with the prior board result in parentheses.

ACTIVITIES BESIDES PLAYING

On BBO you can kibitz star players or random players, and follow their chat with each other, which may occasionally be in foreign languages. You can also be part of the audience watching championship events in BBO's Vugraph Theatre. Chosen expert observers post informed and entertaining remarks about every hand, shown beneath in an ongoing window of commentary and banter. It's a lot like following a live sportscast. In the BBO Vugraph selection of a match in the 2007 Norwegian Team Championships, N–S, at the end of a long session, manage to overbid to 6♥ (auction in upper-right corner). In the screen shown, East is about to win the first trick with the ♦A, and West will win the next trick with the the ♦K, and set the contract. In the commentators' chat booth, goodbye and good wishes are being given.

BBO also furnishes a library archive with many valuable bridge articles and all past Vugraph events, deal by deal. On various Bridge Base Forums, discussions occur among players at all levels.

Running score, with +7.8 IMPs for Author on BD 13

Current hand is Board 14

E–W results at other tables from best to worst

Bridge movie window superimposed on this

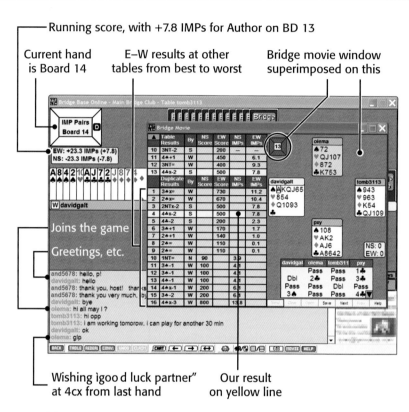

Joins the game

Greetings, etc.

Wishing ìgoo d luck partner" at 4cx from last hand

Our result on yellow line

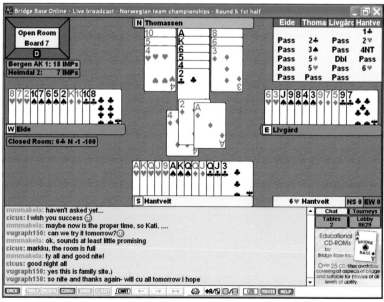

MONEY AND STAKES BRIDGE ON BBO

Besides free, ongoing IMP and match-point play, BBO offers ACBL-sanctioned games that issue masterpoint awards. There is a small card fee to play in these games, for which you need to establish a *Bridge Base Dollars* (BB$) account. You can easily buy these BB$ in small increments, and you can use them also to purchase bridge products from the BBO sites.

BBO has another currency you can purchase: *Money Bridge Dollars* (MB$). You use MB$ for Money Bridge Tournaments (based on your best 100 boards), and for playing in money bridge rooms where you can win or lose real money. These rubber bridge games are at modest stakes, ranging from 1/10 cent per point up to two cents per point. At the highest stake you could lose $100 on a bad evening. You can convert MB$ to BB$, and you can even withdraw MB$ funds (such as your winnings at the rubber bridge tables) for the 3- to 5-percent fee typical to online fund transfers. In some money events, you must play with an automatic partner, called a *robot*, or just *bot*. To buy either type of currency, or purchase bridge products, just click on the Shop Bridge! button.

Player Names at tables

Table host

Scroll button

Kibitzer count per table

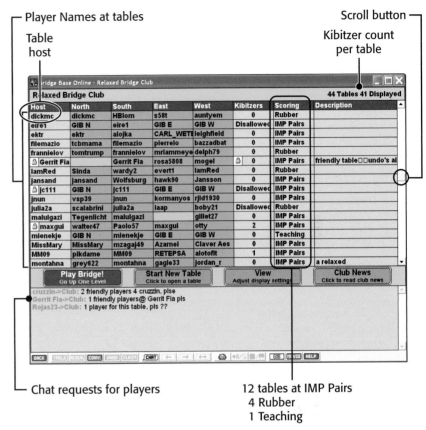

Chat requests for players

12 tables at IMP Pairs
4 Rubber
1 Teaching

You won't need any dollars to compete for the fun of a good game in BBO's Relaxed Bridge Club. Pair games scored at IMPs are the most popular choice there, with a few rubber bridge tables, and even a teaching table!

TIP

For any online bridge player, the biggest fear is losing your Internet connection, even if momentarily. On some sites, you can re-connect right to the spot where you were, with the table awaiting your return. On other sites, you may have to re-connect entirely.

CONTINUED ON NEXT PAGE

OKbridge

Another bridge site with a lot to offer is OKbridge (www.OKbridge.com). It's well geared for players of all levels—from beginner to expert. OKbridge is a membership site whose annual fee of $99 or $149 reflects how much tournament play you intend to do.

SIGN UP AND LOOK FOR A GAME

To sign on for a seven-day free trial, you must submit all of the information that you would give if you were making a full payment. You can create an OKbridge profile and participate just like a full member. Watch, play, look around, and mix with other members. If you choose to withdraw, be sure to inform OKbridge within the seven-day time frame, or else a charge will accrue for a one-year membership.

When looking for a game on OKbridge, you can read Lobby messages to find players at various levels of play. You can also scan table icons or listings for empty seats, and can search for a table or partner according to preferred bidding systems.

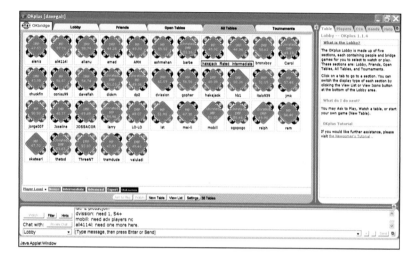

Tables can be viewed by list or icon, and you can just click a button to join as a player or a kibitzer. You can click a table icon or listing for details about who's at the table and the form of bridge that is being played there. You also can choose to *serve*, or host, a table, and choose the form of scoring at the table (IMPs or matchpoints), as well as who joins the table.

The screen capture of the OKbridge lobby shows 4 tables with 1 seat open, 2 tables with 3 seats open, and all other tables full. The table center shows the form of scoring for that table. Players in red rate themselves as intermediate, those in blue are advanced. Players in black are unknown. There's generally an equal representation of each color, with no players identifying themselves as either beginner or expert.

LEHMAN RATINGS ON OKBRIDGE

OKbridge assigns player ratings based on a system that was devised by Bradley Lehman out of an OKbridge online discussion group starting in 1993. Assisting in its development and application were Matthew Clegg and Craig Chase. Players start at 50 percent (an average score), and the bridge results that they achieve send their Lehman number below or above this mark. The Lehman system takes into account past performance in rating a player's mark of achievement. It's easy to find a game at about your own level of play, and to seek players according to these ratings. You can also actually see your Lehman rating change with every deal.

TIP

When you answer to a call for players, or find an empty seat, it's always good etiquette through chat to ask to join the table.

BIDDING ON OKBRIDGE

As a shortcut to choosing bidding agreements with an unknown partner, you can click any of nine popular systems and look at it in summary, or as a completely filled-out convention card. You can also fill out a blank convention card online, almost as if you were at a club game. For existing partnerships, OKbridge provides the resources to work on a convention card together. You can also review the results of boards that you have played previously with any or all partners.

Note: *You've seen the top of the standard ACBL (American Contract Bridge League) convention card in Chapter 15.*

Each OKbridge table has a numbered, metallic duplicate board in the center of the table. You can bid either by clicking in a bidding grid and clicking OK, or by double-clicking (it's your choice). Calls appear on the table in the form of bid-cards that are taken from a bidding box. These details make it feel like you're at an actual club or tournament game.

If you become dummy, you can click to view the whole hand as your partner plays it, or remain in the dark and see the play as it develops.

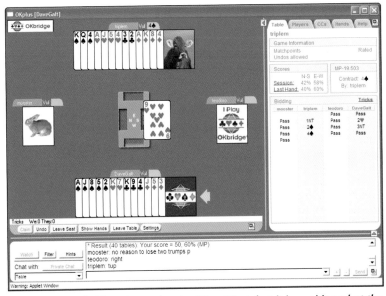

Playing on OKbridge, the author is sitting West, but it is positioned at the bottom of the screen. Opponents have bid to a contract of 4♥. The bidding window showing the remaining available bids will disappear when the opening lead is made.

OTHER FEATURES

OKbridge publications include a regularly e-mailed bridge newsletter called *The Spectator*, as well as archives of bridge hands and articles by well-known bridge authors such as Eddie Kantar, Grant Baze, Billy Miller, and Dr. Prakash Paranjape (known as Panja). Users can comment on columns and in bridge forums.

Newcomers may take a guided tour of OKbridge with someone from the Member Services team, as well as play hands live. A Partnership Desk helps you to find a partner at your level. There's also an OKbridge Store.

Note: *OKbridge has sensible policies for boards that are interrupted through a table crash, or that are skipped. They embrace a zero-tolerance policy for discrimination.*

CONTINUED ON NEXT PAGE

SWAN Bridge

SWAN Bridge (www.swangames.com) bills itself as "The World's Friendliest Internet Bridge Club." Based in Sweden, it covers many European Championship events, and has a wide international membership.

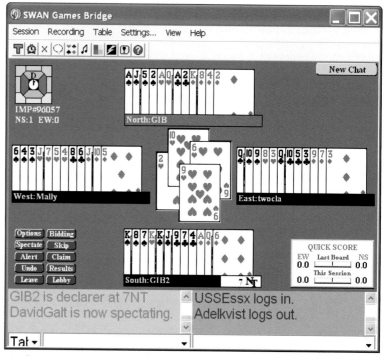

In the screen capture, two bridge robots bid up to a very optimistic 7NT which might succeed with a complex series of possible plays.

MEMBERSHIP

You can have a fine time playing free duplicate bridge on the SWAN site. You pay a small membership fee if you want to play for ACBL masterpoints and SWAN rating points. Payable by credit card, check, or money order, the cost is $2.50 for one week, $8.75 for one month, $22.50 for three months, and $79.95 for one year.

SWAN Bridge lets you select a longer username than some other sites do. Players are listed with their SWAN masterpoint and IMP ratings. Personal settings and appearances give you many options. For example, you can choose to have suits appear in any of four black-red-black-red sequences. Supplied macros can help explain bidding agreements amongst an international membership.

SWAN Bridge offers 12- or 16-board ACBL tournaments three times daily. You only need to sign up at least five minutes before game time. You also need to activate your convention card link so that opponents may see it. Chat between partners is very limited during tournaments.

FEATURES

The screen capture shows a hand already played and now viewed in Review Results mode. As can be seen, East's mild preempt in hearts helped keep North–South out of a sure 3NT or easy-to-make 4♠ contract. This layout lets you review or "post mortem" the hand, with ways to go over the trick-play, see other table results, and discuss.

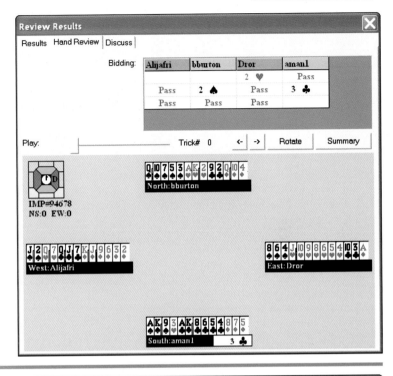

MSN's Game Zone Bridge

A boisterous site for bridge play, with lots of chummy chat, is MSN's Game Zone Bridge (www.zone.msn.com). The site is free but requires that you download MSN's generic Game Zone software. If you have a pre-existing e-mail account under MSN or Hotmail, it is easy to sign up for membership. Otherwise, your computer settings may need to be readjusted in order to download.

Once you've finished downloading, you can play against the computer or play with others in casual or competitive play. Duplicate events are hosted by a director or member, and partners agree to a code or honor system of no private chat—otherwise players could reveal their cards or intentions to their partners via chat. Pairs can post their convention card of bidding agreements. Players remain largely anonymous, although you can supply identifying information in your profile.

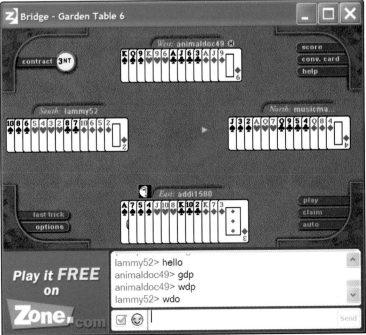

CONTINUED ON NEXT PAGE

Yahoo Bridge

Yahoo Bridge (www.yahoo.com) does not require that you download any software. If you have a Yahoo ID, you can play or kibitz almost immediately. First, you must step past an introductory page containing a lively promotional appeal from a Yahoo games sponsor.

You can click informative Yahoo summaries about the game, including its history, basics, scoring, expert play, and glossary.

While playing Yahoo Bridge, bid grids and a trick review appear in extra windows, and it may sometimes feel like you are juggling these windows while playing. Your score and vulnerability appear in yet another window, and are kept as in rubber bridge.

The low amount of graphics-devoted memory means that little visual space is given over to reviewing or following the auction, seeing the vulnerability, recognizing who is the declarer, and following the trick count. These take getting accustomed to. Also, the review of a hand just played gives no graphics beyond monochrome letters S, H, D, and C—for spades, hearts, diamonds and clubs—and A down to 2 for the card ranks. As usual, the visual and mechanical elements become faster with continued play.

Player identities on Yahoo tend to remain anonymous. Courtesy levels are also less exacting, and an occasional scamp might intrude upon or join a table. Or, someone may suddenly leave in the middle of a hand—of course this can happen on any site. On occasion, the table host may need to click the *boot* button to send a player away from the table.

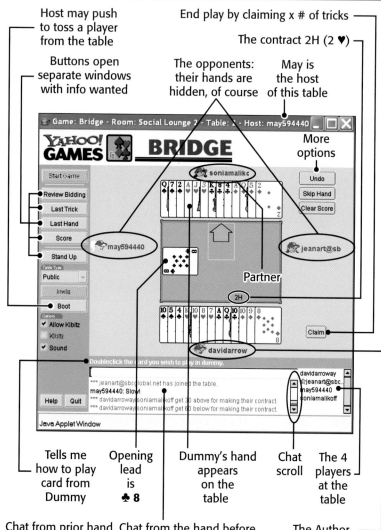

Host may push to toss a player from the table

Buttons open separate windows with info wanted

End play by claiming x # of tricks

The contract 2H (2 ♥)

The opponents: their hands are hidden, of course

May is the host of this table

Tells me how to play card from Dummy

Opening lead is ♣ 8

Dummy's hand appears on the table

Chat scroll

The 4 players at the table

Chat from prior hand. Chat from the hand before, with "may" asking for faster play, and david/soniamalikoff scoring 60 below, 30 above as in rubber bridge.

The Author under Yahoo ID davidarrow, declarer at 2H

South (the author playing rubber bridge under a Yahoo ID), receives West's lead of the ♠8 at his 2♥ contract. The contract was made, and added to the prior hand's 60-point part-score made a game and won the rubber.

Most bridge sites are designed to be very user-friendly, and online players are generally friendly too. You can play online with your favorite partner, or put together a table of people you know. You can also log in on your own and find a game with other players at your level, who might be anywhere on earth, or maybe even in outer space!

Virtually every bridge site offers you an opportunity to chat during play or while waiting around. You can chat with players at your table, chat in a lobby of players, or have a private chat with another player.

With players online from all over the world, you can encounter many different bidding styles. English appears to be a universal chat language, but sometimes you may find yourself kibitzing a table where the chat is in a foreign language, and it can have quite an exotic look. Sites offer you the familiar options of choosing whom you chat with and closing chat windows.

The list on the right gives some common bridge chat shorthand. Of course, abbreviations standard to ordinary chat are part of bridge chat. For example, Dummy may type *brb* "Be right back" when dashing off from the table for a moment.

Bridge Chat Shorthand	
blp	"Bad luck, partner."
bw	Blackwood
gb	"Good bridge" (i.e., down one)
gdo	"Good defense, opponents."
gga	"Good game, all." (said when leaving)
gj	"Good job"
glp	"Good luck, partner!"
nbfab	"Not bad for a beginner."
nh	"Nice hand."
n1	"Need one?" (i.e., a player)
nt	"Nice try."
o, opps	Opponent, opponents
p	Partner
sp	"Sorry, partner."
stay	Stayman
ty	"Thank you."
unt	Unusual notrump
wdp	"Well done, partner."
wpo	"Well played, opponent."
yp	"Your play."

FACT

Because a score of down one can be a good result, especially at duplicate bridge, it's also a way of reporting the outcome of a deal in shorthand. Adding a few words gives ironic shorthand for down two and three.

Agb	Almost good bridge (down two)
Ngb	Nearly good bridge (down two)
Angb	Almost nearly good bridge (down three)

Bridge Resources

WEB SITES

Thousands of Web sites devoted to bridge are maintained by clubs, organizations, enthusiasts, and professionals. Here are just a few links to useful bridge Web sites.

American Bridge Association. www.ababridge.org or www.americanbridge.com

Australian Bridge Federation. www.abf.com.au

Bridge glossary. www.bridgeworld.com

Bridge library. www.prairienet.org/bridge (Karen Walker)

Bridge links. www.homepage.mac.com/bridgeguys

Bridge probabilities. www.rpbridge.net/7z77.htm#02 (Richard Pavlicek)

Lessons, articles, tests, and freeware. www.bridge7.com

University Bridge. www.unibridge.org

BOOKS

Reading about bridge is essential to becoming a good bridge player!

Bergen, Marty. *Points Schmoints!* (Bergen Books, 1995)

Bird, David, and Tim Bourke. *Test Your Bridge Technique.* (Master Point Press, 2004-05)

Colchamiro, Mel. *How You Can Play Like an Expert.* (Magnus Books, 2007)

Darvas, Robert, and Norman de V. Hart. *Right Through the Pack.* (John Wiley & Sons, 1996)

Encyclopedia of Bridge. (Crown Publishers, 1988)

Goren, Charles H. *Goren Settles the Bridge Arguments.* (Ballantine Books, 1985)

Hardy, Max, and Mike Lawrence. *Standard Bridge Bidding for the 21st Century.* (Vivisphere Publishing, 2001)

Kantar, Eddie. *Bridge For Dummies,* 2nd Edition. (Wiley Publishing, Inc., 2006)

Kelsey, Hugh. *Killing Defense.* (Hart Publishing Co., 1972)

Klinger, Ron. *100 Winning Bridge Tips for the Improving Player.* (Houghton Mifflin Co., 1992)

Lawrence, Mike. *Partnership Understandings.* (Baron Barclay Books, 1990)

McPherson, Edward. *The Backwash Squeeze and Other Improbable Feats.* (Harper Collins, 2007)

Mollo, Victor. *Bridge in the Menagerie.* (Batsford, 1996)

Mollo, Victor, and Nico Gardener. *Card Play Technique.* (Anova Books, 2004)

Reese, Terence. *Play These Hands with Me.* (Master Point Press, 2001)

Root, William S. *Playing a Bridge Hand.* (Crown, 1990)

Roth, Alvin. *Picture Bidding: The Art of Painting a Bridge Hand.* (Granovetter Books, 1991)

Rubens, Jeff. *Secrets of Winning Bridge.* (Grosset & Dunlap, 1969)

Schenken, Howard. *The Education of a Bridge Player.* (Simon & Schuster, 1973)

Seagram, Barbara, and Marc Smith. *25 Conventions You Should Know.* (Master Point Press, 1999)

Sontag, Alan. *The Bridge Bum.* (William Morrow, 1977)

Note to Kibitzer: *Look for additional titles by the above authors.*

MAGAZINES
Australian Bridge Magazine

Better Bridge

Bridge Magazine

Bridge Plus

Bridge Today

The Bridge World

The Bulletin of the ACBL

Index

Want instruction in other topics?

Check out these

All designed for visual learners—just like you!

Read Less–Learn More®
Visual®

Teach Yourself **VISUALLY™**
Guitar
Charles Kim.
0-7645-9642-X

Teach Yourself **VISUALLY™**
Knitting
Sharon Turner
0-7645-9640-3

Teach Yourself **VISUALLY™**
Windows XP
2nd Edition
0-7645-7927-4